Swift 4 Programming Cookbook

50 task-oriented recipes to make you productive with Swift 4

Keith Moon

BIRMINGHAM - MUMBAI

Swift 4 Programming Cookbook

First published: September 2017

Production reference: 1260917

Published by Packt Publishing Ltd.
Livery Place
35 Livery Street
Birmingham
B3 2PB, UK.

ISBN 978-1-78646-089-9

www.packtpub.com

Credits

Author
Keith Moon

Reviewer
Giordano Scalzo

Commissioning Editor
Ashwin Nair

Acquisition Editor
Larissa Pinto

Content Development Editor
Onkar Wani

Technical Editor
Akhil Nair

Copy Editor
Shaila Kusanale

Project Coordinator
Ulhas Kambali

Proofreader
Safis Editing

Indexer
Mariammal Chettiyar

Graphics
Abhinash Sahu

Production Coordinator
Shraddha Falebhai

About the Author

Keith Moon is an award-winning iOS developer, author, and speaker based in London. He has worked with some of the biggest companies in the world to create engaging and personal mobile experiences. Keith has been developing in Swift since its release, working on projects both fully Swift, and mixed Swift and Objective-C. Keith has been invited to speak about Swift development in conferences from Moscow to Minsk and London.

I would like to thank my amazing and supportive wife, Alissa. Without her support and patience, this book would not have been possible.

About the Reviewer

Giordano Scalzo is a developer with 20 years of programming experience, since the days of the ZXSpectrum.

He has worked in C++, Java, .NET, Ruby, Python, and in a ton of other languages that he has forgotten the names of.

After years of backend development, over the past five years, Giordano has developed extensively for iOS, releasing more than 20 apps--apps that he wrote for clients, enterprise applications, or on his own.

Currently he is a contractor in London, where through his company Effective Code Ltd, `http://effectivecode.co.uk`, he delivers code for iOS aiming at quality and reliability.

In his spare time, when he is not crafting retro game clones for iOS, he writes his thoughts on `http://giordanoscalzo.com`.

I'd like to thank my better half Valentina, who lovingly supports me in everything I do; without you, none of this would have been possible.
Thanks to my bright future, Mattia and Luca, for giving me lots of smiles and hugs when I needed them.
Finally, my gratitude goes to my mum and my dad, who gave me curiosity and the support to follow my passions, which began one day when they bought me a ZXSpectrum.

www.PacktPub.com

For support files and downloads related to your book, please visit www.PacktPub.com. Did you know that Packt offers eBook versions of every book published, with PDF and ePub files available? You can upgrade to the eBook version at www.PacktPub.com and as a print book customer, you are entitled to a discount on the eBook copy. Get in touch with us at service@packtpub.com for more details.

At www.PacktPub.com, you can also read a collection of free technical articles, sign up for a range of free newsletters and receive exclusive discounts and offers on Packt books and eBooks.

https://www.packtpub.com/mapt

Get the most in-demand software skills with Mapt. Mapt gives you full access to all Packt books and video courses, as well as industry-leading tools to help you plan your personal development and advance your career.

Why subscribe?

- Fully searchable across every book published by Packt
- Copy and paste, print, and bookmark content
- On demand and accessible via a web browser

Customer Feedback

Thanks for purchasing this Packt book. At Packt, quality is at the heart of our editorial process. To help us improve, please leave us an honest review on this book's Amazon page at https://www.amazon.com/dp/1786460890.

If you'd like to join our team of regular reviewers, you can e-mail us at customerreviews@packtpub.com. We award our regular reviewers with free eBooks and videos in exchange for their valuable feedback. Help us be relentless in improving our products!

Table of Contents

Preface

Since Apple announced the Swift programming language at WWDC 2014, it has gone on to become one of the fastest growing programming languages. Swift is modern, open source, and easy to use, and therefore Swift's usefulness can extend beyond Apple's ecosystem, giving it the potential to be used across all platforms and for any scenario.

Swift 4 represents the latest version of this exciting new programming language, giving you the tools to build performant and responsive apps, with safe and clean code.

This book will guide you through Swift's features, building up your knowledge and toolset layer by layer, so you can use Swift to build the next great app or service.

You will be given useful, easy-to-follow recipes for using Swift to accomplish real-world tasks. Each recipe only uses concepts previously covered in the book, so you will never feel lost.

Learn what makes Swift one of the fastest growing and most exciting programming languages available today.

What this book covers

Chapter 1, *Swift Building Blocks*, introduces you to the basic building blocks of Swift 4, its syntax, and the functionalities of basic Swift constructs. Also, this chapter will introduce you to Apple's Xcode 9 IDE and Swift Playgrounds, which provide an ideal way to create, execute, debug, and understand the recipes contained in this book, thus setting you up to initiate the development process. In this chapter, learn to write your first Swift program and understand the various basic elements of the Swift language.

Chapter 2, *Building on the Building Blocks*, teaches the reader to create more complex structures on the basis of the building blocks that you studied in the first chapter and the functionalities provided by the Swift standard library. You will get an understanding of how to bundle the variables into tuples, order the data with the help of an array, and store key-value pairs with Dictionaries. Also, you can learn to use the property observers and control the access to and visibility of your code. Then, you will also learn to extend the functionalities of your codes using the extensions.

Chapter 3, *Data Wrangling with Swift Control Flow,* says that programming is all about making decisions; therefore, this chapter explores how to make a decision on the basis of information gained and how to alter the control flow of the code. You can learn how to conditionally execute code with if/else statements, control the flow of execution of your code with switch statements, and then loop the code by understanding how to use the for and while loops. Then, you will understand how to handle Swift errors with the try, throw, do, and catch statements, and also how a defer statement can be useful to change state once a function's execution is complete or to clean up values that are no longer needed.

Chapter 4, *Generics, Operators, and Nested Types,* provides you with an understanding of two of the advanced features of Swift, which are generics and operators. Using these features, you can learn to build functionalities that are flexible and well defined, and also understand how nested types allow logical grouping, access, and namespacing for your constructs.

Chapter 5, *Beyond the Standard Library,* takes you on a journey to explore the functionalities beyond the standard library, provided by frameworks such as Foundation and UIKit. Learning to use these functionalities will help you make full use of the Swift language.

Chapter 6, *Swift Playgrounds,* gives a total understanding of using Swift Playgrounds and explores advanced features, apart from those explored in the initial chapters, to create fully interactive experiences.

Chapter 7, *Server-Side Swift,* covers a totally different aspect of Swift programming, server-side programming with Swift. Also, you can gain an understanding of how to run Swift on Linux by installing the Swift toolchain, learn to use a web server framework to build a REST API, and host your API via a hosting service. Also, you can learn to accomplish your tasks easily by understanding how to use Vapor, one of the most popular frameworks in Swift 4.

Chapter 8, *Performance and Responsiveness in Swift,* concludes the book by exploring the more advanced concepts of Swift programming to gain an understanding of how certain Swift types are implemented and their performance characteristics. Also, it explains how to perform asynchronous tasks using Grand Central Dispatch. Then, it explores the multithreaded environment available on all Apple platforms and how to enhance the performance profile of your Swift constructs to build a fast and responsive app.

What you need for this book

To follow along with the examples in this book, you will need a computer running macOS 10.12.6 or greater. You also need an Apple ID to download and install Xcode 9 from the Mac App Store. The chapter on server-side Swift also requires Ubuntu 16.04 LTS.

Who this book is for

If you are looking for a book to help you learn about the diverse features offered by Swift 4, along with tips and tricks to efficiently code and build applications, then this book is for you. Basic knowledge of Swift or general programming concepts will be beneficial.

Sections

In this book, you will find several headings that appear frequently (Getting ready, How to do it..., How it works..., There's more..., and See also). To give clear instructions on how to complete a recipe, we use these sections as follows:

Getting ready

This section tells you what to expect in the recipe, and describes how to set up any software or any preliminary settings required for the recipe.

How to do it...

This section contains the steps required to follow the recipe.

How it works...

This section usually consists of a detailed explanation of what happened in the previous section.

There's more...

This section consists of additional information about the recipe in order to make the reader more knowledgeable about the recipe.

See also

This section provides helpful links to other useful information for the recipe.

Conventions

In this book, you will find a number of text styles that distinguish between different kinds of information. Here are some examples of these styles and an explanation of their meaning. Code words in text, database table names, folder names, filenames, file extensions, pathnames, dummy URLs, user input, and Twitter handles are shown as follows:

"Next, we'll create the method that will take an `Int` and return `PoolBallType`".

A block of code is set as follows:

```
func poolBallType(forNumber number: Int) -> PoolBallType {
    if number < 8 {
        return .solid
    } else if number > 8 {
        return .stripe
    } else {
        return .black
    }
}
```

Any command-line input or output is written as follows:

```
brew install postgres
```

New terms and **important words** are shown in bold. Words that you see on the screen, for example, in menus or dialog boxes, appear in the text like this: "The repository landing page provides the structure and location of JSON configuration file under **Configure PostgreSQL**".

Warnings or important notes appear like this.

Tips and tricks appear like this.

Reader feedback

Feedback from our readers is always welcome. Let us know what you think about this book-what you liked or disliked. Reader feedback is important for us as it helps us develop titles that you will really get the most out of. To send us general feedback, simply e-mail feedback@packtpub.com, and mention the book's title in the subject of your message. If there is a topic that you have expertise in and you are interested in either writing or contributing to a book, see our author guide at www.packtpub.com/authors .

Customer support

Now that you are the proud owner of a Packt book, we have a number of things to help you to get the most from your purchase.

Downloading the example code

You can download the example code files for this book from your account at http://www.packtpub.com. If you purchased this book elsewhere, you can visit http://www.packtpub.com/support and register to have the files e-mailed directly to you. You can download the code files by following these steps:

1. Log in or register to our website using your e-mail address and password.
2. Hover the mouse pointer on the **SUPPORT** tab at the top.
3. Click on **Code Downloads & Errata**.
4. Enter the name of the book in the **Search** box.
5. Select the book for which you're looking to download the code files.
6. Choose from the drop-down menu where you purchased this book from.
7. Click on **Code Download**.

You can also download the code files by clicking on the **Code Files** button on the book's webpage at the Packt Publishing website. This page can be accessed by entering the book's name in the **Search** box. Please note that you need to be logged in to your Packt account. Once the file is downloaded, please make sure that you unzip or extract the folder using the latest version of:

- WinRAR / 7-Zip for Windows
- Zipeg / iZip / UnRarX for Mac
- 7-Zip / PeaZip for Linux

The code for the book is also hosted on GitHub at `https://github.com/PacktPublishing/Swift-4-Programming-Cookbook`. We also have other code bundles from our rich catalog of books and videos available at `https://github.com/PacktPublishing/`. Check them out!

Downloading the color images of this book

We also provide you with a PDF file that has color images of the screenshots/diagrams used in this book. The color images will help you better understand the changes in the output. You can download this file from `https://www.packtpub.com/sites/default/files/downloads/Swift4ProgrammingCookbook_ColorImages.pdf`.

Errata

Although we have taken every care to ensure the accuracy of our content, mistakes do happen. If you find a mistake in one of our books-maybe a mistake in the text or the code-we would be grateful if you could report this to us. By doing so, you can save other readers from frustration and help us improve subsequent versions of this book. If you find any errata, please report them by visiting `http://www.packtpub.com/submit-errata`, selecting your book, clicking on the **Errata Submission Form** link, and entering the details of your errata. Once your errata are verified, your submission will be accepted and the errata will be uploaded to our website or added to any list of existing errata under the Errata section of that title. To view the previously submitted errata, go to `https://www.packtpub.com/books/content/support` and enter the name of the book in the search field. The required information will appear under the **Errata** section.

Piracy

Piracy of copyrighted material on the Internet is an ongoing problem across all media. At Packt, we take the protection of our copyright and licenses very seriously. If you come across any illegal copies of our works in any form on the Internet, please provide us with the location address or website name immediately so that we can pursue a remedy. Please contact us at `copyright@packtpub.com` with a link to the suspected pirated material. We appreciate your help in protecting our authors and our ability to bring you valuable content.

Questions

If you have a problem with any aspect of this book, you can contact us at `questions@packtpub.com`, and we will do our best to address the problem.

1
Swift Building Blocks

In this chapter, we will cover the following recipes:

- Your first Swift program
- Strings, Ints, Floats, and Bools
- Optionals, unwrap, and force unwrap
- Functions
- Object classes
- Structs
- Enumerations
- Closures
- Protocols

Introduction

Since Apple announced the Swift programming language at WWDC 2014, it has gone on to become one of the fastest growing programming language. TIOBE is a company that measures software quality and publishes a ranking index of programming language usage. At the time of writing, Swift ranks the 12th most popular language on this index and has overtaken Objective-C (visit `http://www.tiobe.com/tiobe_index`).

Swift is a modern, general purpose programming language that focuses on type safety, and an expressive and concise syntax. Seen as a replacement for the aging Objective-C, its use among Mac and iOS developers has skyrocketed, ensuring its place as the future of development on Apple's platforms.

While occupying this niche would alone ensure Swift's place as a useful and important programming language. Apple's decision to open source Swift's runtime and compiler have allowed Swift's influence to extend beyond Apple's ecosystem, giving it the potential to be used across all platforms and for any scenario.

Since open sourcing the Swift toolchain, Apple has provided support for running your Swift code on Linux. In the later chapters, we will investigate using a Swift server to execute your code. In addition, the release of the Swift Playgrounds iPad app, which happened alongside iOS 10, turns your tablet into a lightweight **Integrated Development Environment (IDE)**. However, the simplest way to get up and running with Swift is still on Mac and with Apple's Xcode IDE. Therefore, this book will assume that this is also the development environment of the reader. Xcode also provides a perfect way to explore the structure and syntax of the Swift standard library, foundation, and any other framework available for iOS or Mac development in the form of its Playgrounds feature.

An **Swift Playgrounds** is a simplified environment for executing Swift code. For our purposes, Playgrounds provide an ideal way to create, execute, debug, and understand the recipes contained in this book. As such, it will also be assumed that the reader is using an Xcode Playground to implement the recipes contained in this book, unless otherwise stated.

Swift 3, released in 2016, presented a major step forward in standardizing the language syntax and, as a result, migrating code written in Swift 2 to Swift 3 was not always an easy task. Swift 4, by contrast, has been designed to be source compatible with Swift 3; therefore, the task of migrating between Swift 3 and Swift 4 should be minimal. Swift 4 has been available in a prerelease form since the beta release of Xcode 9, and will be finalized with the release of Xcode 9 and iOS 11. This book will use Swift 4 throughout, and differences from Swift 3 will be highlighted.

In this chapter, we will look at the building blocks of the Swift language, examining the syntax and functionality of the basic Swift constructs that everything else is based on.

All the code for this chapter can be found in GitHub repository at `https://github.com/SwiftProgrammingCookbook/SwiftBuildingBlocks`.

Your first Swift program

In the first recipe, we will get up and running with Swift using a Swift Playground, and we will run our first piece of Swift code.

Getting ready

To run our first Swift program, we need to download and install our IDE. During the beta of Apple's Xcode 9, it is available as a direct download from Apple's developer website at http://developer.apple.com/download, access to this beta will require a free Apple developer account. Once the beta has ended and Xcode 9 is publicly available, it will also be available from the Mac App Store. By obtaining it from the Mac App Store, you will be informed of updates automatically, so this is the preferred route once Xcode 9 is out of beta.

Downloading Xcode

Follow these steps to download Xcode from the Mac App Store:

1. Open up the Mac App Store, either from the dock or via Spotlight:

2. Search for **xcode**:

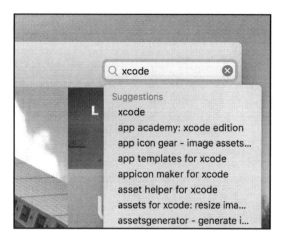

3. Click on **Install**:

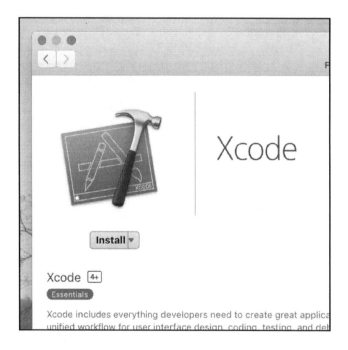

Xcode is a large download (over 4 GB). So, depending on your internet connection, this can take a while.

4. The progress can be monitored from Launchpad:

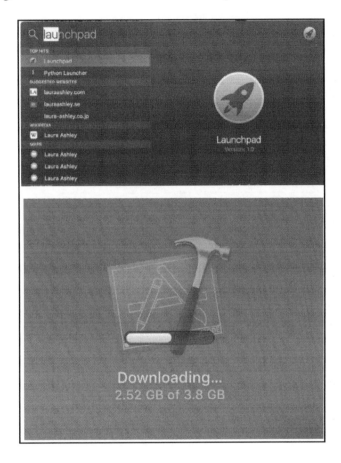

Follow these steps to get Xcode as a direct download:

1. Go to the Apple Developer download page at `http://developer.apple.com/download`:

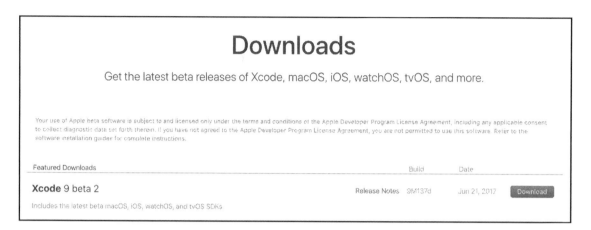

2. Click on the **Download** button to download Xcode within a `.xip` file:

3. Double-click on the downloaded file to unpack the Xcode application.

4. Drag the Xcode application into your `Applications` folder:

How to do it...

With Xcode downloaded, let's create our first Swift playground:

1. Launch Xcode from the icon in your dock.
2. From the welcome screen, choose **Get started with a playground**:

3. From the template chooser, select the **blank** template from the **iOS** tab:

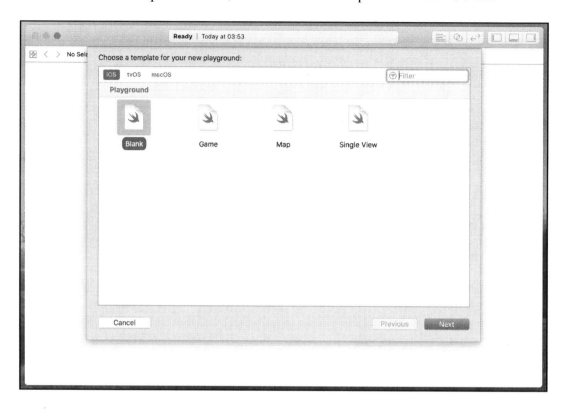

4. Choose a name for your playground and a location to save it:

 Xcode Playgrounds can be based on one of the three different Apple platforms: **iOS**, **tvOS**, and **macOS** (the operating system formerly known as **OSX**). Playgrounds provide full access to the frameworks available to either iOS, tvOS, or macOS, depending on which you choose. An iOS playground will be assumed for the entirety of this book, chiefly because this is the platform of choice of the author. Where recipes do have UI components, the iOS platform will be used until stated otherwise.

5. You are now presented with a view that looks like this:

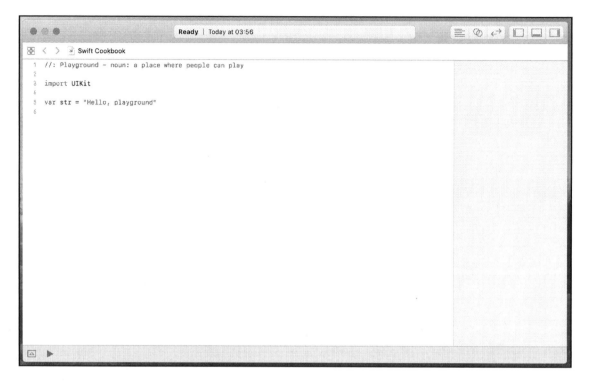

6. Let's replace the word `playground` with `Swift!`.
7. Click on the blue play icon in the bottom left-hand corner of the window to execute the code in the playground:

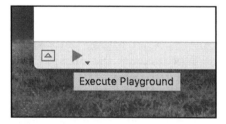

8. Congratulations! You have just run some Swift code.

9. On the right-hand side of the window, you will see the output of each line of code in the playground. We can see that our line of code has output "**Hello, Swift!**":

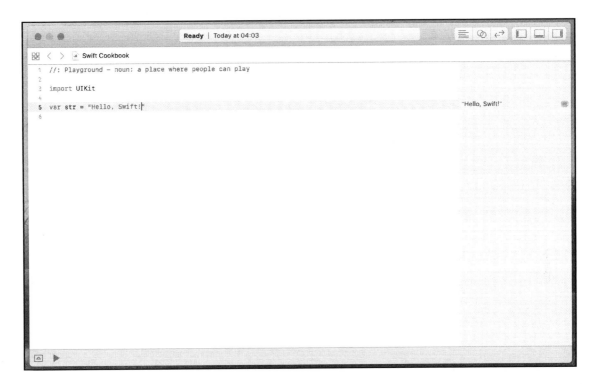

There's more...

If you put your cursor over the output on the right-hand side, you will see two buttons: one that looks like an eye and another that is a rounded square:

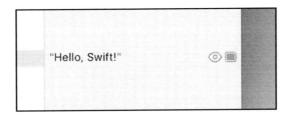

Click on the eye button to get a **Quick Look** box of the output. This isn't that useful for just a string, but can be useful for more visual output, such as colors and views:

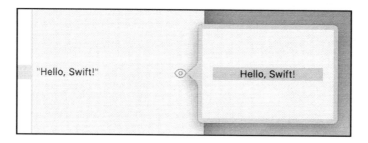

Click on the square button, and a box will be added in-line, under your code, showing the output of the code. This can be really useful if you want to see how the output changes as you change the code:

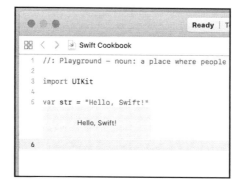

See also

We will learn more about playgrounds and how we can take them further in Chapter 6, *Swift Playgrounds*.

Strings, Ints, Floats, and Bools

Some of the most basic operations in Swift, and any programming language, involve manipulating text and numbers, and determining true/false answers.

Getting ready

Let's take a look at the basic types in Swift that enable us to perform these operations. As we do that, we will learn how to assign constants and variables, and touch on Swift's static typing and mutability system.

How to do it...

Let's execute some Swift code that explores the basic types, and then we can walk through it step by step:

1. Type the following into a new Playground file:

```swift
let phrase: String = "The quick brown fox jumps over the lazy dog"
let numberOfFoxes: Int = 1
let numberOfAnimals: Int = 2

let averageCharactersPerWord: Float = (3+5+5+3+5+4+3+4+3) / 9
print(averageCharactersPerWord) // 43

/*
phrase = "The quick brown ? jumps over the lazy ?" // Doesn't
compile
*/

var anotherPhrase = phrase
anotherPhrase = "The quick brown 🦊 jumps over the lazy 🐶"
print(phrase) // "The quick brown fox jumps over the lazy dog"
print(anotherPhrase) // "The quick brown 🦊 jumps over the lazy 🐶"

var phraseInfo = "The phrase" + " has: "
print(phraseInfo) // "The phrase has: "

phraseInfo = phraseInfo + "\(numberOfFoxes) fox and
\(numberOfAnimals) animals"
print(phraseInfo) // "The phrase has: 1 fox and 2 animals"

print("Number of characters in phrase: \(phrase.count)")

let multilineExplanation = """
Why is the following phrase often used?
"The quick brown fox jumps over the lazy dog"
This phrase contains every letter in the alphabet.
"""
```

```
let phrasesAreEqual = phrase == anotherPhrase
print(phrasesAreEqual) // false

let phraseHas43Characters = phrase.count == 40 + 3
print(phraseHas43Characters) // true
```

2. Execute the playground to verify that it compiles and runs without any errors. Your playground should look like the following screenshot, with an output for each line in the timeline on the right-hand side and printed values in the console at the bottom:

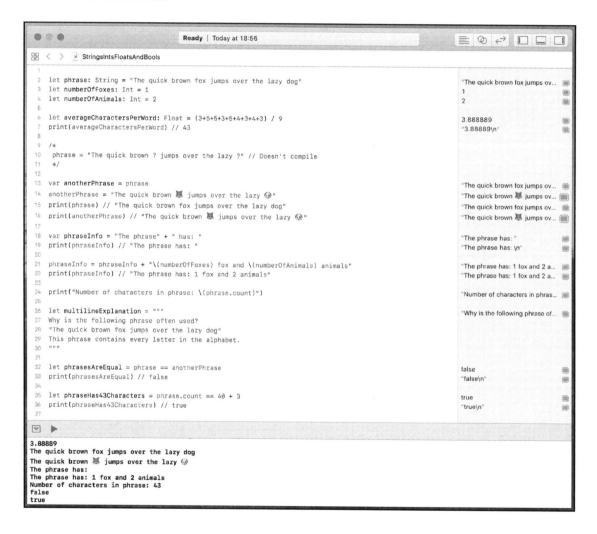

How it works...

Let's step through the preceding code line by line to understand it:

```
let phrase: String = "The quick brown fox jumps over the lazy dog"
```

We designate that we want to assign a constant by using the `let` keyword, and we give that constant a name--`phrase`. After the `:`, we define the type of constant we want to assign; in this case, we want to assign a `String` (`String` is how most programming languages refer to text). The `=` sign indicates that we are assigning a value to the constant we have defined, and `The quick brown fox jumps over the lazy dog` is a `String` literal, which means that it's an easy way to construct a string. So, we are assigning the `String` literal on the right-hand side of the `=` sign to the constant on the left-hand side of the `=` sign:

```
let numberOfFoxes: Int = 1
let numberOfAnimals: Int = 2
```

Now, we will assign some more constants, but this time they are `Int`, or integers:

```
let averageCharactersPerWord: Float = (3+5+5+3+5+4+3+4+3) / 9
```

Rather than assigning a value directly, we can assign the outcome from a mathematical expression to the constant. This constant is a `Float` or floating point number; in other words, it can store fractions rather than integers:

```
print(averageCharactersPerWord)
```

The `print` function allows us to see the output from any expression printed to the console or displayed in the playground. The playground has displayed the output of the statement as `3.88889`. The actual value of the mathematical expression we performed is `3.88888888...` with an infinite number of 8s. However, the print function has rounded this up to just five decimal places. This potential difference between the true value of a floating point number and how it's represented by the Swift language is important to remember when dealing with floats:

```
phrase = "The quick brown ? jumps over the lazy ?" // Doesn't compile
```

The playground doesn't produce an output for this line because it is commented out. The `/*` syntax before the line and the `*/` syntax after the line denote that this is a comment block, so the Swift compiler should ignore anything typed in this block.

Remove /* and */ (you'll see that // Doesn't compile is still highlighted in green; this is because // denotes that anything after this, on the same line, is also a comment); now try and run the code. The code cannot run because the compiler has detected a problem with this line, so let's look at the line to determine the issue.

On the left-hand side of the = sign, we have phrase, which we declared earlier, and now we are trying to assign a new value to it. We can't do this because we defined phrase as a constant using the let keyword. We should only use let for things we know will not change. If we want to define something that can change, we declare it as a variable using the var keyword:

```
var anotherPhrase = phrase
```

Here, we take our constant phrase and assign it to the anotherPhrase variable. This ability to define something as unchanging, or **immutable,** is an important concept in Swift, and we will revisit in the later chapters:

```
anotherPhrase = "The quick brown 🦊 jumps over the lazy 🐶"
```

Since anotherPhrase is a variable, we can assign a new value to it. Strings in Swift are fully *Unicode compliant,* so we can have some fun and use emojis instead of words:

```
print(phrase) // "The quick brown fox jumps over the lazy dog"
print(anotherPhrase) // "The quick brown 🦊 jumps over the lazy 🐶"
```

In the preceding lines, we have done the following:

- Defined a string called phrase
- Defined a string called anotherPhrase as having the same value as phrase
- Changed the value of anotherPhrase
- Printed the value of phrase and anotherPhrase

When we do this, we see that only anotherPhrase prints the new value that was assigned, even though the values of phrase and anotherPhrase were initially the same. Although phrase and anotherPhrase had the same value, they do not have an intrinsic connection; so, when anotherPhrase is assigned a new value, this does not affect phrase.

Strings can be easily combined using the + operator; this gives the expected result:

```
var phraseInfo = "The phrase" + " has: "
print(phraseInfo) // "The phrase has: "
```

You will often want to create strings by including values derived from other expressions. We can do this with String interpolation. The values inserted after \(and before) can be anything that can be represented as a string, including other Strings, Ints, Floats, or expressions:

```
phraseInfo = phraseInfo + "\(numberOfFoxes) fox and \(numberOfAnimals)
animals"
print(phraseInfo) // "The phrase has: 1 fox and 2 animals"
```

Multiline string literals can be defined using """ at the beginning and end of the string. The contents of the multiline string must be on a separate line from the start and end signifiers; there is no need to escape and use " within the string as you would need to do in a single-line string:

```
let multilineExplanation = """
Why is the following phrase often used?
"The quick brown fox jumps over the lazy dog"
This phrase contains every letter in the alphabet.
"""
```

Multiline string literals were introduced with Swift 4 and are not available in Swift 3.

Strings in Swift are collections, which are containers of elements; in this case, a string is a collection of characters. We will cover collections in more depth in a later recipe, but for now, it's enough to know that your collections can tell you how many elements they contain through their count property. We use this to output the number of characters in the phrase:

```
print("Number of characters in phrase: \(phrase.count)")
```

The concept of strings acting as collections was introduced with Swift 4. In Swift 3, you could not get a string's character count directly; instead, you could access the character array within the String and get its count property. This means that the preceding print statement would be print("Number of characters in phrase: \(phrase.characters.count)"). In Swift 4, String still has a character array, and therefore code written for Swift 3 will continue to work in Swift 4.

Boolean values represent either true or false. Here, we are assigning the result of the `phrase == anotherPhrase` equality expression to the `phrasesAreEqual` constant. The `==` operator compares the values on the left- and right-hand side of the operator:

```
let phrasesAreEqual: Bool = phrase == anotherPhrase
print(phrasesAreEqual) // false
```

As we discussed earlier, although we assigned `anotherPhrase` the value of `phrase` initially, we then assigned a new, different value to `anotherPhrase`; therefore, phrase does not equal `anotherPhrase`, and the expression assigns the Boolean value of `false`:

```
let phraseHas43Characters: Bool = phrase.characters.count == 40 + 3
print(phraseHas43Characters) // true
```

Each side of the `==` operator can be any expression that evaluates to match the type of the other side. In this case, the character count of `phrase` equals 43, so the constant is assigned the value of `true`.

There's more...

While we defined constants and variables earlier, we also defined the type of thing we are assigning to explicitly. For example, consider the following:

```
let clearlyAString: String = "This is a string literal"
```

Swift is a statically typed language, which means any constant or variable that we define has to have a specific type, which cannot be changed. However, in the preceding line, the `clearlyAString` constant is clearly a String! The right-hand side of the expression is a String literal, and therefore we know that the left-hand side will be a String. More importantly, the compiler also knows this. Swift is all about being concise, so since the type can be inferred by the compiler, we do not need to explicitly state it. Try the following instead, and see whether you can run the code:

```
let clearlyAString = "This is a string literal"
```

In fact, all the type declaration that we have made so far can be removed! So, go back through the code we have already written and remove all type declarations (`:String`, `:Int`, `:Float`, and `:Bool`), as they can all be inferred.

See also

Further information about these base types in Swift can be found in Apple's documentation of the Swift language:

- **Ints, Floats, and Bools**:

  `http://swiftbook.link/docs/the-basics`

- **Strings and characters**:

  `http://swiftbook.link/docs/strings`

Optionals, unwrap, and force unwrap

In the real world, we don't always know the answer to a problem, and problems can occur if we blindly assume that someone does. The same is true in programming languages, especially when dealing with external systems that we may not control. In many languages, including Objective-C (until recently), there was no way to indicate that something being declared may not exist at the time you attempt to access it. This would lead to either fragile code that could have broken if a `nil` unexpectedly found its way in or tests being run all over the code to ensure that a value did exist where it was needed, which added complexity and increased the boilerplate code that had to be written.

 The `nil` or `null` term is used in programming languages to denote the absence of a value, not to be confused with the number 0 as the value or the empty (zero length) string "", they would be something, this... is nothing. Swift uses `nil`, and this can be assigned to a variable to remove any value currently assigned, replacing it with nil or nothing.

With a focus on Swift being type-safe and making it easier to write safe code, this ambiguity had to be addressed, and the Swift language does this with the use of optionals.

Getting started

Enter the following into the playground:

```
var dayOfTheWeek: String = "Monday"
dayOfTheWeek = "Tuesday"
dayOfTheWeek = "Wednesday"
dayOfTheWeek = nil
```

When you try to run the code, you'll see that the compiler has raised an error and will not let you assign `nil` to the `dayOfTheWeek` variable. Quite right too--the day of the week might change, but there will never not be a current day of the week.

As we declared the type to be `String`, that is what the compiler expects, and `nil` is not a `String`, so it can't be assigned to this variable.

The same is true even if you remove the type declaration and have the compiler infer it, as we did in the preceding recipe. This is the type inferred at the point the variable is declared, and since it is being assigned a string value, the type of `String` is inferred. All other uses of this variable are checked against this inferred type of `String`.

Delete the last line, as the compiler issue will prevent us from running further code in the playground.

How to do it...

We will look at a different scenario where it is appropriate to have an optional variable. Melody and Finn are playing a game. In each round, Finn will hold his hand behind his back and choose a number of fingers to hold up, Melody will guess how many, and Finn will show her how many fingers he had chosen to hold up.

To help keep track of the game, Melody stores how many fingers Finn has held up in a variable. When Finn shows his hand, Melody can enter a value for the number of fingers, but when Finn's hands are behind his back, Melody doesn't know how many fingers Finn is holding up, and so can't store a value for how many fingers are being held up.

Let's enter the following code:

```
// Start of the game
var numberOfFingersHeldUpByFinn: Int?
// Finn's hand behind his back
numberOfFingersHeldUpByFinn = nil
// Finn shows his hand
numberOfFingersHeldUpByFinn = 3
```

```
// Finn puts hand back behind his back
numberOfFingersHeldUpByFinn = nil
// Finn shows his hand
numberOfFingersHeldUpByFinn = 1
print(numberOfFingersHeldUpByFinn)
// End of the game
let lastNumberOfFingersHeldUpByFinn: Int = numberOfFingersHeldUpByFinn!
```

Unlike the day of the week example, this code compiles without issues, despite the fact that we assign `nil` to the variable.

How it works...

We know that there will be time during the game when we don't know how many fingers are being held up, so the variable is optional--it may be an `Int` or it maybe `nil`. You will remember from earlier that `nil` does not mean `0`. It is entirely possible that the other player may be holding up zero fingers (that is, a clenched fist) as this is a valid answer. In this scenario, `nil` represents a lack of knowledge about the number of fingers. To declare this variable as optional, we define the expected type, but with an additional `?`:

```
var numberOfFingersHeldUpByFinn: Int?
```

In Swift, this is referred to as an optionally wrapped `Int`. We have wrapped the `Int` type in the concept of being optional. I am emphasizing this term **wrapping** because we will need to **unwrap** this optional type later on. At the start of the game, we don't know how many fingers are being held up, so we assign `nil` to this variable, which is allowable for optional variables:

```
numberOfFingersHeldUpByFinn = nil
```

Once Finn's hand is shown and we know how many fingers he has held up, we can assign that `Int` value to the variable:

```
numberOfFingersHeldUpByFinn = 3
```

Since the variable type is an optional `Int`, the valid values are either an `Int` or `nil`; if we try something of another type, we will get a compiler error:

```
numberOfFingersHeldUpByFinn = "three" // Doesn't compile because "three"
isn't an Int or nil
```

As we discussed earlier, Swift has a static type system, so the type of a variable can't be changed after it is declared. Therefore, although we have assigned a value of the `Int` type to the variable, this hasn't changed the variable type to the non-optional `Int`; its type remains `Int?`, an optional `Int`. Since the type is still optional, we can assign it a `nil` value when Finn puts his hands behind his back again:

```
numberOfFingersHeldUpByFinn = nil
```

When we print an optional variable, the output tells us that it is optional, for example, `Optional(1)`:

```
numberOfFingersHeldUpByFinn = 1
print(numberOfFingersHeldUpByFinn)
```

You will notice that the compiler highlights an issue that says **Expression implicitly coerced from 'Int?' to 'Any'** on the print line. We see this because we are passing an option call to the print comment, which is expecting a non-optional value. To solve this issue, we can provide a value to use if our optional value happens to be nil; there is actually a really concise way to do this. The `??` operator can be can be applied after an optional value, and the value to the right of the operator will be used if the optional value is `nil`; this is called the **nil coalescing operator**:

```
print(numberOfFingersHeldUpByFinn ?? "Unknown")
```

At the end of the game, we want to store the number of fingers that Finn held up during the last round of the game. Since we know that we will play at least one round of the game, we know that there must be a value for the last number of fingers that were held up. Therefore, we declare the `lastNumberOfFingersHeldUpByFinn` variable as a non-optional `Int`:

```
let lastNumberOfFingersHeldUpByFinn: Int = numberOfFingersHeldUpByFinn!
```

However, our `numberOfFingersHeldUpByFinn` variable is an optional `Int`. This is a problem for the compiler and the safeness and stability of our code as we would be applying a value that can be `nil` at runtime to a variable that is not allowed to be `nil`. If you remove `!` from the preceding statement, that's what we will be doing, and the compiler will complain:

```
let lastNumberOfFingersHeldUpByFinn: Int = numberOfFingersHeldUpByFinn //
Does not compile
```

To get around this issue, we need to declare that although we initially declared this variable as optional, we know there is a value assigned to it, so we want to declare that this is now non-optional, which is denoted by the `!`.

In Swift terminology, we are unwrapping the optionality of the variable. Once it is unwrapped, and therefore non-optional, we can assign it to the `lastNumberOfFingersHeldUpByFinn` variable, which is also non optional.

Beware! Use of this forced unwrapping can be risky. When you forcibly unwrap an optional, as we just did, you are declaring to the compiler that you are sure that there will be a value in that variable at that point in the execution of the code. If for some reason you don't, and the variable is nil, you will get an error at runtime and your execution will terminate. If this code is running in an app, then the app will crash. We will see safer ways to unwrap an optional value in the later chapters.

Take the counting fingers game described earlier. Imagine that we ended the game before playing the first round:

```
// Start of the game
var numberOfFingersHeldUpByFinn: Int?
// Hand behind his back
numberOfFingersHeldUpByFinn = nil
print (numberOfFingersHeldUpByFinn) // nil
// End of the game
let lastNumberOfFingersHeldUpByFinn: Int = numberOfFingersHeldUpByFinn!
```

This code will compile and run, but will crash at runtime because at the point that `numberOfFingersHeldUpByFinn` is assigned to `lastNumberOfFingersHeldUpByFinn`, the value of `numberOfFingersHeldUpByFinn` is nil.

There's more...

So far, we have seen non-optional variables, where a value of the correct type must be provided, and optional variables, where the value can either be the underlying type or nil. In a perfect world, this would be all we need. However, we may often find ourselves in the situation where we need to define a variable that we know should have a non-nil value, and, when it comes to be used, will have a value, but at the point of declaration, we don't know exactly what that value is. For these situations, we can declare a variable as an **implicitly unwrapped optional (IUO)** in Swift.

Run the following code in the playground:

```
var legalName: String!
// At birth
legalName = nil
// At birth registration
legalName = "Alissa Jones"
// At enrolling in school
print(legalName)
// At enrolling in college
print(legalName)
// Registering Marriage
legalName = "Alissa Moon"
// When meeting new people
print(legalName)
```

In this example, we have a person's legal name, which is used at many points during their life, for instance, when registering for educational institutions. It can be changed, either by legal request or through marriage, and yet you would never expect someone's legal name to not exist. However, that is exactly what happens when someone is born! When a person is born (or initialized!), they don't have a legal name until their birth is registered. So, if we were trying to model this in code, a person's legal name could be represented as an **IUO**.

In code, we declare a variable to be an IUO by placing a ! sign after the type:

```
let legalName: String!
```

 IUOs present the same risk as forced unwrapping. You are promising that, although it's possible for the variable to be `nil`, when something tries to access it, a value will be there. If there isn't, the execution will terminate and your app will crash.

There is some subtlety to how IUOs behave when they are assigned to other variables and the type is inferred. Put the following into the playground, as it's best illustrated with code:

```
var input: Int! = 5 // Int!
print(input) // 5
var output1 = input // Int?
print(output1 as Any) // Optional(5)
var output2 = input + 1 // Int
print(output2) // 5
```

When an IUO is assigned to a new variable, the compiler can't be sure that there is a non-nil value assigned. So, if an IUO is assigned to a new variable, as is the case with output1 here, the compiler plays it safe and infers that the type of this new variable is an optional. If, however, the value of the IUO has been unwrapped, then the compiler knows that it has a non-nil value, and will infer a non-optional type. When assigning output2 earlier, the value of the input is unwrapped in order to add 1 to it; therefore, the type of output2 is inferred to be the non-optional Int.

See also

Further information about **optionals** can be found in Apple's documentation of the Swift language at
https://developer.apple.com/library/ios/documentation/Swift/Conceptual/Swift_Programming_Language/TheBasics.html.

Functions

Functions are a building block of almost all programming languages, allowing functionality to be defined and reused. Swift's syntax provides an expressive way to define your functions, creating concise and readable code.

How to do it...

Let's look at how functions are defined in Swift:

```
func nameOfFunction(parameterLabel1 parameter1: ParameterType1,
parameterLabel2 parameter2: ParameterType2,...) -> OutputType {
    // Function's implementaion
    // If the function has an output type,
    // the function must return a valid value
    return output
}
```

Let's look at this in more detail to see how a function is defined:

- `func` : This indicates that you are declaring a function.
- `nameOfFunction` : This will be the name of your function, and by convention is written in camel case (this means that each word, apart from the first, is capitalized and all spaces are removed). This should describe what the function does, and should provide some context to the value returned by the function, if one is returned. This will be how you will invoke the method from elsewhere in your code, so bear that in mind when naming it.
- `parameterLabel1 parameter1: ParameterType1` : This is the first input, or parameter, into the function. You can specify as many parameters as you like, separated by commas. Each parameter has a parameter name (`parameter1`) and type (`ParameterType1`); the parameter name is how the value of the parameter will be made available to your function's implementation. You can optionally provide a parameter label in front of the parameter name (`parameterLabel1`), which will be used to label the parameter when your function is used (at the call site).
- `-> OutputType` : This indicates that the function returns a value and indicates the type of that value. If no value will be returned, this can be omitted. In the following code illustration, the curly brackets indicate the start and end of the function's implementation; anything within them will be executed when the function is called:

```
{
    // Function's implementaion
}
```

- `return output` : If the function returns a value, you type `return` and then the value to return. This ends the execution of the function; any code written after the return statement is not executed.

Now, let's put this into action.

How it works...

Imagine that we are building a contacts app to hold the details of your family and friends, and we want to create a string of a contact's full name. Let's explore some of the ways functions can be used:

```
// Input parameters and output
func fullName(givenName: String, middleName: String, familyName: String) ->
```

```
String {
    return "\(givenName) \(middleName) \(familyName)"
}
```

The preceding function takes three string parameters and outputs a string that puts all these together with spaces in between and returns the resulting string. The only thing this function does is take some inputs and produce an output without causing any side effects; this type of function is often called a **pure function**. To call this function, we enter the name of the function followed by the input parameters within `()` brackets, where each parameter value is preceded by its label:

```
let myFullName = fullName(givenName: "Keith", middleName: "David",
familyName: "Moon")
print(myFullName) // Keith David Moon
```

Since the function returns a value, we can assign the output of this function to a constant or a variable, just like any other expression:

```
// Input parameters, with a side effect and no output
func printFullName(givenName: String, middleName: String, familyName:
String) {
    print("\(givenName) \(middleName) \(familyName)")
}
```

The next function takes the same input parameters, but its goal is not to return a value. Instead, it prints out the parameters as one string separated by spaces:

```
printFullName(givenName: "Keith", middleName: "David", familyName: "Moon")
```

We can call this function in the same way as the preceding function, although it can't be assigned to anything since it doesn't have a return value:

```
// No inputs, with an output
func authorsFullName() -> String {
    return fullName(givenName: "Keith", middleName: "David", familyName:
"Moon")
}
```

The preceding function takes no parameters as everything it needs to perform its task is contained within it, although it does output a string. This function calls the `fullName` function we defined earlier, taking advantage of its ability to produce a full name when given the component names; reusing is the most useful feature that functions provide:

```
let authorOfThisBook = authorsFullName()
```

Since `authorsFullName` takes no parameters, we can execute it by entering the function name followed by empty brackets `()`, and since it returns a value, we can assign the outcome of `authorsFullName` to a variable:

```
// No inputs, no ouput
func printAuthorsFullName() {
    let author = authorsFullName()
    print(author)
}
```

Our final example takes no parameters and returns no value:

```
printAuthorsFullName()
```

You can call this function in the same way as the previous functions with no parameters, but there is no return value to assign.

As you can see from the preceding examples, having input parameters and providing an output value are not required when defining a function.

There's more...

Now, let's look at a couple of ways to make your use of functions more expressive and concise.

Default parameter values

One convenience in Swift is that you can specify default values for parameters, which allows you to omit the parameter when calling. Let's take the preceding example situation, where we are creating a contact app to hold information about our family and friends. Many of your family members are likely to have the same family name as you, so you can set your family name as the default value for that parameter so that you only need specify the family name if it is different from the default.

Let's enter the following code into a playground:

```
func fullName(givenName: String, middleName: String, familyName: String =
"Moon") -> String {
    return "\(givenName) \(middleName) \(familyName)"
}
```

Defining a default value looks similar to assigning a value to the `familyName: String = "Moon"` parameter. When calling the function, the parameter with the default value does not have to be given:

```
let keith = fullName(givenName: "Keith", middleName: "David")
let alissa = fullName(givenName: "Alissa", middleName: "May")
let laura = fullName(givenName: "Laura", middleName: "May", familyName:
"Jones")
print(keith) // Keith David Moon
print(alissa) // Alissa May Moon
print(laura)  // Laura May Jones
```

Parameter overloading

Unlike Objective-C, Swift supports parameter overloading, which allows for functions to have the same name and only be differentiated by the parameters that they take.

Let's learn more about parameter overloading by entering the following code into a playground:

```
func combine(_ givenName: String, _ familyName: String) -> String {
    return "\(givenName) \(familyName)"
}

func combine(_ integer1: Int, _ integer2: Int) -> Int {
    return integer1+integer2
}

let combinedString = combine("Finnley", "Moon")
let combinedInt = combine(5, 10)
print(combinedString) // Finnley Moon
print(combinedInt) // 15
```

Both the preceding functions have the name `combine`, but one takes two **Strings** as parameters and the other takes two **Ints**. Therefore, when we come to call the function, the compiler knows which implementation we intended by the values we pass as parameters.

We've introduced something new in the preceding function declarations--anonymous parameter labels, `_ givenName: String`.

When we declare the parameters, we use an underscore _ for the parameter label; this indicates that we don't want a parameter name shown when calling the function. This should only be used if the purpose of the parameters is clear without the labels, as is the case in the preceding example--`combine("Finnley", "Moon")`.

See also

Further information about functions can be found in Apple's documentation of the Swift language at `http://swiftbook.link/docs/functions`.

Object classes

Object-oriented programming is currently the dominant programming paradigm. At the core of this paradigm is the *object class*. Objects allow us to encapsulate data and functionality, which can then be stored and passed around.

Getting ready

Let's build some class objects. Then, we'll break down the components of the class to understand how it is defined and used.

How to do it...

Let's start by entering the following code into the playground:

```swift
class Person {
    let givenName: String
    let middleName: String
    let familyName: String
    var countryOfResidence: String = "UK"
    init(givenName: String, middleName: String, familyName: String) {
        self.givenName = givenName
        self.middleName = middleName
        self.familyName = familyName
    }
    var displayString: String {
        return "\(fullName()) - Location: \(countryOfResidence)"
    }
    func fullName() -> String {
        return "\(givenName) \(middleName) \(familyName)"
    }
}

final class Friend: Person {
    var whereWeMet: String?
    override var displayString: String {
```

```
            return "\(super.displayString) - \(whereWeMet ?? "Don't know where
    we met")"
        }
    }

    final class Family: Person {
        let relationship: String
        init(givenName: String, middleName: String, familyName: String =
    "Moon",
        relationship: String) {
            self.relationship = relationship
            super.init(givenName: givenName, middleName: middleName,
    familyName:
            familyName)
        }
        override var displayString: String {
            return "\(super.displayString) - \(relationship)"
        }
    }

    let steve = Person(givenName: "Steven", middleName: "Paul", familyName:
    "Jobs")
    let dan = Friend(givenName: "Daniel", middleName: "James", familyName:
    "Woodel")
    dan.whereWeMet = "Worked together at BBC News"
    let finnley = Family(givenName: "Finnley", middleName: "David",
    relationship: "Son")
    let dave = Family(givenName: "Dave", middleName: "deRidder", familyName:
    "Jones", relationship: "Father-In-Law")
    dave.countryOfResidence = "US"

    print(steve.displayString) // Steven Paul Jobs
    print(dan.displayString) // Daniel James Woodel - Worked together at BBC
    News
    print(finnley.displayString) // Finnley David Moon - Son
```

How it works...

Classes are defined with the `class` keyword, class names start with a capital letter by convention, and the implementation of the class is contained, or "scoped", within curly brackets:

```
class Person {
    //...
}
```

An object can have property values, which are contained within the object. These properties can have initial values, as `countryOfResidence` does in the following code, although bear in mind that constants (defined with `let`) cannot be changed once the initial value has been set:

```
class Person {
    let givenName: String
    let middleName: String
    let familyName: String
    var countryOfResidence: String = "UK"
    //...
}
```

If your class were to just have the preceding property definitions, the compiler would raise a warning, as `givenName`, `middleName`, and `familyName` are defined as non-optional strings, but we have not provided any way to populate those values.

The compiler needs to know how the object will be initialized, so that we can be sure that all the non-optional properties will indeed have values:

```
class Person {
    let givenName: String
    let middleName: String
    let familyName: String
    var countryOfResidence: String = "UK"
    init(givenName: String, middleName: String, familyName: String) {
        self.givenName = givenName
        self.middleName = middleName
        self.familyName = familyName
    }
    //...
}
```

The `init` is a special method (functions defined within objects are called methods) that's called when the object is initialized. In the `Person` object of the preceding code, we expect `givenName`, `middleName`, and `familyName` to be passed in when the object is initialized, and we assign those provided values to the object's properties. The `self.` prefix is used to differentiate between the property and the value passed in as they have the same name.

We do not need to pass in a value for `countryOfResidence` as we defined an initial value when the property was defined. This isn't ideal, though, as when we initialize a `Person` object, it will always have the `countryOfResidence` variable set to `"UK"`, and we will have to change that value after initializing. Another way to do this would be to use a default parameter value, as seen in the previous recipe. Amend the `Person` object initialization to the following:

```
class Person {
    let givenName: String
    let middleName: String
    let familyName: String
    var countryOfResidence: String
    init(givenName: String, middleName: String, familyName: String,
countryOfResidence:
      String = "UK") {
        self.givenName = givenName
        self.middleName = middleName
        self.familyName = familyName
        self.countryOfResidence = countryOfResidence
    }
    //...
}
```

Now, you can provide a country of residence in the initialization or omit it to use the default value:

```
class Person {
    //...
    var displayString: String {
        return "\(fullName()) - Location: \(countryOfResidence)"
    }
    //...
}
```

The property declaration for displayString is different from the others. Rather than having a value assigned to it, it is followed by an expression contained within curly braces. This is a computed property; its value is not static, but is determined by the given expression every time the property is accessed. Any valid expressions can be used to compute the property, but must return a value that matches the property type that is declared. The compiler will enforce this, and you can't omit the variable type for computed properties.

Since the value of the property is determined at the time of access, it follows that computed properties are read-only:

```
class Person {
    //...
    func fullName() -> String {
        return "\(givenName) \(middleName) \(familyName))"
    }
    //...
}
```

Objects can do work based on the information they contain, and this work can be defined in methods. Methods are just functions that are contained within classes and have access to all the object's properties. All the abilities of a function are available, which we explored in the last recipe, including optional inputs and outputs, default parameter values, and parameter overloading:

```
final class Friend: Person {
    var whereWeMet: String?
    //...
}
```

Having defined a `Person` object, we want to extend the concept of `Person` to define a friend. A friend is also a person, so it stands to reason that anything a `Person` object can do, a `Friend` object can also do. We model this inherited behavior by defining `Friend` as a subclass of `Person`. We define the class that our `Friend` class inherits from after the class name, separated by `:`.

By inheriting from `Person`, our `Friend` object inherits all the properties and methods from its superclass. We can add any extra functionality we require--in this case, a property holding details of where we met this friend.

The `final` prefix tells the compiler that we don't intend for this class to be subclassed; it is the final class in the inheritance hierarchy. This allows the compiler to make some optimizations as we know it won't be extended:

```
final class Friend: Person {
    //...
    override var displayString: String {
        return "\(super.displayString) - \(whereWeMet ?? "Don't know where
we met")"
    }
}
```

In addition to implementing new functionalities, we can override functionalities from the superclass using the `override` keyword. In the preceding code, we override the `displayString` computed property from `Person` as we want to add the `"where we met"` information. Within the computed property, we want to get the superclass's implementation; we do this by referencing `super` and `.`, and then referencing the property. We can do the same to access the superclass's methods:

```
final class Family: Person {
    let relationship: String
    init(givenName: String, middleName: String, familyName: String =
"Moon", relationship: String) {
        self.relationship = relationship
```

```
        super.init(givenName: givenName, middleName: middleName,
familyName: familyName)
    }
    //...
}
```

Our `Family` class also inherits from `Person`, and we want to add a `relationship` property, which we want to form part of the initialization, so we can declare a new `init` that also takes a relationship value.

There's more...

Class objects are **reference types** that refer to the way they are stored and referenced internally. To see how these reference type semantics work, consider the following code:

```
class MovieReview {
    let movieTitle: String
    var starRating: Int // Rating out of 5
    init(movieTitle: String, starRating: Int) {
        self.movieTitle = movieTitle
        self.starRating = starRating
    }
}

// Write a review
let shawshankReviewOnYourWebsite = MovieReview(movieTitle: "Shawshank
Redemption", starRating: 3)

// Post it to social media
let reviewLinkOnTwitter = shawshankReviewOnYourWebsite
let reviewLinkOnFacebook = shawshankReviewOnYourWebsite

print(reviewLinkOnTwitter.starRating) // 3
print(reviewLinkOnFacebook.starRating) // 3

// Reconsider my review
shawshankReviewOnYourWebsite.starRating = 5

// The change visible from anywhere with a reference to the object
print(reviewLinkOnTwitter.starRating) // 5
print(reviewLinkOnFacebook.starRating) // 5
```

We created a review object and assigned that review to two separate constants. As an object is a reference type, it is a reference to the object that is stored in the constant, rather than a new copy of the object. Therefore, when we reconsider our review and rightly give *The Shawshank Redemption* five stars, we are changing the underlying object, and all references that access that underlying object will see that the starRating property has changed.

See also

- Further information about classes can be found in Apple's documentation of the Swift language at http://swiftbook.link/docs/classes-and-structures.

- In Chapter 8, *Performance and Responsiveness in Swift*, we will examine reference semantics in more detail, and see how it affects performance.

Structs

Objects are great for encapsulating data and functionality behind a unifying and referenceable concept, such as a person. However, not everything is an object; we may have a set of data that is logically grouped together, but that isn't much more than that. It's not more than the sum of its parts--it is the sum of its parts.

For this, there are structs. Short for structure, structs can be found in the C programming language and were, therefore, available in Objective-C, which was built on top of C. If you are familiar with iOS/macOS development, CGRect is an example of a C struct.

Structs are **value types**, as opposed to classes, which are reference types, and as such behave differently when passed around. In this recipe, we will examine how structs work in Swift, and learn when and how to use them.

Getting ready

This recipe will build on top of the previous recipes, so open the playground you have used for the previous recipes. Don't worry if you haven't tried out the previous recipes; this one will contain all the code you need.

How to do it...

We have already defined a `Person` object as having three separate string properties relating to the person's name; however, these three separate strings don't exist in isolation from each other--they together define a person's name. Currently, to get a person's name, you have to access three separate properties and combine them. Let's tidy this up by defining a person's name as its own `struct`. Enter the following code into the playground and run the playground:

```swift
struct PersonName {
    let givenName: String
    let middleName: String
    var familyName: String
    func fullName() -> String {
        return "\(givenName) \(middleName) \(familyName)"
    }
    mutating func change(familyName: String) {
        self.familyName = familyName
    }
}
var alissasName = PersonName(givenName: "Alissa", middleName: "May",
familyName: "Jones")
```

How it works...

Defining a struct is very similar to defining an object class, and that is intentional. Much of the functionality available to a class is also available to a struct.

Within the `PersonName` struct, we have properties for the three components of the name and the `fullName` method we saw earlier to combine the three name components into a full name string.

Next, we have a method to change the family name property, which is why we defined the familyName property as a var variable instead of a let constant. This method assigns a new value to a property of the struct; it is **mutating**, or changing, the struct, and therefore needs to be marked with the mutating keyword. This keyword is enforced by the compiler to remind us that when we mutate a struct, a new copy of the original struct is created with the new value. This is known as **value-type semantics**.

To see this in action, consider the following code:

```
let alissasBirthName = PersonName(givenName: "Alissa", middleName: "May",
familyName: "Jones")
print(alissasName.fullName()) // Alissa May Jones
var alissasCurrentName = alissasBirthName
print(alissasName.fullName()) // Alissa May Jones
```

So far, so good. We have created a PersonName struct and assigned it to a constant called alissasBirthName and a variable called alissasCurrentName.

When we change or "mutate" the alissasCurrentName variable, only this variable is changed; alissasBirthName is a copy, and so it doesn't have the amended family name, even though they were assigned from the same source:

```
alissasCurrentName.change(familyName: "Moon")
print(alissasBirthName.fullName()) // Alissa May Jones
print(alissasCurrentName.fullName()) // Alissa May Moon
```

There's more...

Now that we have a PersonName struct, let's amend our Person class so that it can use it:

```
class Person {
    let birthName: PersonName
    var currentName: PersonName
    var countryOfResidence: String
    init(name: PersonName, countryOfResidence: String = "UK") {
        birthName = name
        currentName = name
        self.countryOfResidence = countryOfResidence
    }
    var displayString: String {
        return "\(currentName.fullName()) - Location:
\(countryOfResidence)"
    }
}
```

We've added the `birthName` and `currentName` properties of our new `PersonName` struct type, and we initiate them with the same value when the `Person` object is initiated. Since a person's birth name won't change, we define it as a constant, but their current name can change, so it's defined as a variable.

Now, let's create a new `Person` object:

```
var name = PersonName(givenName: "Alissa", middleName: "May", familyName:
"Jones")
let alissa = Person(name: name)
print(alissa.currentName.fullName()) // Alissa May Jones
```

Since our `PersonName` struct has value semantics, we can use this to enforce the behavior that we expect our model to have. We would expect to not be able to change a person's birth name, and if you try, you will find that the compiler won't let you.

As we discussed earlier, changing the family name mutates the struct, and so a new copy is made. However, we defined `birthName` as a constant, which can't be changed, so the only way we would be able to change the family name would be to change our definition of `birthName` from `let` to `var`:

```
alissa.birthName.change(familyName: "Moon") // Does not compile. Compiler
tells you to change let to var
```

When we change the `currentName` to have a new family name, which we can do, since we defined it as a `var`, it changes the `currentName` property, but not the `birthName` property, even though these were assigned from the same source:

```
print(alissa.birthName.fullName()) // Alissa May Jones
print(alissa.currentName.fullName()) // Alissa May Jones
alissa.currentName.change(familyName: "Moon")
print(alissa.birthName.fullName()) // Alissa May Jones
print(alissa.currentName.fullName()) // Alissa May Moon
```

We have used a combination of objects and structs to create a model that enforces our expected behavior.

See also

- Further information about structs can be found in Apple's documentation of the Swift language at `http://swiftbook.link/docs/classes-and-structures`.

- In Chapter 8, *Performance and Responsiveness in Swift*, we will examine value semantics in more detail, and see how it affects performance.

Enumerations

Enumerations are a programming construct that let you define a value type with a finite set of options. Most languages have enumerations (usually abbreviated to **enums**), including C and, by extension, Objective-C.

An example of an enum from the iOS/macOS SDK is NSComparisonResult, which you would use when sorting items. When comparing for the purposes of sorting, there are only three possible results from a comparison:

- ascending : The items are ordered in ascending order
- descending : The items are ordered in descending order
- same : The items are the same

There are a finite number of possible options for a comparison result; therefore, it's a perfect candidate for being represented by an enum:

```
enum ComparisonResult : Int {
    case orderedAscending
    case orderedSame
    case orderedDescending
}
```

Swift takes the enum concept and elevates it to a first class type. As we will see, this makes enums a very powerful tool for modeling your information.

This recipe will examine how and when to use enums in Swift.

Getting ready

This recipe will build on top of the earlier recipes, so open the playground you have used for the previous recipes. Don't worry if you haven't tried out the previous recipes; this one will contain all the code you need.

How to do it...

Earlier, we created a `Person` object to represent people in our model and a `PersonName` struct to hold information about a person's name. Now, let's turn our attention to a person's title, for example, Mr., Mrs., and so on, which precede someone's full name. There are a small and finite number of common titles that a person may have; therefore, an `enum` is a great way to model this information.

Enter the following into the playground:

```
enum Title {
    case mr
    case mrs
    case mister
    case miss
    case dr
    case prof
    case other
}
```

We define our enumeration with the `enum` keyword and provide a name for the enum. As with classes and structs, the convention is that this starts with a capital letter, and the implementation is defined within curly brackets. We define each enum option with the `case` keyword, and the convention since Swift 3 is that these start with a lowercase character. Now that we have defined our enum, let's see how to assign it:

```
let title1 = Title.mr
```

Enums can be assigned by specifying the enum type, then a dot, and then the case. However, if the compiler can infer the enum type, we can omit the type and just provide the case, preceded by a dot:

```
let title2: Title
title2 = .mr
```

How it works...

When used in C and Objective-C, enums are defined as a type definition on top of an integer, with each case being given a defined integer value. In Swift, enums do not need to represent integers under the hood; in fact, they do not need to be backed by any type, and can exist as their own abstract concepts. Consider the following example:

```
enum CompassPoint {
    case North, South, East, West
```

```
    }
```

Note that we can define multiple cases on the same line by separating them with commas.

For `Title`, an integer-based enum doesn't seem appropriate; however, a string-based one may be. So, let's declare our enum to be string based:

```
enum Title: String {
    case mr = "Mr"
    case mrs = "Mrs"
    case mister = "Master"
    case miss = "Miss"
    case dr = "Dr"
    case prof = "Prof"
    case other // Inferred as "other"
}
```

The enum's raw type is declared after its name and a `:` separator. The raw types that can be used to back the enum are limited to types that can be represented as a literal; this includes Swift base types--`String`, `Int`, `Float`, and `Bool`.

These types can be used to back an enum because they conform to a protocol, called `RawRepresentable`. We will cover protocols later in the chapter.

Cases can be assigned a value of the raw type; however, certain types can be inferred, and so do not need to be explicitly declared. For Int-backed enums, the inferred values are sequentially assigned starting at `0`:

```
enum Rating: Int {
    case worst   // Infered as 0
    case bad     // Infered as 1
    case average // Infered as 2
    case good    // Infered as 3
    case best    // Infered as 4
}
```

For string-based enums, the inferred value is the name of the case, so the `other` case in our `Title` enum is inferred to be other.

We can get the underlying value of the enum in its raw type by accessing its `rawValue` property:

```
let title1 = Title.mr
print(title1.rawValue) // "Mr"
```

There's more...

As I mentioned in the introduction to this recipe, Swift treats enums as a first-class type, and therefore they can have functionalities that are not available to enums in most programming languages. These functionalities include having computed variables and methods.

Methods and computed variables

Say that it is important for us to know whether a person's title relates to a professional qualification that the person holds. Let's add a method to our enum to provide that information:

```
enum Title: String {
    case mr = "Mr"
    case mrs = "Mrs"
    case mister = "Master"
    case miss = "Miss"
    case dr = "Dr"
    case prof = "Prof"
    case other // Inferred as "other"
    func isProfessional() -> Bool {
        return self == Title.dr || self == Title.prof
    }
}
```

For the list of titles that we have defined, `Dr` and `Prof` relate to professional qualifications, so we have our method return `true` if self (the instance of the enum type this method is called on) is equal to the `dr` case, or equal to the `prof` case.

This functionality feels more appropriate as a computed property since whether it `isProfessional` or not is intrinsic to the enum itself, and we don't need to do much work to determine the answer. So, let's change this into a property:

```
enum Title: String {
    case mr = "Mr"
    case mrs = "Mrs"
```

```
        case mister = "Master"
        case miss = "Miss"
        case dr = "Dr"
        case prof = "Prof"
        case other // Inferred as "other"
        var isProfessional: Bool {
            return self == Title.dr || self == Title.prof
        }
    }
```

Now, we can determine whether a title is a professional title by accessing the computed property on it:

```
let loganTitle = Title.mr
let xavierTitle = Title.prof
print(loganTitle.isProfessional) // false
print(xavierTitle.isProfessional) // true
```

We can't store new information on an enum, but being able to define methods and computed properties that provide extra information about the enum is really powerful.

Associated values

Our string-based enum seems perfect for our title information, except that we have a case called other. If the person has a title that we hadn't considered when defining the enum, we can select other, but that doesn't capture what the other title is. We will need to define a whole other property to hold the value of the other title, but there would be nothing to force it to be used when the other case is selected, and nothing to stop it from being used when a different Title case is selected.

Swift enums have a solution for this situation--**associated values**; we can choose to associate a value with each enum case, allowing us to bind a non-optional string to our other case.

Let's rewrite our Title enum to use an associated value:

```
enum Title {
    case mr
    case mrs
    case mister
    case miss
    case dr
    case prof
    case other(String)
}
```

We have defined the `other` case to have an associated value by putting the value's type in brackets after the case declaration. We do not need to add associated values wholesale to every case; other case declarations can have associated values of a different type, or none at all.

 Enums containing associated values cannot have a raw type as they are now too complex to be represented by one of these base types, so our `Title` enum is no longer string-based.

Let's look at how we assign an enum case with an associated type:

```
let mister: Title = .mr
let dame: Title = .other("Dame")
```

The associated value is declared in brackets after the case, and the compiler enforces that the type matches the type declared in our enum definition. As we declared the `other` case to have a non-optional string, we are ensuring that a title of `other` cannot be selected without providing details of what the other title is, and we don't have an unneeded property hanging around when anything else is selected.

See also

Further information about enums can be found in Apple's documentation of the Swift language at `http://swiftbook.link/docs/enums`.

Closures

Closures are also referred to as **anonymous functions**, and this is the best way to explain them. Closures are functions that optionally take a set of input parameters, and they optionally return an output, the same as other functions. However, rather than having a function name, closures behave like other primary types--they can be assigned, stored, passed around, and used as the input and output to functions and other closures.

Getting ready

We will continue to build on our contacts app example from earlier in this chapter, so you should use the same playground as in the previous recipes. Don't worry if you haven't followed the previous recipes; all the code needed is listed here, so you can enter this in a new playground.

How to do it...

If you are implementing this in a new playground, enter the following:

```swift
struct PersonName {
    let givenName: String
    let middleName: String
    var familyName: String
    func fullName() -> String {
        return "\(givenName) \(middleName) \(familyName)"
    }
    mutating func change(familyName: String) {
        self.familyName = familyName
    }
}

class Person {
    let birthName: PersonName
    var currentName: PersonName
    var countryOfResidence: String
    init(name: PersonName, countryOfResidence: String = "UK") {
        birthName = name
        currentName = name
        self.countryOfResidence = countryOfResidence
    }
    var displayString: String {
        return "\(currentName.fullName()) - Location:
\(countryOfResidence)"
    }
}
```

You will need to go back over the previous recipes to see how these were created.

Now, let's put a number of closure types in the playground so we examine them:

```
// No input, no output
let printAuthorsDetails: () -> Void = {
    let name = PersonName(givenName: "Keith", middleName: "David",
familyName: "Moon")
    let author = Person(name: name)
    print(author.displayString)
}
printAuthorsDetails() // "Keith David Moon - Location: UK"

// No input, Person output
let createAuthor: () -> Person = {
    let name = PersonName(givenName: "Keith", middleName: "David",
familyName: "Moon")
    let author = Person(name: name)
    return author
}
let author = createAuthor()
print(author.displayString) // "Keith David Moon - Location: UK"

// String inputs, no output
let printPersonsDetails: (String, String, String) -> Void = { givenName,
middleName, familyName in
    let name = PersonName(givenName: givenName, middleName: middleName,
familyName: familyName)
    let author = Person(name: name)
    print(author.displayString)
}
printPersonsDetails("Kathyleen", "Mary", "Moon") // "Kathleen Mary Moon -
Location: UK"

// String inputs, Person output
let createPerson: (String, String, String) -> Person = { givenName,
middleName, familyName in
    let name = PersonName(givenName: givenName, middleName: middleName,
familyName: familyName)
    let person = Person(name: name)
    return person
}
let melody = createPerson("Melody", "Margaret", "Moon")
print(melody.displayString) // "Melody Margaret Moon - Location: UK"
```

How it works...

Let's take a look at the different types of closures we just implemented:

```
// No input, no output
let printAuthorsDetails: () -> Void = {
    let name = PersonName(givenName: "Keith", middleName: "David",
familyName: "Moon")
    let author = Person(name: name)
    print(author.displayString)
}
```

As a first-class type in Swift, closures can be assigned to constants or variables, and constants and variables need a type. To define a closure's type, we need to specify the input parameter types and the output type, and for the closure in the preceding code, the type is `() -> Void`. The `Void` type is another way of saying nothing, so this closure takes no inputs and returns nothing, and the closure's functionality is defined within the curly brackets, as with other functions.

Now that we have this closure defined and assigned to the `printAuthorsDetails` constant, we can execute it as follows, which will cause this author's details to be printed:

```
printAuthorsDetails() // "Keith David Moon - Location: UK"
```

The next closure type takes no input parameters, but returns a `Person` object, as you can see with the `() -> Person` type definition:

```
// No input, Person output
let createAuthor: () -> Person = {
    let name = PersonName(givenName: "Keith", middleName: "David",
familyName: "Moon")
    let author = Person(name: name)
    return author
}
let author: Person = createAuthor()
print(author.displayString) // "Keith David Moon - Location: UK"
```

Since it has an output, the execution of the closure returns a value and can be assigned to a variable or constant. In the preceding code, we execute the `createAuthor` closure and assign the output to the `author` constant. Since we defined the closure type as `() -> Person`, the compiler knows that the output type is a `Person` and therefore the type of the constant can be inferred, so we don't need to explicitly declare it. Let's remove the explicit type declaration:

```
let author = createAuthor()
print(author.displayString) // "Keith David Moon - Location: UK"
```

Next, let's take a look at a closure that takes input parameters:

```
// String inputs, no output
let printPersonsDetails: (String, String, String) -> Void = { given,
middle, family in
    let name = PersonName(givenName: given, middleName: middle, familyName:
family)
    let author = Person(name: name)
    print(author.displayString)
}
printPersonsDetails("Kathleen", "Mary", "Moon") // "Kathleen Mary Moon -
Location: UK"
```

You will remember, from the recipe on functions, that we can define parameter labels, which define how the parameters are referenced when the function is used, and parameter names, which define how the parameter is referenced from within the function. In closures, these are defined a bit differently:

- Parameter labels cannot be defined for closures, so, when calling a closure, the order and parameter type have to be used to determine what values should be provided as parameters:

  ```
  (String, String, String) -> Void
  ```

- Parameter names are defined inside the curly brackets, followed by the `in` keyword:

  ```
  given, middle, family in
  ```

Putting it all together, we can define and execute a closure with inputs and an output, as follows:

```
// String inputs, Person output
let createPerson: (String, String, String) -> Person = { given, middle,
family in
    let name = PersonName(givenName: given, middleName: middle, familyName:
family)
    let person = Person(name: name)
    return person
}
let melody = createPerson("Melody", "Margaret", "Moon")
print(melody.displayString) // "Melody Margaret Moon - Location: UK"
```

There's more...

We've seen how we can store closures, but we can also use them as method parameters. This pattern can be really useful when we want to be notified when a long-running task is completed.

Let's imagine that we want to save the details of our `person` object to a remote database, maybe for backup or use on other devices. We'll amend our `Person` class to include this save functionality, and in the process, see how we can pass in a closure, store it, and execute it at a later time.

Add the following code to our `Person` class:

```
class Person {
    //....
    var saveHandler: ((Bool) -> Void)?
    func saveToRemoteDatabase(handler: @escaping (Bool) -> Void) {
        saveHandler = handler
        // Send person information to remove database
        // Once remote save is complete, it calls saveComplete(Bool)
    }
    func saveComplete(success: Bool) {
        saveHandler?(success)
    }
}
```

We define an optional variable to hold onto the save handler during the long-running save operation. Our closure will take a `Bool` to indicate whether the save was a success:

```
var saveHandler: ((Bool) -> Void)?
```

Let's define a method to save our `Person` object, which takes a closure as a parameter:

```
func saveToRemoteDatabase(handler: @escaping (Bool) -> Void) {
    saveHandler = handler
    // Send person information to remove database
    // Once remote save is complete, it calls saveComplete(Bool)
}
```

Our function stores the given closure in the variable, and then starts the process to save to the remote database (the actual implementation of this is outside the scope of this recipe). This save process will call the `saveComplete` method when completed. We added a modifier, `@escaping`, just before the closure type definition. This tells the compiler that, rather than using the closure within this method, we intend to store the closure and use it later. The closure will be *escaping* the scope of this method. This modifier is needed to prevent the compiler from doing certain optimizations that would be possible if the closure was *nonescaping*.

With the save operation complete, we can execute the `saveHandler` variable, passing in the success boolean. However, since we stored the closure as optional, we need to unwrap it by adding a `?` after the variable name. If `saveHandler` has a value, the closure will be executed; if it is `nil`, the expression is ignored:

```
func saveComplete(success: Bool) {
    saveHandler?(success)
}
```

Now that we have a function that takes a closure, let's see how we call it:

```
let dave = createPerson("David", "Ernest", "Moon")
dave.saveToRemoteDatabase(handler: { success in
    print("Saved finished. Successful: \(success))")
})
```

Swift provides a more concise way to provide closures to functions. When a closure is the last (or only) parameter, Swift allows it to be provided as a **trailing closure**--that is, the parameter name can be dropped and the closure can be specified after the parameter brackets. So we can, instead, do the following:

```
dave.saveToRemoteDatabase { success in
    print("Saved finished. Successful: \(success))")
}
```

See also

Further information about closures can be found in Apple's documentation of the Swift language at `http://swiftbook.link/docs/closures`.

Protocols

Protocols are a way to describe the interface that a type provides; they can be thought of as a contract, defining how you can interact with instances of that type. They are a great way to abstract the "what" something does from "how" it does it. As we will see in the subsequent chapters, Swift adds functionalities to protocols, which make them even more useful and powerful.

Getting ready

We will continue to build on examples from the previous recipes, but don't worry if you haven't followed these yet as all the code you need is listed in the upcoming sections.

How to do it...

In the last recipe, we added a method to our `Person` class to save it to a remote database. This is a very useful functionality, and as we add more and more features to our app, we will likely have more types where we will want to save instances of that type to a remote database. Let's create a protocol to define how we will interface with anything that can be saved in this way:

```
protocol Saveable {
    var saveNeeded: Bool { get set }
    func saveToRemoteDatabase(handler: @escaping (Bool) -> Void)
}
```

How it works...

Protocols are defined with the `protocol` keyword, and the implementation is contained within curly brackets. It is conventional to begin a protocol name with a capital letter, and to name a protocol as either something that the type **is** or something that it **does**; in this protocol, we are declaring that any type implementing it is **saveable.**

Types implementing this protocol have two parts of the interface to implement.

The `Saveable` protocol declares that anything implementing it needs to have a variable called `saveNeeded`, which is a `Bool`. This property will indicate that the information held in the remote database is out of date and a save is needed. In addition to the usual property declaration, a protocol requires us to define whether the property can be accessed (`get`) and changed (`set`), which is added in curly brackets after the type declaration. Removing the set keywords makes it a read-only variable. Consider the given example:

```
var saveNeeded: Bool { get set }
```

 Defining a protocol property as read-only doesn't prevent an implementing type from allowing the property to be set, just that the setting of that property isn't defined in the interface.

The second part of our protocol definition is to describe the method we can call to save the information to the remote database. This `func` declaration is exactly the same as other function declarations we have seen; however, the implementation of the function, usually contained in the curly brackets, is omitted as this is provided by the implementing type:

```
func saveToRemoteDatabase(handler: @escaping (Bool) -> Void)
```

Now that we have defined our protocol, we need to implement the `Saveable` protocol on our `Person` class that we have been using throughout this chapter:

```
class Person: Saveable {
    //....
    var saveHandler: ((Bool) -> Void)?
    func saveToRemoteDatabase(handler: @escaping (Bool) -> Void) {
        saveHandler = handler
        // Send person information to remove database
        // Once remote save is complete, it calls saveComplete(Bool)
    }
    func saveComplete(success: Bool) {
        saveHandler?(success)
    }
}
```

We conform to a protocol, and in a similar way, we declare that an object inherits from another object, by adding the protocol name after the type name, separated by `:`. By adding this conformance, the compiler will complain that our `Person` object doesn't implement part of the protocol as we haven't declared a `saveNeeded` property, so let's add that:

```
class Person: Saveable {
    //....
    var saveHandler: ((Bool) -> Void)?
```

```
    var saveNeeded: Bool = true
    func saveToRemoteDatabase(handler: @escaping (Bool) -> Void) {
        saveHandler = handler
        // Send person information to remove database
        // Once remote save is complete, it calls saveComplete(Bool)
    }
    func saveComplete(success: Bool) {
        saveHandler?(success)
    }
}
```

We'll add a default value of true since when an instance of this object is created, it won't be in the remote database, and so it will need saving.

There's more...

Protocol conformance can be applied to classes, structs, enums, and even other protocols, allowing an instance to be stored and passed without needing to know how it's implemented under the hood. This provides many benefits, including testing using mock objects and changing implementations without changing how and where the implementations are used.

Let's add a feature to our app that lets us set a reminder for a contact's birthday, which we will also want to save to our remote database.

We can use class inheritance to give our reminder the save functionality, but a reminder should not have the same features and functionality as a person, and our process for saving a reminder may be different to that used for a person.

Instead, we can create our Reminder object and have it conform to the Saveable protocol:

```
class Reminder: Saveable {
    var dateOfReminder: String // There is a better to store dates, but
this suffice currently.
    var reminderDetail: String // eg. Alissa's birthday
    init(date: String, detail: String) {
        dateOfReminder = date
        reminderDetail = detail
    }
    var saveHandler: ((Bool) -> Void)?
    var saveNeeded: Bool = true
    func saveToRemoteDatabase(handler: @escaping (Bool) -> Void) {
        saveHandler = handler
        // Send reminder information to remove database
        // Once remote save is complete, it calls saveComplete(success:
```

```
Bool)
    }
    func saveComplete(success: Bool) {
        saveHandler?(success)
    }
}
```

Our `Reminder` object conforms to `Saveable` and implements all the requirements.

We now have two objects that represent very different things and have different functionalities, but they both implement `Saveable`, and therefore we can treat them in a common way.

To see this in action, let's create an object that will manage the saving of information in our app:

```
class SaveManager {
    func save(_ thingToSave: Saveable) {
        thingToSave.saveToRemoteDatabase { success in
            print("Saved! Success: \(success))")
        }
    }
}
let colin = createPerson("Colin", "Alfred", "Moon") // This closure was
covered in the previous recipe
let birthdayReminder = Reminder(date: "27/11/1982", detail: "Colin's
Birthday")
let saveManager = SaveManager()
saveManager.save(colin)
saveManager.save(birthdayReminder)
```

In the preceding example, our `SaveManager` doesn't know the underlying types that it is being passed, but it doesn't need to. It receives instances that conform to the `Saveable` protocol, and can, therefore, use the interface provided by `Saveable` to save each object.

See also

Further information about protocols can be found in Apple's documentation of the Swift language at `http://swiftbook.link/docs/protocols`.

2
Building on the Building Blocks

In this chapter, we will cover the following recipes:

- Bundling variables into tuples
- Ordering your data with arrays
- Containing your data with sets
- Storing key-value pairs with Dictionaries
- Subscripts for custom types
- Changing your name with typealias
- Getting property changing notifications using property observers
- Controlling access with access control
- Extending functionality with extensions

Introduction

The last chapter gave us the basic types that form the building blocks of the Swift language. Now we will build on top of this knowledge to create more complex structures using functionalities provided by the Swift standard library.

All the code for this chapter can be found in the GitHub repository at `https://github.com/SwiftProgrammingCookbook/BuildingOnTheBuildingBlocks`.

Bundling variables into tuples

A **tuple** is a combination of two or more values that can be treated as one. If you have ever wished you could return more than one value from a function or method, you should find tuples very interesting.

Getting ready

Create a new playground and add the following statement:

```
import Foundation
```

This example uses one function from Foundation. We will delve into Foundation in more detail in `Chapter 5`, *Beyond the Standard Library*, but for now, we just need to import it.

How to do it...

Let's say that we are building an app that pulls together movie ratings from multiple sources and presents them together to help the user decide which movie to see. These sources may use different rating systems, for instance, the number of stars out of 5, points out of 10, or a rating as a percentage, and so on. We want to normalize the ratings before we can display them side by side; this will allow them to be compared directly. We want all the ratings to be represented as a number of stars out of 5, so we will have our function return the number of whole stars out of 5, which we will use to display the correct number of stars in our UI.

Our UI also includes a label that will read **x Star Movie**, where **x** is the number of stars. It would be good if our function returned both the number of stars and a string that we can put in the UI. We can use a tuple to do this.

Enter the following into your playground:

```
func normalisedStarRating(forRating rating: Float,
                          ofPossibleTotal total: Float) -> (Int, String) {
    let fraction = rating / total
    let ratingOutOf5 = fraction * 5
    let roundedRating = round(ratingOutOf5) // Rounds to the nearest
integer.
    let numberOfStars = Int(roundedRating) // Turns a Float into an Int
    let ratingString = "\(numberOfStars) Star Movie"
    return (numberOfStars, ratingString)
}
```

```
let ratingValueAndDisplayString = normalisedStarRating(forRating: 5,
ofPossibleTotal: 10)

let ratingValue = ratingValueAndDisplayString.0
print(ratingValue) // 3 - Use to show the right number of stars

let ratingString = ratingValueAndDisplayString.1
print(ratingString) // "3 Star Movie" - Use to put in the label
```

How it works...

A tuple is declared as a comma-separated list of the types it contains, within brackets, for example, `(Int, String)`, as shown in the preceding code. The preceding function, `normalisedStarRating`, normalizes the rating and creates `numberOfStars` as the closest number of stars, and `ratingString` as a display string. These values are then combined into a tuple and returned by placing them, separated by a comma, within brackets as `(numberOfStars, ratingString)`:

```
let ratingValueAndDisplayString = normalisedStarRating(forRating: 5,
ofPossibleTotal: 10)
```

Calling our function returns a tuple that we store in a constant called `ratingValueAndDisplayString`. We can access the tuple's components by accessing the zero-based numbered member of the tuple:

```
let ratingValue = ratingValueAndDisplayString.0
print(ratingValue) // 3 - Use to show the right number of stars

let ratingString = ratingValueAndDisplayString.1
print(ratingString) // "3 Star Movie" - Use to put in the label
```

There is another way to retrieve the values out of a tuple, and it can be achieved as the value is assigned. By specifying a tuple of variable names, each value of the tuple will be assigned to the respective variable name. Consider the following example:

```
let (nextValue, nextString) = normalisedStarRating(forRating: 8,
ofPossibleTotal: 10)
print(nextValue)  // 4
print(nextString) // "4 Star Movie"
```

There's more...

Accessing a tuple's components via a number is not ideal as we have to remember the order of the tuple members to ensure that we are accessing the correct one; this is even more confusing when the members are of the same type. To provide some context, we can add labels to the tuple members to identify them when they are accessed. Tuple labels are defined in a similar way to parameter labels, preceding the type and separated by a : . Let's add labels to both the tuple declaration and the tuple construction, and when accessed:

```
func normalisedStarRating(forRating rating: Float,
                          ofPossibleTotal total: Float)
                       -> (starRating: Int, displayString: String) {
    let fraction = rating / total
    let ratingOutOf5 = fraction * 5
    let roundedRating = round(ratingOutOf5) // Rounds to the nearest
integer.
    let numberOfStars = Int(roundedRating) // Turns a Float into an Int
    let ratingString = "\(numberOfStars) Star Movie"
    return (starRating: numberOfStars, displayString: ratingString)
}

let ratingValueAndDisplayString = normalisedStarRating(forRating: 5,
ofPossibleTotal: 10)

let ratingValue = ratingValueAndDisplayString.starRating
print(ratingValue) // 3 - Use to show the right number of stars

let ratingString = ratingValueAndDisplayString.displayString
print(ratingString) // "3 Stars" - Use to put in the label
```

Now, at the point of access, we can be sure that we have the right tuple member.

See also

Further information about tuples can be found in Apple's documentation of the Swift language at
https://developer.apple.com/library/ios/documentation/Swift/Conceptual/Swift_Programming_Language/Types.html.

Ordering your data with arrays

In this chapter, and the last, we were introduced to many different Swift constructs: **classes**, **structs**, **enums**, **closures**, **protocols**, and **tuples**. Yet, rarely will we be dealing with these on their own; we will likely have many instances of these constructs, and we need a way to collect multiple instances in useful data structures. We will examine three collection data structures provided by Swift: **arrays**, **sets**, and **Dictionaries** (often called **hash tables** in other languages):

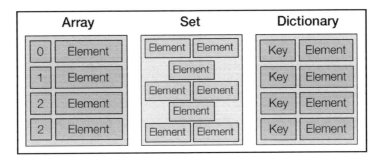

In the next few recipes, we'll look at how to use them to store and access elements, and examine their relative characteristics.

How to do it...

First, let's investigate **arrays**, which are an ordered list of elements. Enter the following into a new playground to see how we can create arrays and manipulate the elements in them:

```
var moviesToWatch: Array<String> = Array()
moviesToWatch.append("The Shawshank Redemption")
moviesToWatch.append("Ghostbusters")
moviesToWatch.append("Terminator 2")
print(moviesToWatch[0]) // "The Shawshank Redemption"
print(moviesToWatch[1]) // "Ghostbusters"
print(moviesToWatch[2]) // "Terminator 2"
print(moviesToWatch.count) // 3

moviesToWatch.insert("The Matrix", at: 2)
print(moviesToWatch.count) // 4
print(moviesToWatch)
// The Shawshank Redemption
// Ghostbusters
// The Matrix
// Terminator 2
```

```
let firstMovieToWatch = moviesToWatch.first
print(firstMovieToWatch as Any) // Optional("The Shawshank Redemption")
let lastMovieToWatch = moviesToWatch.last
print(lastMovieToWatch as Any) // Optional("Terminator 2")
let secondMovieToWatch = moviesToWatch[1]
print(secondMovieToWatch) // "Ghostbusters"

moviesToWatch[1] = "Ghostbusters (1984)"
print(moviesToWatch.count) // 4
print(moviesToWatch)
// The Shawshank Redemption
// Ghostbusters (1984)
// The Matrix
// Terminator 2

let spyMovieSuggestions: [String] = ["The Bourne Identity", "Casino
Royale", "Mission Impossible"]

moviesToWatch = moviesToWatch + spyMovieSuggestions
print(moviesToWatch.count) // 7
print(moviesToWatch)
// The Shawshank Redemption
// Ghostbusters (1984)
// The Matrix
// Terminator 2
// The Bourne Identity
// Casino Royale
// Mission Impossible

var starWarsTrilogy = Array<String>(repeating: "Star Wars: ", count: 3)
starWarsTrilogy[0] = starWarsTrilogy[0] + "A New Hope"
starWarsTrilogy[1] = starWarsTrilogy[1] + "Empire Strikes Back"
starWarsTrilogy[2] = starWarsTrilogy[2] + "Return of the Jedi"
print(starWarsTrilogy)
// Star Wars: A New Hope
// Star Wars: Empire Strikes Back
// Star Wars: Return of the Jedi

moviesToWatch.replaceSubrange(2...4, with: starWarsTrilogy)
print(moviesToWatch.count) // 7
print(moviesToWatch)
// The Shawshank Redemption
// Ghostbusters (1984)
// Star Wars: A New Hope
// Star Wars: Empire Strikes Back
// Star Wars: Return of the Jedi
// Casino Royale
// Mission Impossible
```

```
moviesToWatch.remove(at: 6)
print(moviesToWatch.count) // 6
print(moviesToWatch)
// The Shawshank Redemption
// Ghostbusters (1984)
// Star Wars: A New Hope
// Star Wars: Empire Strikes Back
// Star Wars: Return of the Jedi
// Casino Royale
```

How it works...

When creating an array, we need to specify the type of the elements that we will be storing in the array; this is declared in angular brackets as part of the array's type declaration:

```
var moviesToWatch: Array<String> = Array()
moviesToWatch.append("The Shawshank Redemption")
moviesToWatch.append("Ghostbusters")
moviesToWatch.append("Terminator 2")
```

This uses a language feature called **generics**, which we will cover in detail in `Chapter 4,` *Generics, Operators, and Nested Types*.

The `append` method on the array will add a new element to the end of the array. Now that we have put some elements in the array, let's access those elements:

```
print(moviesToWatch[0]) // "The Shawshank Redemption"
print(moviesToWatch[1]) // "Ghostbusters"
print(moviesToWatch[2]) // "Terminator 2"
```

Elements in an array are numbered with a zero-based index, so the first element in the array is at index 0, the second at index 1, the third at index 2, and so on. We can access the elements in the array using a subscript, in which we provide the index of the element we want to access; a subscript is specified in square brackets after the array instance's name.

There is nothing to stop us from entering an index in the subscript that doesn't exist in the array, and this will cause a crash. Instead, we can use some index helper methods on `Array` to ensure that we have an index that is valid for this array. Enter the following at the end of the playground:

```
let index5 = moviesToWatch.index(moviesToWatch.startIndex,
                                 offsetBy: 5,
                                 limitedBy: moviesToWatch.endIndex)
print(index5 as Any) // Optional 5
```

```
let index10 = moviesToWatch.index(moviesToWatch.startIndex,
                                   offsetBy: 10,
                                   limitedBy: moviesToWatch.endIndex)
print(index10 as Any) // nil
```

The `index` method lets us specify an offset, but binds it to the start and end index of the array. This will return the valid index if it is within the bound, or `nil` if it is not, since by the end of the playground, the `moviesToWatch` array has 6 elements, in which case retrieving index 5 is successful, but index 10 returns `nil`.

In the next chapter, we will cover how to make decisions based on whether this index exists, but for now, it's just useful to know that this method is available:

```
print(moviesToWatch.count) // 3
```

Arrays have a `count` property that will tell us how many elements they store, so when we add an element, this value will change:

```
moviesToWatch.insert("The Matrix", at: 2)
```

Elements can be inserted at any place in the array using the same zero-based index that we used in the preceding code. So, by inserting `"The Matrix"` at index 2, it will be placed at the third position in our array, and all elements at position 2 or greater will be moved down by 1.

This increases the array's count:

```
print(moviesToWatch.count) // 4
```

The array also provides some helpful computed properties for accessing elements at either end of the array:

```
let firstMovieToWatch = moviesToWatch.first
print(firstMovieToWatch as Any) // Optional("The Shawshank Redemption")
let lastMovieToWatch = moviesToWatch.last
print(firstMovieToWatch as Any) // Optional("Terminator 2")
let secondMovieToWatch = moviesToWatch[1]
print(secondMovieToWatch) // "Ghostbusters"
```

These properties are optional values as the array may be empty, and if it is, these will be `nil`. Conversely, accessing an element via the index subscript returns a non-optional value, as the assumption is made that if you have a valid index, you will get a valid value.

Along with retrieving values via the subscript, we can assign values to an array subscript:

```
moviesToWatch[1] = "Ghostbusters (1984)"
```

This will replace the element at the given index with the new value.

In the preceding code, we created an empty array and then appended values to it. But, we can also create an array that already contains values using an array literal:

```
let spyMovieSuggestions: [String] = ["The Bourne Identity", "Casino
Royale", "Mission Impossible"]
```

An array type can be specified with the element type enclosed by square brackets, and the array literal can be defined by comma-separated elements within square brackets. So, we can define an array of integers like this:

```
let fibonacci: [Int] = [1, 1, 2, 3, 5, 8, 13, 21, 34, 55]
```

As we have seen earlier, the compiler can often infer the type from the value we assign, and when the type is inferred, we don't need to specify it. In both the preceding arrays, spyMovieSuggestions and fibonacci, all the elements in the array are of the same type, String and Int respectively; so the array's type can be inferred, and therefore omitted, as follows:

```
let spyMovieSuggestions = ["The Bourne Identity", "Casino Royale", "Mission
Impossible"]
let fibonacci = [1, 1, 2, 3, 5, 8, 13, 21, 34, 55]
```

Arrays can be combined using the + operator:

```
moviesToWatch = moviesToWatch + spyMovieSuggestions
```

This will create a new array by appending the elements in the second array to the first:

```
var starWarsTrilogy = Array<String>(repeating: "Star Wars: ", count: 3)
```

The array provides a convenience initializer that will fill an array with elements. Let's access, append, and assign all of them in a single line:

```
starWarsTrilogy[0] = starWarsTrilogy[0] + "A New Hope"
starWarsTrilogy[1] = starWarsTrilogy[1] + "Empire Strikes Back"
starWarsTrilogy[2] = starWarsTrilogy[2] + "Return of the Jedi"
```

The array also provides a helper for replacing a range of values with the values contained in another array:

```
moviesToWatch.replaceSubrange(2...4, with: starWarsTrilogy)
```

Here, we have specified a range using . . . to indicate a range between two integer values, inclusive of those values. So this range contains the integers 2, 3, and 4.

This way to specify a range will be used in the subsequent chapters. Alternatively, you can specify a range that goes up to, but not including, the top of the range, known as a half-open range:

```
moviesToWatch.replaceSubrange(2..<5, with: starWarsTrilogy)
```

We've added elements, accessed them, and replaced them; let's see how to delete elements from an array:

```
moviesToWatch.remove(at: 6)
```

Provide the index of the element to the `remove` method, and the element at that index will be removed from the array, with all the subsequent elements moving up one place to fill the empty space. This will reduce the array's count by 1.

There's more...

If you are familiar with Objective-C, you will have used NSArray, which provides similar functionalities to a Swift array. You may also remember that NSArray is immutable--that is, its contents can't be changed once it's created--and NSMutableArray should be used instead if you want to change an array's contents. You will, therefore, be forgiven for wondering whether there is an immutable version of Array in Swift, and there is, but it's not a separate type. You create an immutable array simply by declaring it as a constant:

```
let evenNumbersTo10 = [2, 4, 6, 8, 10]
evenNumbersTo10.append(12) // Doesn't compile
```

To understand why this is the case, it's important to know that array is a value type, as are the other collection types in Swift.

As we saw in the last chapter, a value type is immutable in nature and creates a changed copy whenever it is mutated. Therefore, by assigning the array to a constant using let, we prevent any new value from being assigned, making mutating the array impossible.

See also

Further information about arrays can be found in Apple's documentation of the Swift language at `https://developer.apple.com/library/ios/documentation/Swift/Conceptual/Swift_Programming_Language/CollectionTypes.html`.

- Arrays use generics to define the element type they contain. Generics are discussed in detail in `Chapter 4`, *Generics, Operators, and Nested Types*.

Containing your data with sets

The next collection type we will look at is a **set**. Sets differ from arrays in two important ways. The elements in a set are stored *unordered*, and each unique element is only held once. In this recipe, we will look at how we can create and manipulate sets.

How to do it...

Let's take a look at the following steps:

1. First, let's look at how sets only store unique elements:

```
let fibonacciArray: Array<Int> = [1, 1, 2, 3, 5, 8, 13, 21, 34]
let fibonacciSet: Set<Int> = [1, 1, 2, 3, 5, 8, 13, 21, 34]
print(fibonacciArray.count) // 10
print(fibonacciSet.count) // 9
```

2. Elements can be inserted and removed, and you can check whether a set contains an element using the following:

```
var animals: Set<String> = ["cat", "dog", "mouse", "elephant"]
animals.insert("rabbit")
print(animals.contains("dog")) // true
animals.remove("dog")
print(animals.contains("dog")) // false
```

3. Next, we'll look at some useful set manipulation methods--union, intersection, symmetric difference, and subtract:

```
let evenNumbers = Set<Int>(arrayLiteral: 2, 4, 6, 8, 10)
let oddNumbers: Set<Int> = [1, 3, 5, 7, 9]
let squareNumbers: Set<Int> = [1, 4, 9]
let triangularNumbers: Set<Int> = [1, 3, 6, 10]

let evenOrTriangularNumbers =
evenNumbers.union(triangularNumbers) // 2, 4, 6, 8, 10, 1, 3,
unordered
print(evenOrTriangularNumbers.count) // 7

let oddAndSquareNumbers =
oddNumbers.intersection(squareNumbers) // 1, 9, unordered
print(oddAndSquareNumbers.count) // 2

let squareOrTriangularNotBoth =
squareNumbers.symmetricDifference(triangularNumbers) // 4, 9,
3, 6, 10, unordered
print(squareOrTriangularNotBoth.count) // 5

let squareNotOdd = squareNumbers.subtracting(oddNumbers) // 4
print(squareNotOdd.count) // 1
```

How it works...

Sets are created in almost the same way as arrays, and like arrays, we have to specify the element type that we will be storing in them:

```
let fibonacciArray: Array<Int> = [1, 1, 2, 3, 5, 8, 13, 21, 34]
let fibonacciSet: Set<Int> = [1, 1, 2, 3, 5, 8, 13, 21, 34]
```

Arrays and sets store their elements differently. If you provide the multiple elements of the same value to an array, it will store them multiple times; however, a set will only store one version of each unique element. So in the preceding Fibonacci number sequence, an array will store two elements for the first two values, but a set will only store one element for the first two values:

```
print(fibonacciArray.count) // 10
print(fibonacciSet.count) // 9
```

This ability to store elements uniquely is due to a requirement that a set has; its element type must conform to the Hashable protocol. This protocol requires a hashValue property to be provided as an Int, and the set uses this hashValue to do its uniqueness comparison. Both the Int and String types conform to Hashable, and any custom types that will be stored in a set will also need to conform to Hashable.

Set's insert, remove, and contains methods work as you would expect, with the compiler enforcing that the correct types are provided. This compiler type checking is due to the **generics** constraints that all the collections types have. We will cover generics in more detail in Chapter 4, *Generics, Operators and Nested Types*.

Union

The union method returns a set with all the unique elements from the set that the method is called on and the set provided as a parameter:

```
let evenOrTriangularNumbers = evenNumbers.union(triangularNumbers)
// 2,4,6,8,10,1,3,unordered
```

The following image depicts the **Union** of **Set A** and **Set B**:

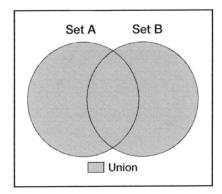

Intersection

The intersection method returns a set of unique elements that were contained in both the set that the method is called on and the set provided as a parameter:

```
let oddAndSquareNumbers = oddNumbers.intersection(squareNumbers) // 1, 9,
unordered
```

This method was renamed in Swift 3; prior to that, it was named `intersect`.

The following image depicts the **Intersection** of **Set A** and **Set B**:

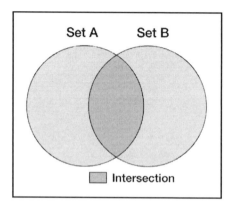

Symmetric difference

The `symmetricDifference` method returns a set of unique elements that are in either the set the method is called on, or the set provided as a parameter, but not elements that are in both:

```
let squareOrTriangularNotBoth =
squareNumbers.symmetricDifference(triangularNumbers)
// 4, 9, 3, 6, 10, unordered
```

 This method was renamed in Swift 3; prior to that, it was named `exclusiveOr`.

The following image depicts the **Symmetric Difference** of **Set A** and **Set B**:

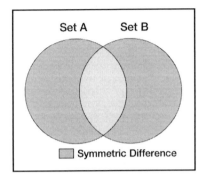

Subtracting

The subtracting method returns a unique set of elements that are in the set the method is called on, but not in the set passed as a parameter. Unlike the other set manipulation methods mentioned, this will not necessarily return the same value if you swap the set that the method is called on with the set provided as a parameter:

```
let squareNotOdd = squareNumbers.subtracting(oddNumbers) // 4
```

 This method was renamed in Swift 3; prior to that, it was called subtract.

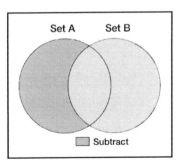

There's more...

In addition to set manipulation methods, we have a number of methods to determine information about set membership.

Let's take a look at the following code:

```
let animalKingdom: Set<String> = ["dog", "cat", "pidgeon",
                                  "chimpanzee", "snake", "kangaroo",
                                  "giraffe", "elephant", "tiger",
                                  "lion", "panther"]
let vertebrates: Set<String> = ["dog", "cat", "pidgeon",
                                "chimpanzee", "snake", "kangaroo",
                                "giraffe", "elephant", "tiger",
                                "lion", "panther"]
let reptile: Set<String> = ["snake"]
let mammals: Set<String> = ["dog", "cat", "chimpanzee",
                            "kangaroo", "giraffe", "elephant",
                            "tiger", "lion", "panther"]
let catFamily: Set<String> = ["cat", "tiger", "lion", "panther"]
let domesticAnimals: Set<String> = ["cat", "dog"]

print(mammals.isSubset(of: animalKingdom)) // true
print(mammals.isSuperset(of: catFamily)) // true

print(vertebrates.isStrictSubset(of: animalKingdom)) // false
print(mammals.isStrictSubset(of: animalKingdom)) // true
print(animalKingdom.isStrictSuperset(of: vertebrates)) // false
print(animalKingdom.isStrictSuperset(of: domesticAnimals))  // true

print(catFamily.isDisjoint(with: reptile)) // true
```

Now, let's look at how the preceding code functions.

The `isSubset` method will return true if all elements in the set that the method is called on are contained within the set passed as a parameter:

```
print(mammals.isSubset(of: animalKingdom)) // true
```

The following image depicts **Set B** as the **subset** of **Set A**:

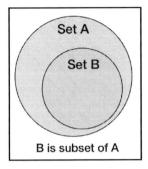

This will also return true if the two sets are equal (contain the same elements). If you want a true value only if the set that the method is called on is a subset and *not* equal, then you can use isStrictSubset:

```
print(vertebrates.isStrictSubset(of: animalKingdom)) // false
print(mammals.isStrictSubset(of: animalKingdom)) // true
```

The isSuperset method will return true if all elements in the set passed as a parameter are within the set that the method is called on:

```
print(mammals.isSuperset(of: catFamily)) // true
```

The following image depicts **Set A** as the **superset** of **Set B**:

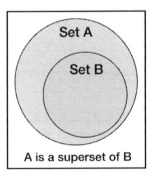

This will also return true if the two sets are equal (contain the same elements). If you want a true value only if the set that the method is called on is a superset and not equal, then you can use `isStrictSuperset`:

```
print(animalKingdom.isStrictSuperset(of: vertebrates))     // false
print(animalKingdom.isStrictSuperset(of: domesticAnimals)) // true
```

The `isDisjoint` method will return true if there are no common elements between the set that the method is called on and the set passed as a parameter:

```
print(catFamily.isDisjoint(with: reptile)) // true
```

The following image shows that **Set A** and **Set B** are **disjoint**:

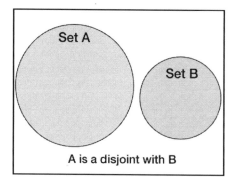

As with arrays, a set can be declared immutable by assigning it to a `let` constant instead of a `var` variable:

```
let planets: Set<String> = ["Mercury", "Venus", "Earth",
                            "Mars", "Jupiter", "Saturn",
                            "Uranus", "Neptune", "Pluto"]
planets.remove("Pluto") // Doesn't compile
```

This is because a set, like the other collection types, is a value type. Removing an element would mutate the set, which creates a new copy, but a `let` constant can't have a new value assigned to it, so the compiler prevents any mutating operations.

See also

- Further information about arrays can be found in Apple's documentation of the Swift language at `https://developer.apple.com/library/ios/documentation/Swift/Conceptual/Swift_Programming_Language/CollectionTypes.html`.

- Arrays use generics to define the element type it contains. Generics are discussed in detail in `Chapter 4`, *Generics, Operators, and Nested Types*.

Storing key-value pairs with Dictionaries

The last collection type we will look at is the **Dictionary**, which is a familiar construct in programming languages, where it is sometimes referred to as a **hash table**. A dictionary holds a collection of pairings between a key and a value. The **key** can be any element that conforms to the `Hashable` protocol (just like elements in a set), and the `value` can be any type. The contents of a Dictionary are not stored in order, unlike an array; instead, the *key* is used both when storing a value and as a lookup when retrieving a value.

Getting ready

In this recipe, we will use a Dictionary to store details of people at a place of work. We need to store and retrieve a person's information based on their role in the organization, like a company directory. To hold our person's information, we will use a modified version of our `Person` class from `Chapter 1`, *Swift Building Blocks*.

Enter the following code into a new playground:

```
struct PersonName {
    let givenName: String
    let familyName: String
}

enum CommunicationMethod {
    case phone
    case email
    case textMessage
    case fax
    case telepathy
    case subSpaceRelay
    case quantumEntanglement
}
```

```
class Person {
    let name: PersonName
    let preferredCommunicationMethod: CommunicationMethod
    convenience init(givenName: String,
                     familyName: String,
                     commsMethod: CommunicationMethod) {
        let name = PersonName(givenName: givenName, familyName: familyName)
        self.init(name: name, commsMethod: commsMethod)
    }
    init(name: PersonName, commsMethod: CommunicationMethod) {
        self.name = name
        preferredCommunicationMethod = commsMethod
    }
}
```

How to do it...

Let's use the `Person` object we have just defined to build up our workplace directory using a Dictionary. Then we will break down how we went about it:

1. First, create a Dictionary for the employee directory:

```
var crewDirectory = Dictionary<String, Person>()
```

2. Next, we will populate our Dictionary with employee details:

```
crewDirectory["Captain"] = Person(givenName: "Jean-Luc",
                                  familyName: "Picard",
                                  commsMethod: .phone)

crewDirectory["First Officer"] = Person(givenName: "William",
                                        familyName: "Riker",
                                        commsMethod: .email)

crewDirectory["Chief Engineer"] = Person(givenName: "Georgi",
                                         familyName: "LaForge",
                                         commsMethod:
.textMessage)

crewDirectory["Second Officer"] = Person(givenName: "Data",
                                         familyName: "Soong",
                                         commsMethod: .fax)

crewDirectory["Councillor"] = Person(givenName: "Deanna",
                                     familyName: "Troy",
                                     commsMethod: .telepathy)
```

```
crewDirectory["Security Officer"] = Person(givenName: "Tasha",
                                            familyName: "Yar",
                                            commsMethod:
.subSpaceRelay)

crewDirectory["Chief Medical Officer"] = Person(givenName:
"Beverly",
                                                familyName:
"Crusher",
                                                commsMethod:
.quantumEntanglement)
```

3. Now that we have our employee directory, we will want to present a list of all the employee roles that exist at the workplace to our users so that they can decide who to get more information about:

```
let roles = Array(crewDirectory.keys)
print(roles)
```

4. When the user picks one of the roles, we can use that to retrieve the person's details from the company directory:

```
let firstRole = roles.first! // Chief Medical Officer
let cmo = crewDirectory[firstRole]! // Person: Beverly Crusher
print("\(firstRole): \(cmo.name.givenName)
\(cmo.name.familyName)")
// Chief Medical Officer: Beverly Crusher
```

5. We can replace a value in the Dictionary by assigning a new value against an existing key:

```
print(crewDirectory["Security Officer"]!.name.givenName) //
Tasha

crewDirectory["Security Officer"] = Person(givenName: "Worf",
                                           familyName: "Son of
Mogh",
                                           commsMethod:
.subSpaceRelay)

print(crewDirectory["Security Officer"]!.name.givenName) //
Worf
```

6. The previous value for the key is discarded when a new value is set.

How it works...

As with the other collection types, we provide details of the Swift types that a Dictionary will hold when we create it. However, we now have to provide two types: the first is the type of the key (which must conform to `Hashable`), and the second is the type of the value:

```
var crewDirectory = Dictionary<String, Person>()
```

As with an array, we can specify a Dictionary type using square brackets and create one using a Dictionary literal, where : separates the key and value:

```
let intByName: [String: Int] = ["one": 1, "two": 2, "three": 3]
```

Therefore, we can change our Dictionary definition to be as follows:

```
var crewDictionary: [String: Person] = [:]
```

The `[:]` symbol denotes an empty Dictionary as a Dictionary literal.

Elements are added to a Dictionary using subscript. Unlike an array, which takes an `Int` index in the subscript, a Dictionary takes the key and pairs the given value with the given key:

```
crewDirectory["Captain"] = Person(givenName: "Jean-Luc",
                                  familyName: "Picard",
                                  commsMethod: .phone)
```

If no value currently exists, the assigned value will be added; if a value already exists for the given key, the old value will be replaced with the new value and the old value will be discarded.

There are properties on the Dictionary that will provide all the keys, as well as all the values--albeit separately as a collection, which can be used to create an array:

```
let roles = Array(crewDirectory.keys)
print(roles)
```

To display all the Dictionary's keys, as provided by the `keys` property, we can either use it to create an array, as shown in the preceding code, or iterate over the collection directly. We will cover iterating over a collection's values in the next chapter; for now, we will create an array.

In Swift 3, the `keys` property in Dictionary provided `LazyMapCollection`, which computed its elements lazily. In Swift 4, this has been changed, and `keys` is now a custom `Collection`.

Next, we use one of the values from an array of keys with the crew to retrieve the full details about the associated `Person`:

```
let firstRole = roles.first! // Chief Medical Officer
let cmo = crewDirectory[firstRole]! // Person: Beverly Crusher
```

We get the first element using the `first` property, but as this is an optional type, we need to force unwrap it using `!`. We can pass the `firstRole`, which is now a non-optional `String` to the Dictionary subscript to get the `Person` object associated with that key. Since we could have used a key that doesn't exist, the return type from the subscript is optional (`Person?`), so it also needs to be force unwrapped to print its values.

 Force unwrapping is justifiable here because we know that the Dictionary is not empty, and we know that the string we provide to the subscript has an associated value. Ideally, we wouldn't force unwrap these values, but instead check if they were nil, and only unwrap if they are not nil. We will cover how to do this in the next chapter.

There's more...

One problem with our approach to using a Dictionary for our employee directory is that our key can be any `String`, so it's very easy to mistype an employee's role or look for a role that you expect to exist, but doesn't. However, our key doesn't have to be a `String`; it can be anything that conforms to the `Hashable` protocol. So, we'll improve our implementation using something that is `Hashable` and more suited to our model as a key.

We have a finite set of employee roles in our model, and an **enumeration** is perfect for representing a finite number of options, so let's define our roles as an enum:

```
enum Role: String {
    case captain = "Captain"
    case firstOfficer = "First Officer"
    case secondOfficer = "Second Officer"
    case chiefEngineer = "Chief Engineer"
    case councillor = "Councillor"
    case securityOfficer = "Security Officer"
    case chiefMedicalOfficer = "Chief Medical Officer"
}
```

Now, let's change our Dictionary definition to use this new enum as a key, and insert our employees using the enum values:

```
var crewDirectory = Dictionary<Role, Person>()

crewDirectory[.captain] = Person(givenName: "Jean-Luc",
                                 familyName: "Picard",
                                 commsMethod: .phone)

crewDirectory[.firstOfficer] = Person(givenName: "William",
                                      familyName: "Riker",
                                      commsMethod: .email)

crewDirectory[.chiefEngineer] = Person(givenName: "Georgi",
                                       familyName: "LaForge",
                                       commsMethod: .textMessage)

crewDirectory[.secondOfficer] = Person(givenName: "Data",
                                       familyName: "Soong",
                                       commsMethod: .fax)

crewDirectory[.councillor] = Person(givenName: "Deanna",
                                    familyName: "Troy",
                                    commsMethod: .telepathy)

crewDirectory[.securityOfficer] = Person(givenName: "Tasha",
                                         familyName: "Yar",
                                         commsMethod: .subSpaceRelay)

crewDirectory[.chiefMedicalOfficer] = Person(givenName: "Beverly",
                                             familyName: "Crusher",
                                             commsMethod:
.quantumEntanglement)
```

You will also need to change all the other uses of crewDirectory to use the new enum-based key.

Let's take a look at how and why this works. We created Role as a String-based enum:

```
enum Role: String {
    //...
}
```

Defining it this way has two benefits:

- We intend to display these roles to the user, so we will need a string representation of the Role enum no matter how we defined it.

- Enums have a little bit of protocol and generics magic in them, which means that if an enum is backed by a type that implements the `Hashable` protocol (as `String` does), the enum also automatically implements the `Hashable` protocol. Therefore, defining `Role` as being `String` based satisfies the Dictionary requirement of a key being `Hashable` without us having to do any extra work.

With our `crewDictionary` now defined as having a `Role`-based key, all subscript operations have to use a value in the role enum:

```
crewDirectory[.captain] = Person(givenName: "Jean-Luc",
                                 familyName: "Picard",
                                 commsMethod: .phone)
let cmo = crewDirectory[.chiefMedicalOfficer]
```

The compiler enforces this, so it's no longer possible to use an incorrect role when interacting with our employee directory. This pattern of using Swift's constructs and type system to enforce the correct use of your model is something we should strive to do as we pick the types we use to define our model.

See also

- Further information about Dictionaries can be found in Apple's documentation of the Swift language at `https://developer.apple.com/library/ios/documentation/Swift/Conceptual/Swift_Programming_Language/CollectionTypes.html`.

Subscripts for custom types

From the last few recipes on collection types, we have seen, that their elements are accessed through subscripts. However, it's not just collection types that can have subscripts; your own custom types can provide subscript functionality too.

Getting ready

Let's create a simple game of *tic-tac-toe*, also known as *Noughts and Crosses*. To do this, we need a three-by-three grid of positions, with each position being filled by either a nought from Player 1, a cross from Player 2, or nothing. We can store these positions in an array of arrays.

The initial game setup code uses the constructs we covered earlier, so we won't go into its implementation. Enter the following code into a new playground so that we can see how subscripts can improve its usage:

```
enum GridPosition: String {
    case player1 = "o"
    case player2 = "x"
    case empty = " "
}

struct TicTacToe {
    var gridStorage: [[GridPosition]] = []
    init() {
        gridStorage.append(Array(repeating: .empty, count: 3))
        gridStorage.append(Array(repeating: .empty, count: 3))
        gridStorage.append(Array(repeating: .empty, count: 3))
    }
    func gameStateString() -> String {
        var stateString = "-------------\n"
        stateString += printableString(forRow: gridStorage[0])
        stateString += "-------------\n"
        stateString += printableString(forRow: gridStorage[1])
        stateString += "-------------\n"
        stateString += printableString(forRow: gridStorage[2])
        stateString += "-------------\n"
        return stateString
    }
    func printableString(forRow row: [GridPosition]) -> String {
        var rowString = "| \(row[0].rawValue) "
        rowString += "| \(row[1].rawValue) "
        rowString += "| \(row[2].rawValue) |\n"
        return rowString
    }
}
```

How to do it...

We will run through how we can use the tic-tac-toe game defined earlier, and how it can be improved using a subscript. Then, we will examine how this works:

1. Let's create an instance of our `TicTacToe` grid:

```
var game = TicTacToe()
```

2. For a player to make a move, we need to change the `GridPosition` value assigned to the relevant place in the array of arrays, which is used to store the grid positions. Player 1 will place a nought in the middle position of the grid, which would be row position 1, column position 1 (since it's a zero-based array):

```
// Move 1
game.gridStorage[1][1] = .player1
print(game.gameStateString())
/*
-------------
|   |   |   |
-------------
|   | o |   |
-------------
|   |   |   |
-------------
*/
```

3. Next, Player 2 places their cross in the top-right position, which is row position 0, column position 2:

```
// Move 2
game.gridStorage[0][2] = .player2
print(game.gameStateString())
/*
-------------
|   |   | x |
-------------
|   | o |   |
-------------
|   |   |   |
-------------
*/
```

4. We can make moves in our game, but we are doing so by adding information directly to the `gridStorage` array, which isn't ideal. The player shouldn't need to know how the moves are stored, and we should be able to change how we store the game information without having to change how the moves are made. To solve this, let's create a subscript to our game object so that making a move in the game is just like assigning a value to an array.

5. Add the following subscript method to the `TicTacToe` struct:

```
struct TicTacToe {
    var gridStorage: [[GridPosition]] = []
    //...
    subscript(row: Int, column: Int) -> GridPosition {
        get {
            return gridStorage[row][column]
        }
        set(newValue) {
            gridStorage[row][column] = newValue
        }
    }
    //...
}
```

6. So now, we can change how each player makes their move, and finish the game:

```
// Move 1
game[1, 1] = .player1
print(game.gameStateString())
/*
 -------------
 |   |   |   |   |
 -------------
 |   | o |   |   |
 -------------
 |   |   |   |   |
 -------------
 */

// Move 2
game[0, 2] = .player2
print(game.gameStateString())
/*
 -------------
 |   |   | x |   |
 -------------
 |   | o |   |   |
 -------------
 |   |   |   |   |
 -------------
 */

// Move 3
game[0, 0] = .player1
print(game.gameStateString())
/*
```

```
    ------------
   | o |   | x |
    ------------
   |   | o |   |
    ------------
   |   |   |   |
    ------------
 */

// Move 4
game[1, 2] = .player2
print(game.gameStateString())
/*
    ------------
   | o |   | x |
    ------------
   |   | o | x |
    ------------
   |   |   |   |
    ------------
 */

// Move 5
game[2, 2] = .player1
print(game.gameStateString())
/*
    ------------
   | o |   | x |
    ------------
   |   | o | x |
    ------------
   |   |   | o |
    ------------
 */
```

7. Just like in an array, we can use a subscript to access the value as well as assign a value to it:

```
let topLeft = game[0, 0]
let middle = game[1, 1]
let bottomRight = game[2, 2]
let player1HasWon =
(topLeft==.player1)&&(middle==.player1)&&(bottomRight==.player1)
```

How it works...

Subscript functionality can be defined within a class, struct, or enum, or declared within a protocol as a requirement. To do this, we define `subscript` (which is a reserved keyword that activates the functionality) with input parameters and an output type:

```
subscript(row: Int, column: Int) -> GridPosition
```

This subscript definition works like a computed property, where `get` can be defined to allow you to access values through subscript, and `set` can be defined to assign values using subscript:

```
subscript(row: Int, column: Int) -> GridPosition {
    get {
        return gridStorage[row][column]
    }
    set(newValue) {
        gridStorage[row][column] = newValue
    }
}
```

Any number of input parameters can be defined, and these should be provided as comma-separated values in the subscript:

```
game[1, 2] = .player2 // Assigning a value
let topLeft = game[0, 0] // Accessing a value
```

There's more...

Just like parameters defined in a function, subscript parameters can have additional labels. If defined, these become required at the call site, so the subscript we added can alternatively be defined as follows:

```
subscript(atRow row: Int, atColumn column: Int) -> GridPosition
```

In this case, using the subscript will look like the following:

```
game[atRow: 1, atColumn: 2] = .player2 // Assigning a value
let topLeft = game[atRow: 0, atColumn: 0] // Accessing a value
```

See also

- Further information about subscripts can be found in Apple's documentation of the Swift language at
  `https://developer.apple.com/library/ios/documentation/Swift/Conceptual/Swift_Programming_Language/Subscripts.html`.

Changing your name with typealias

The **typealias** declaration allows you to create an alias for a `type`; it does exactly what it says on the tin. You can specify a name that can be used in place of any given type definition. If this type is quite complex, a typealias can be a useful way to simplify its use.

How to do it...

Let's take look at the following steps to understand how to use typealias:

1. First, let's create something to store in an array--in this instance, a `Pug` struct:

```
struct Pug {
    let name: String
}
```

2. Now we can create an array that will contain instances of a `Pug` struct:

```
let pugs = [Pug]()
```

 As you may or may not know, the collective noun for a group of pugs is called a **grumble**.
https://www.reference.com/pets-animals/call-group-pugs-1bb3e75b6 008897b

3. So we can set up a `typealias` to define an array of pugs as a `Grumble`:

```
typealias Grumble = [Pug]
```

4. With this defined, we can substitute `Grumble` wherever we would use `[Pug]`:

```
var grumble = Grumble()
```

5. However, this isn't some new type--it is just an array with all the same functionalities:

```
let marty = Pug(name: "Marty McPug")
let wolfie = Pug(name: "Wolfgang Pug")
let poppy = Pug(name: "Poppy")
let rudy = Pug(name: "Rudy")
grumble.append(marty)
grumble.append(wolfie)
grumble.append(poppy)
grumble.append(rudy)
```

There's more...

The preceding example allows us to use types in a more natural and expressive way. In addition, we can use a `typealias` to simplify a more complex type that may be used at multiple places.

To see how this might be useful, we can build an object that will fetch program information from some service. Enter the following into a new playground:

```
enum Channel {
    case BBC1
    case BBC2
    case BBCNews
    //...
}

class ProgrammeFetcher {
    func fetchCurrentProgrammeName(forChannel channel: Channel,
                                   resultHandler: (String?, Error?) ->
Void) {
        // ...
        // Do the work to get the current programme
        // ...
        let programmeName = "Sherlock"
        resultHandler(programmeName, nil)
    }
    func fetchNextProgrammeName(forChannel channel: Channel,
                                resultHandler: (String?, Error?) -> Void) {
        // ...
        // Do the work to get the next programme
        // ...
        let programmeName = "Luther"
        resultHandler(programmeName, nil)
    }
```

```
}
```

In the `ProgrammeFetcher` object, we have two methods that take a channel and a result handler block; this result handler block has the following definition, which we have to define twice, once for each method:

```
(String?, Error?) -> Void
```

Instead, we can define this block definition with a typealias as `FetchResultHandler` and replace each method definition with reference to this `typealias`.

Let's replace the existing `ProgrammeFetcher` definition with the following:

```swift
class ProgrammeFetcher {
    typealias FetchResultHandler = (String?, Error?) -> Void
    func fetchCurrentProgrammeName(forChannel channel: Channel,
                               resultHandler: FetchResultHandler) {
        // Get next programme
        let programmeName = "Sherlock"
        resultHandler(programmeName, nil)
    }
    func fetchNextProgrammeName(forChannel channel: Channel,
                           resultHandler: FetchResultHandler) {
        // Get next programme
        let programmeName = "Luther"
        resultHandler(programmeName, nil)
    }
}
```

Not only does this save us from defining the block twice, it is also a better description of the function that the block performs.

Using the method with a `typealias` -defined block works exactly the same as if it didn't have a `typealias`:

```swift
let fetcher = ProgrammeFetcher()
fetcher.fetchCurrentProgrammeName(forChannel: .BBC1,
                              resultHandler: { programmeName, error in
    print(programmeName as Any)
})
```

See also

Further information about typealiases can be found in Apple's documentation of the Swift language at `https://developer.apple.com/library/ios/documentation/Swift/ Conceptual/Swift_Programming_Language/Declarations.html`.

Getting property changing notifications using property observers

You may often find that you would like to know when a property changes its value; maybe you want to update the value of another property, or inform a delegate. In Objective-C, this was often accomplished by writing your own getter and setter, or using **Key-Value observing (KVO)**, but we have native support for property observers in Swift.

Getting ready

To examine property observers, we should create an object with a property that we want to observe. Let's create an object to manage users and a property to hold the current user's name:

```
class UserManager {
    var currentUserName: String = "Emmanuel Goldstein"
}
```

We want to present some friendly messages when the current user changes, and we'll use property observers to do it.

How to do it...

Amend the `currentUserName` property definition to be the following:

```
class UserManager {
    var currentUserName: String = "Emmanuel Goldstein" {
        willSet (newUserName) {
            print("Goodbye to \(currentUserName)")
            print("I hear \(newUserName) is on their way!")
        }
        didSet (oldUserName) {
            print("Welcome to \(currentUserName)")
            print("I miss \(oldUserName) already!")
```

```
        }
      }
   }
```

Now, we can create an instance of the `UserManager` and change the current username, which will generate the friendly messages:

```
let manager = UserManager()

manager.currentUserName = "Dade Murphy"
// Goodbye to Emmanuel Goldstein
// I hear Dade Murphy is on their way!
// Welcome to Dade Murphy
// I miss Emmanuel Goldstein already!

manager.currentUserName = "Kate Libby"
// Goodbye to Dade Murphy
// I hear Kate Libby is on their way!
// Welcome to Kate Libby
// I miss Dade Murphy already!
```

How it works...

Property observers can be added within curly brackets after the property declaration, and there are two types: `willSet` and `didSet`.

The `willSet` observer will be called before the property is set, and will be provided with the value that will be set on the property. This new value can be given a name within brackets; we have named it `newUserName`, in our case:

```
willSet (newUserName) {
    //...
}
```

The `didSet` observer will be called after the property is set, and it will be provided with the value that the property had before being set. This old value can be given a name within brackets; we have named it `oldUserName`, in our case:

```
didSet (oldUserName) {
    //...
}
```

There's more...

The new value and old value that are passed into the property observers have implicit names, so there is no need to explicitly name them. The willSet observer is passed something with an implicit name of newValue, and the didSet observer is passed something with an implicit name of oldValue; let's remove our explicit names and use the implicit value names:

```
class UserManager {
    var currentUserName: String = "Emmanuel Goldstein" {
        willSet {
            print("Goodbye to \(currentUserName)")
            print("I hear \(newValue) is on their way!")
        }
        didSet {
            print("Welcome to \(currentUserName)")
            print("I miss \(oldValue) already!")
        }
    }
}
```

See also

- Further information about property observers can be found in Apple's documentation of the Swift language at https://developer.apple.com/library/mac/documentation/Swift/Conceptual/Swift_Programming_Language/Properties.html.

Controlling access with access control

Swift provides fine-grained access control, allowing you to specify the visibility that your code has to the other areas of code. This enables you to be explicit about the interface you provide to other parts of the system, encapsulating implementation logic and helping to separate the areas of concern.

Swift has five access levels:

- **Private**: Only accessible within the existing scope (defined by curly brackets) or extensions in the same file
- **File private**: Accessible to anything in the same file, but nothing outside the file

- **Internal**: Accessible to anything in the same module, but nothing outside the module
- **Public**: Accessible both inside and outside the module, but cannot be subclassed or overwritten outside of the defining module
- **Open**: Accessible everywhere, with no restrictions on its use

These can be applied to types, properties, and functions.

 Swift 4 extends the behavior of the private access level, as compared to Swift 3. In Swift 3, anything that was declared private was only available within the scope in which it was defined; however, in Swift 4, anything declared private will also be available within extensions to the type it was declared within, as long as the extensions are in the same file. We will talk about extensions in the next recipe.

Getting ready

To explore each of these access levels, we need to step outside our playground comfort zone and create a module. To hold our module and a playground that can use it, we will need to create an Xcode workspace:

1. In Xcode, select **File** | **New** | **Workspace...** from the menu, as shown in the following screenshot:

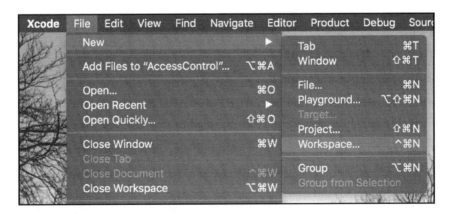

2. Give your Workspace a name, such as `AccessControl`, and choose a save location.

3. You will now see an empty workspace:

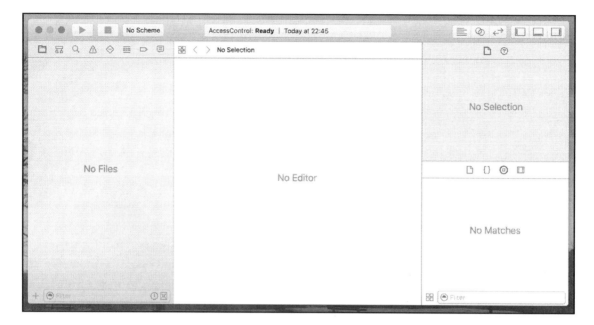

In this workspace, we need to create a module, which represents something that tightly controls the information it exposes and the information that it keeps hidden. So, we will make a module to represent Apple, the company.

4. Create a new project from the Xcode menu by selecting **File** | **New** | **Project...**, as illustrated in the following screenshot:

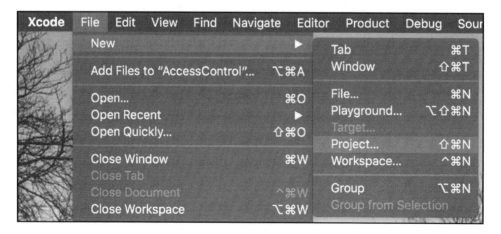

5. From the template selector, select **Cocoa Touch Framework**:

6. Name the project `AppleInc`:

7. Choose a location and at the bottom of the window, ensure that **Add to:** is set to be the workspace we just created:

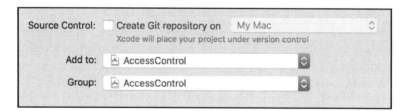

8. Now that we have a module, let's set up a playground to use it in. From the Xcode menu, select **File** | **New** | **Playground...**, as in the following screenshot:

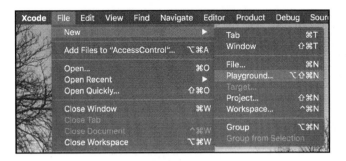

9. Give the playground a name and save location:

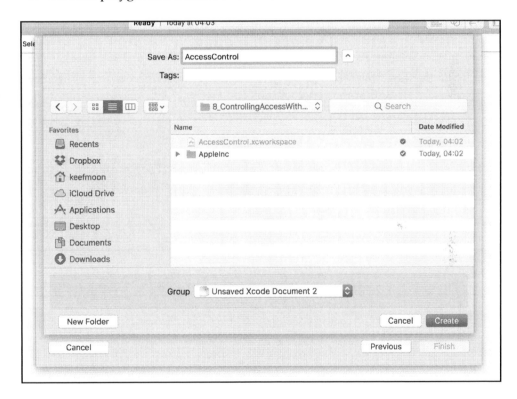

10. This playground will not be added to the workspace automatically; you will need to locate the playground you just created and drag it into the file explorer pane on the left-hand side of your workspace.

11. Press the run button on the Xcode toolbar to build the `AppleInc` module:

12. Select the playground from the file navigator and add an import statement at the top of the file:

```
import AppleInc
```

We are now ready to look into the different access controls that are available.

How to do it...

Let's investigate the most restrictive of the access controls--private. Structures marked private are only visible within the scope of the type they are defined in and that type's extensions in the same file. We know that Apple has supersecret areas where it works on its new products, so let's create one:

1. Select the `AppleInc` group in the file navigator and create a new file by selecting **File** | **New** | **File...** from the menu. Let's call it `SecretProductDepartment`.

2. In the new file, add the following code:

```
class SecretProductDepartment {
    private var secretCodeWord = "Titan"
    private var secretProducts = ["iPhone 8",
                                  "Apple Car",
                                  "Apple Brain Implant",
                                  "Apple Spaceship"]
    func nextProduct(givenCodeWord codeWord: String) -> String?
    {

        let codeCorrect = codeWord == secretCodeWord
        return codeCorrect ? secretProducts.first : nil
    }
}
```

3. When you buy an iPhone in the Apple Store, it's not made in-store; it's made in a factory that the public doesn't have access to. So let's model that using `fileprivate`.

4. Next, let's look at the `fileprivate` access control. Structures marked as `fileprivate` are only visible within the file that they are defined in, so a collection of related structures defined in the same file will be visible to each other, but anything outside the file will not see these structures.

5. Create a new file called `AppleStore`, and add the following code to the file:

```
public enum DeviceModel {
    case iPhoneSE
    case iPhone6
    case iPhone6Plus
    case iPhone6S
    case iPhone6SPlus
}

public class AppleiPhone {
    public let model: DeviceModel
    fileprivate init(model: DeviceModel) {
        self.model = model
    }
}

fileprivate class Factory {
        func makeiPhone(ofModel model: DeviceModel) ->
AppleiPhone {
        return AppleiPhone(model: model)
    }
}

public class AppleStore {
    private var factory = Factory()
    public func selliPhone(ofModel model: DeviceModel) ->
AppleiPhone {
        return factory.makeiPhone(ofModel: model)
    }
}
```

6. To investigate the `public` access control, we will be defining something that is visible outside the defining module, but cannot be subclassed or overridden. Apple itself is the perfect candidate to model this behavior on as certain parts of it are visible to the public, but it closely guards its image and brand, and so *subclassing* Apple to alter and customize it will not be allowed.

7. Create a new file called `Apple`, and add the following code to the file:

```
public class Person {
    public let name: String
    public init(name: String) {
        self.name = name
    }
}

public class Apple {
    public private(set) var ceo: Person
    private var employees = [Person]()
    public let store = AppleStore()
    private let secretDepartment = SecretProductDepartment()
    public init() {
        ceo = Person(name: "Tim Cook")
        employees.append(ceo)
    }
    public func newEmployee(person: Person) {
        employees.append(person)
    }
    func weeklyProductMeeting() {
        var superSecretProduct =
secretDepartment.nextProduct(givenCodeWord: "Not sure...
Abracadabra?") // nil
        // Try again
        superSecretProduct =
secretDepartment.nextProduct(givenCodeWord: "Titan") // "iPhone
8"
        print(superSecretProduct as Any)
    }
}
```

8. Lastly, we have the open access control. Structures defined as open are available outside the module and can be subclassed and overridden without restriction. To explain this last control, we want to model something that exists within Apple's domain, but is completely open and free from restrictions, so we can use the Swift language itself!

9. Swift has been open sourced by Apple, so while they maintain the project, the source code is fully available for others to take, modify, and improve.

10. Create a new file called `SwiftLanguage`, and add the following code to the file:

```
open class SwiftLanguage {
    open func versionNumber() -> Float {
        return 4.0
    }
```

```
open func supportedPlatforms() -> [String] {
    return ["iOS", "macOSX", "tvOS", "watchOS", "Linux"]
}
}
```

We now have a module that uses Swift's access controls to provide interfaces that match our model and provide the appropriate visibility.

How it works...

Let's examine our `SecretProductDepartment` class to see how the visibility matches our model:

```
internal class SecretProductDepartment {
    private var secretCodeWord = "Titan"
    private var secretProducts = ["iPhone 8",
                                  "Apple Car",
                                  "Apple Brain Implant",
                                  "Apple Spaceship"]
    func nextProduct(givenCodeWord codeWord: String) -> String? {
        let codeCorrect = codeWord == secretCodeWord
        return codeCorrect ? secretProducts.first : nil
    }
}
```

The `SecretProductDepartment` class is declared without an access control keyword, and when no access control is specified, the default control of `internal` is applied. Since we want the secret product department to be visible within Apple, but not from outside Apple, this is the correct access control.

The two properties of the `secretCodeWord` and `secretProducts` classes are marked as private, hiding their value and existence from anything outside the `SecretProductDepartment` class. To see the restriction in action, add the following to the same file, but outside the class:

```
let inSecureCodeWord = SecretProductDepartment().secretCodeWord
```

When you try to build the module, you are told that `secretCodeWord` is not accessible due to the `private` protection level.

While the properties are not directly accessible, we can provide an interface that allows the information to be provided in a controlled way, which is what the `nextProduct` method provides:

```
func nextProduct(givenCodeWord codeWord: String) -> String? {
    let codeCorrect = codeWord == secretCodeWord
    return codeCorrect ? secretProducts.first : nil
}
```

If the correct code word is passed, it will provide the name of the next product from the secret department, but the details of all other products, and the code word itself, are hidden. Since this method doesn't have a specified access control, it is set as the default of `internal`.

 It's not possible for contents within a structure to have a more permissive access control than the structure itself. For instance, we can't define the `nextProduct` method as being `public` because this is more permissive than the class it is defined in, which is only `internal`.
With further thought, this is obvious as you cannot create an instance of an internal class outside of the defining module, so how can you possibly call a method on a class instance that you can't even create?

Next, let's look at the `AppleStore.swift` file we created. The purpose here is to provide people outside of Apple the ability to purchase an iPhone through the Apple Store, but to restrict the creation of iPhones to just the factories where they are built, and restrict access to those factories to just the Apple Store:

```
public enum DeviceModel {
    case iPhoneSE
    case iPhone6
    case iPhone6Plus
    case iPhone6S
    case iPhone6SPlus
}

public class AppleiPhone {
    public let model: DeviceModel
    fileprivate init(model: DeviceModel) {
        self.model = model
    }
}

public class AppleStore {
    private var factory = Factory()
    public func selliPhone(ofModel model: DeviceModel) -> AppleiPhone {
        return factory.makeiPhone(ofModel: model)
```

```
        }
    }
```

Since we want to be able to sell the iPhone outside of the `AppleInc` module, the `DeviceModel` enum and the `AppleiPhone` and `AppleStore` classes are all declared as public. This has the benefit of making them available outside the module, but preventing them from being subclassed and modified, and given how Apple protects the look and feel of their phones and stores, this seems correct for this model.

The Apple Store needs to get the iPhones from somewhere, and that is the factory:

```
fileprivate class Factory {
    func makeiPhone(ofModel model: DeviceModel) -> AppleiPhone {
        return AppleiPhone(model: model)
    }
}
```

By making the `Factory` class `fileprivate`, it is only visible within this file, which is perfect because we only want the Apple Store to be able to use the factory to create iPhones.

We have also restricted the iPhone's initialization method to be only accessible from structures in this file:

```
fileprivate init(model: DeviceModel)
```

The resulting iPhone is public, but only structures within this file can create the iPhone class objects in the first place. In this case, that is done by the factory.

Next, let's look at the `Apple.swift` file:

```
public class Person {
    public let name: String
    public init(name: String) {
        self.name = name
    }
}

public class Apple {
    public private(set) var ceo: Person
    private var employees = [Person]()
    public let store = AppleStore()
    private let secretDepartment = SecretProductDepartment()
    public init() {
        ceo = Person(name: "Tim Cook")
        employees.append(ceo)
    }
    public func newEmployee(person: Person) {
```

```
        employees.append(person)
    }
    func weeklyProductMeeting() {
        var superSecretProduct =
secretDepartment.nextProduct(givenCodeWord: "Not sure... Abracadabra?") //
nil
        // Try again
        superSecretProduct = secretDepartment.nextProduct(givenCodeWord:
"Titan") // "iPhone 8"
        print(superSecretProduct)
    }
}
```

We make both the `Person` and `Apple` classes public, along with the `newEmployee` method, allowing new employees to join the company. The CEO, however, is defined to be both public and private:

```
public private(set) var ceo: Person
```

We are able to set a separate, more restrictive access control for setting a property than the one that was set for getting it. This has the effect of making it a read-only property from outside the defining structure. This provides the access we require, since we want the CEO to be visible outside of the `AppleInc` module, but we want to only be able to change the CEO from within Apple.

The final access control is open, which we applied to the `SwiftLanguage` class:

```
open class SwiftLanguage {
    open func versionNumber() -> Float {
        return 4.0
    }
    open func supportedPlatforms() -> [String] {
        return ["iOS", "macOSX", "tvOS", "watchOS", "Linux"]
    }
}
```

By declaring the class and methods as open, we are allowing them to be subclassed, overridden, and modified by anyone, including those outside the `AppleInc` module. With the Swift language being fully open source, this matches what we are trying to achieve.

There's more...

With our module fully defined, let's see how things look from outside the module. We need to build the module to make it available to the playground. Now, select the playground; it should have a statement that imports the `AppleInc` module:

```
import AppleInc
```

First, let's look at the most accessible class that we created--`SwiftLanguage`. Add the following to the playground:

```
class WinSwift: SwiftLanguage {
    override func versionNumber() -> Float {
        return 5.0
    }
    override func supportedPlatforms() -> [String] {
        var supported = super.supportedPlatforms()
        supported.append("Windows")
        return supported
    }
}
```

Since `SwiftLanguage` is `open`, we can subclass it to add more supported platforms and increase the version number.

Next, let's create an instance of the `Apple` class and see how we can interact with it:

```
let apple = Apple()

let keith = Person(name: "Keith Moon")
apple.newEmployee(person: keith)

print("Current CEO: \(apple.ceo.name)")
let jony = Person(name: "Jony Ive")
apple.ceo = jony // Doesn't compile
```

We can create `Person` and provide it to Apple as a new employee since the `Person` class and the `newEmployee` method are declared as public. We can retrieve information about the CEO, but we aren't able to set a new CEO as we defined the property to be private (set).

Another of the public interfaces provided by the module is the ability to buy an iPhone from the Apple Store:

```
// Buy new iPhone
let boughtiPhone = apple.store.selliPhone(ofModel: .iPhone6S)
// This works

// Try and create your own iPhone
let buildAndPhone = AppleiPhone(model: .iPhone6S) // Doesn't compile
```

We can retrieve a new iPhone from the Apple Store because we declared the `selliPhone` method as `public`, but we can't create a new iPhone directly as the iPhone's `init` method is declared as `fileprivate`.

See also

Further information about access control can be found in Apple's documentation of the Swift language at
`https://developer.apple.com/library/ios/documentation/Swift/Conceptual/Swift_Programming_Language/AccessControl.html`.

Extending functionality with extensions

Extensions let us add functionalities to the existing classes, structs, enums, and protocols. This can be especially useful when the original type is provided by an external framework, and therefore you aren't able to add a functionality directly.

Getting ready

Imagine that we often need to obtain the first word from a given string. Rather than repeatedly writing the code to split the string into words and then retrieving the first word, we can extend the functionality of `String` to provide its own first word.

How to do it...

Let's extend the functionality of `String`, and then we will examine how it works:

1. Add the following code to the playground:

```
extension String {
    func firstWord() -> String {
        let firstSpace = characters.index(of: " ") ??
characters.endIndex
        let firstName = String(characters.prefix(upTo:
firstSpace))
        return firstName
    }
}
```

2. Now we can use this new method on `String` to get the first word from a phrase:

```
let llap = "Live long, and prosper"
let firstWord = llap.firstWord()
print(firstWord) // Live
```

How it works...

We can define an extension using the extension keyword and then specify the type we want to extend. How we will extend the type is defined within curly brackets:

```
extension String {
    //...
}
```

Methods and computed properties can be defined in extensions in the same way that they are within classes, structs, and enums. Here, we add a `firstWord` function to the `String` struct:

```
extension String {
    func firstWord() -> String {
        let firstSpace = index(of: " ") ?? endIndex
        let firstName = String(prefix(upTo: firstSpace))
        return firstName
    }
}
```

The implementation of the `firstWord` method is not important to this recipe, so we'll just touch on it briefly.

In Swift 4, `String` is a collection, so we can use the collection methods to find the first index of an empty space. However, this could be nil since the string may contain only one word or no characters at all, so if the index is nil, we will use the `endIndex` instead. This is a function of the `??` operator, the nil coalescing operator, which we briefly mentioned earlier. It will assign the value on the left-hand side of the operator, unless it is nil, in which case it will assign the value on the right-hand side.

Then, we use the index of the first space to retrieve the substring up to the index, and create and return a `String` from this.

> Much of this behavior is new in Swift 4. `String` is a collection in Swift 4, but it would have been necessary to access String's `characters` array to perform the `String` manipulation in Swift 3. Also new to Swift 4 is the fact that methods that return a substring from the original string actually return a new `SubString` type. This new type can be used in many of the same ways as String, and can be used to create a `String`.

Extensions can implement anything that uses the existing functionality, but they can't store information in a new property; therefore, computed properties can be added, but stored properties cannot. Let's change our `firstWord` method to be a computed property instead:

```
extension String {
    var firstWord: String {
        let firstSpace = characters.index(of: " ") ?? characters.endIndex
        let firstName = String(characters.prefix(upTo: firstSpace))
        return firstName
    }
}
```

There's more...

Extensions can also be used to add protocol conformance, so let's create a protocol that we want to add conformance to. The protocol declares that something can be represented as an `Int`:

```
protocol IntRepresentable {
    var intValue: Int { get }
}
```

We can extend `Int` and have it conform to `IntRepresentable` by returning itself:

```
extension Int: IntRepresentable {
    var intValue: Int {
        return self
    }
}
```

Next, we'll extend `String`, and we'll use an `Int` constructor that takes a `String` and returns an `Int` if the `String` contains digits that represent an integer:

```
extension String: IntRepresentable {
    var intValue: Int {
        return Int(self) ?? 0
    }
}
```

We can also extend our own custom types and add conformance to the same protocol, so let's create an `enum` that can be `IntRepresentable`:

```
enum CrewComplement: Int {
    case enterpriseD = 1014
    case voyager = 150
    case deepSpaceNine = 2000
}
```

Conformance to `IntRepresentable` can be added by providing the `rawValue`:

```
extension CrewComplement: IntRepresentable {
    var intValue: Int {
        return rawValue
    }
}
```

We now have `String`, `Int`, and `CrewComplement` all conforming to `IntRepresentable`, and since we didn't define `String` or `Int`, we have only been able to add conformance through the use of extensions. This common conformance allows us to treat them as the same type:

```
var intableThings = [IntRepresentable]()
intableThings.append(55)
intableThings.append(1200)
intableThings.append("5")
intableThings.append("1009")
intableThings.append(CrewComplement.enterpriseD)
intableThings.append(CrewComplement.voyager)
intableThings.append(CrewComplement.deepSpaceNine)
```

```
let over1000 = intableThings.flatMap { $0.intValue > 1000 ? $0.intValue:
nil }
print(over1000)
```

See also

Further information about extensions can be found in Apple's documentation of the Swift language at
https://developer.apple.com/library/mac/documentation/Swift/Conceptual/Swift_Pr
ogramming_Language/Extensions.html.

3

Data Wrangling with Swift Control Flow

In this chapter, we will cover the following recipes:

- Making decisions with if/else
- Switch it up
- For the love of loops
- While loops
- Try, throw, do, and catch - Swift error handling
- Checking up front with Guard
- Doing it later with defer
- Bailing out with fatalError and precondition

Introduction

Programming is all about making decisions. The purpose of most code involves taking information, inspecting it, making decisions, and producing an output. So far, we have seen a lot of ways to represent information, but in this chapter, we will explore how to make decisions based on that information and alter the control flow of the code.

All the code for this chapter can be found in following GitHub repository:

`https://github.com/SwiftProgrammingCookbook/DataWranglingWithSwiftControlFlow`

Making decisions with if/else

The if/else statement is a cornerstone of almost every programming language. It enables code to be executed conditionally, based on the outcome of a Boolean statement.

Getting ready

If you have ever played pool, you'll know that the aim of the game (when playing standard 8-ball pool) is to pot all the balls of one type and then to pot the black ball. When using American pool balls, they are numbered 1-15, and have a different pattern depending on their type. Balls 1-7 have a solid color, balls 9-15 are white with a colored stripe around them, and ball 8 is black.

Let's write a function that will take the number on the pool ball and return to us the type of ball it is.

How to do it...

Let's take a look at these steps to write this function, and then we will review how it works:

1. First, let's create enum to describe the possible types:

```
enum PoolBallType {
    case solid
    case stripe
    case black
}
```

2. Next, we'll create the method that will take an Int and return PoolBallType:

```
func poolBallType(forNumber number: Int) -> PoolBallType {
    if number < 8 {
        return .solid
    } else if number > 8 {
        return .stripe
    } else {
        return .black
    }
}
```

3. Now we can use this function and test that we get the expected results:

```
let two = poolBallType(forNumber: 2) // .solid
let eight = poolBallType(forNumber: 8) // .black
let twelve = poolBallType(forNumber: 12) // .stripe
```

How it works...

Within the function, we define three code paths: if, else if, and else:

```
if <#a boolean expression#> {
    <#executed if boolean expression above is true#>
} else if <#other boolean expression#> {
    <#executed if other boolean expression above is true#>
} else {
    <#executed if neither boolean expressions are true#>
}
```

First, we want to determine whether the ball is solid. Since we know that the balls numbered 1-7 are solid, we can test whether the ball number is less than 8, with number<8. If this is true, we return the .solid case of our enum.

If that is false, the else if Boolean expression is evaluated. As balls 9-15 are striped, we can test whether the ball number is more than 8, with number > 8. If this is true, we return the .stripe case of our enum.

Lastly, if both the preceding Boolean expressions are false, we return the .black case of our enum.

The else if and else blocks are optional, and you can declare multiple else if to cover additional conditions. Let's expand our preceding example with an extra else if to better decide the pool ball type.

As we stated previously, pool balls are numbered between 1 and 15, but we don't take into account those upper and lower bounds in our implementation, so if we were to provide the function with ball number 0, it would return .solid, and if we were to provide ball number 16, it would return .stripe, which doesn't accurately reflect our intention:

```
let zero = poolBallType(forNumber: 0) // .solid
let sixteen = poolBallType(forNumber: 16) // .stripe
```

Let's modify our function to only return a pool ball type if the number is between 1 and 15, and return nil otherwise:

```swift
func poolBallType(forNumber number: Int) -> PoolBallType? {
    if number > 0 && number < 8 {
        return .solid
    } else if number > 8 && number < 16 {
        return .stripe
    } else if number == 8 {
        return .black
    } else {
        return nil
    }
}
```

Now we have four code branches in our `if` statement, and we can use the AND operator, `&&`, to combine Boolean statements; the OR operator, `||`, is also available.

With our improved function, providing a number outside of the expected range will produce a nil:

```swift
let two = poolBallType(forNumber: 2) // .solid
let eight = poolBallType(forNumber: 8) // .black
let twelve = poolBallType(forNumber: 12) // .stripe
let zero = poolBallType(forNumber: 0) // nil
let sixteen = poolBallType(forNumber: 16) // nil
```

There's more...

Let's take a look at some of the other ways we can use if/else statements.

Conditional unwrap

The function we created earlier returns an optional value, so if you want to do anything useful with the resulting value, we need to `unwrap` the optional. So far, the only way to do this is by force unwrapping, which will cause a crash if the value is nil.

Instead, we can use an `if` statement to *conditionally unwrap* the optional, turning it into a more useful, non-optional value.

Let's create a function that will print information about a pool ball of a given number. If the provided number is valid for a pool ball, it will print the ball's number and type; otherwise, it will print a message explaining that it is not a valid number.

Since we will want to print the value of the `PoolBallType` enum, let's make it String backed, which will make printing its value easier:

```
enum PoolBallType: String {
    case solid
    case stripe
    case black
}
```

Now, let's write the function to print the pool ball details:

```
func printBallDetails(ofNumber number: Int) {
    let possibleBallType = poolBallType(forNumber: number)
    if let ballType = possibleBallType {
        print("\(number) - \(ballType.rawValue)")
    } else {
        print("\(number) is not a valid pool ball number")
    }
}
```

The first thing we do in our `printBallDetails` function is to get the ball type for the given number:

```
let possibleBallType = poolBallType(forNumber: number)
```

In our improved version of this function, this returns an optional version of the `PoolBallType` enum. We want to include the `rawValue` of the returned `enum` as part of printing the ball details, but we need to unwrap it to do that:

```
if let ballType = possibleBallType {
    print("\(number) - \(ballType.rawValue))")
}
```

In this `if` statement, instead of defining a Boolean expression, we are assigning our optional value to a constant; the `if` statement uses this to *conditionally unwrap* the optional. The value of the optional is checked to see whether it is `nil`; if it is not `nil`, then the value is unwrapped and assigned to the constant as a non-optional value; that constant is now available within the scope of the curly brackets following the `if` statement. We use that `ballType` non-optional value to obtain the raw value for the print statement.

Since the `if` branch of the `if-else` statement is followed when the optional value is non-nil, the `else` branch is followed when the optional value is nil:

```
else {
    print("\(number) is not a valid pool ball number")
}
```

Since this means that the given number is not valid for a pool ball, we print a relevant message.

Now we can insert any integer and print ball correct details:

```
printBallDetails(ofNumber: 2)   // 2 - solid
printBallDetails(ofNumber: 8)   // 8 - black
printBallDetails(ofNumber: 12)  // 12 - stripe
printBallDetails(ofNumber: 0)   // 0 is not a valid pool ball number
printBallDetails(ofNumber: 16)  // 16 is not a valid pool ball number
```

Chain unwrapping Optionals

The ability of `if` statements conditional unwrap Optionals can be chained together to produce some useful and concise code. The following example is a bit contrived, but it illustrates how we can use a single `if` statement to unwrap a chain of optional values.

When you play a game of pool, called a *frame*, the type of the first ball you pot becomes the type you need to pot for the rest of the frame, and your opponent has to pot the opposite type.

Let's define a frame of pool and say that we want to track what type of ball each player will be potting:

```
class PoolFrame {
    var player1BallType: PoolBallType?
    var player2BallType: PoolBallType?
}
```

We will also create a `PoolTable` object that has an optional `currentFrame` property, which will contain information about the current frame if one is in progress:

```
class PoolTable {
    var currentFrame: PoolFrame?
}
```

So, we have a pool table that has an optional frame and a frame that has optional ball type for each player.

Now, let's write a function that prints the ball type for player 1 in the current frame. However, it is possible that the current frame is `nil` because there is no frame currently being played, or that player 1's ball type is `nil` because a ball hasn't been potted. Therefore, we need to account for either of those being `nil`:

```
func printBallTypeOfPlayer1(forTable table: PoolTable) {
    if let frame = table.currentFrame, let ballType = frame.player1BallType
{
        print(ballType.rawValue)
    } else {
        print("Player 1 doesn't yet have a ball type or there is no current
frame")
    }
}
```

Our function is given `PoolTable`, and to print player 1's ball type, we first need to check and unwrap the `currentFrame` property, and then we need to check and unwrap the current frame's `player1BallType` property.

We can do this by nesting our `if` statements as follows:

```
func printBallTypeOfPlayer1(forTable table: PoolTable) {
    if let frame = table.currentFrame {
        if let ballType = frame.player1BallType {
            print(ballType.rawValue)
        } //... handle else
    } //... handle else
}
```

Instead, we can handle this chained unwrapping in one `if` statement by performing the unwrapping statement sequentially, separated by commas, and each statement can access the unwrapped values from the previous statements:

```
func printBallTypeOfPlayer1(forTable table: PoolTable) {
    if let frame = table.currentFrame, let ballType = frame.player1BallType
{
        print("\(ballType)")
    } //... handle else
}
```

The first statement unwraps the `currentFrame` property, and the second statement uses that unwrapped frame to unwrap player 1's ball type.

Let's use the functions we've just created:

```
//
// Table with no frame in play
//
let table = PoolTable()
table.currentFrame = nil
printBallTypeOfPlayer1(forTable: table)
// Player 1 doesn't yet have a ball type or there is no current frame

//
// Table with frame in play, but no balls potted
//
let frame = PoolFrame()
frame.player1BallType = nil
frame.player2BallType = nil
table.currentFrame = frame
printBallTypeOfPlayer1(forTable: table)
// Player 1 doesn't yet have a ball type or there is no current frame

//
// Table with frame in play, and a ball potted
//
frame.player1BallType = .solid
frame.player2BallType = .stripe
printBallTypeOfPlayer1(forTable: table)
// solid
```

Enum with associated values

As we saw in the enumeration recipe from Chapter 1, *Swift Building Blocks*, enums can have associated values, and we can use an if statement to both check an enum's case and extract the associated value in one expression.

Let's create an enum to represent the result of the pool game, with each case having an associated message:

```
enum Result {
    case win(congratulationsMessage: String)
    case lose(commiserationsMessage: String)
}
```

Next, we'll create a function that takes a `Result` and prints either the congratulatory message or the commiseration message:

```
func printMessage(forResult result: Result) {
    if case Result.win(congratulationsMessage: let winString) = result {
        print("You won! \(winString)")
    } else if case Result.lose(commiserationsMessage: let loseString) =
result {
        print("You lost :( \(loseString)")
    }
}
```

Calling this function will print the result, followed by the relevant message:

```
let result = Result.win(congratulationsMessage: "You're simply the best!")
printMessage(forResult: result) // You won! You're simply the best!
```

The `if` case block will be executed if the value on the right-hand side matches the case on the left-hand side. In addition, you can specify a local constant for the associated value (`winString` in the following example), which is then available within the subsequent block:

```
if case Result.win(congratulationsMessage: let winString) = result {
    print("You won! \(winString)")
}
```

See also

Further information about if/else can be found in Apple's documentation of the Swift language at
https://developer.apple.com/library/ios/documentation/Swift/Conceptual/Swift_Programming_Language/Statements.html.

Switch it up

Switch statements allow you to control the flow of execution by testing one specific value in multiple ways. In Objective-C, and other languages, Switch statements can only be used on values that can be represented by an integer, and are most commonly used to make decisions based on enumeration cases.

As we have seen, **enumerations** have become a lot more powerful in Swift, as they can be based on more than just integers, and so too can switch statements.

Switch statements in Swift can be used on any type and have advanced pattern-matching functionality, as we will see.

Getting ready

If you are old enough to remember the early days of the home computer, you may also remember text-based adventures. These were simple games that usually described a scene and then let you move around by typing if you want to move north, south, east, or west. You would find and pick up items, and could often combine them to solve puzzles.

How to do it...

Let's create parts of a text-based adventure to see how we can use switch statements to make decisions:

1. First, let's define an `enum` to represent the directions we can travel in:

```
enum CompassPoint {
    case north
    case south
    case east
    case west
}
```

2. Next, let's create a function that describes what the player of the text adventure will see when they look in that direction:

```
func lookTowards(_ direction: CompassPoint) {
    switch direction {
    case .north:
        print("To the north lies a winding road")
    case .south:
        print("To the south is the Prancing Pony tavern")
    case .east:
        print("To the east is a blacksmith")
    case .west:
        print("The the west is the town square")
    }
}

lookTowards(.south) // To the south is the Prancing Pony tavern
```

3. In our text adventure, users can pick up items and attempt to combine them to produce new items and solve problems. Let's define our available items as an `enum`:

```
enum Item {
    case key
    case lockedDoor
    case openDoor
    case bluntKnife
    case sharpeningStone
    case sharpKnife
}
```

4. Now, we'll write a function that takes two items and tries to combine them into a new item. If the items cannot be combined, it will return nil:

```
func combine(_ firstItem: Item, with secondItem: Item) -> Item?
{
    switch (firstItem, secondItem) {
    case (.key, .lockedDoor):
        print("You have unlocked the door!")
        return .openDoor
    case (.bluntKnife, .sharpeningStone):
        print("Your knife is now sharp")
        return .sharpKnife
    default:
        print("\(firstItem) and \(secondItem) cannot be
combined)")
        return nil
    }
}
let door = combine(.key, with: .lockedDoor) // openDoor
let oilAndWater = combine(.bluntKnife, with: .lockedDoor) //
nil
```

5. In our text adventure, the player will meet different characters and can interact with them; so first, let's define the characters that the player can meet:

```
enum Character: String {
    case wizard
    case bartender
    case dragon
}
```

6. Now, let's write a function that will allow the player to say something, and optionally provide a character to say it to. The interaction that will occur will depend on what say is and the character it is said to:

```swift
func say(_ textToSay: String, to character: Character? = nil) {
    switch (textToSay, character) {
    case ("abracadabra", .wizard?):
        print("The wizard says, \"Hey, that's my line!\"")
    case ("Pour me a drink", .bartender?):
        print("The bartender pours you a drink")
    case ("Can I have some of your gold?", .dragon?):
        print("The dragon burns you to death with his firey
breath")
    case (let textSaid, nil):
        print("You say \"\(textSaid)\", to no-one.")
    case (_, let anyCharacter?):
        print("The \(anyCharacter) looks at you, blankly)")
    }
}
say("Is anybody there?") // You say "Is anybody there?", to no-
one.
say("Pour me a drink", to: .bartender) // The bartender pours
you a drink
say("Can I open a tab?", to: .bartender) // The bartender looks
at you, blankly
```

How it works...

Within the lookTowards function, we want to print a different message for each possible CompassPoint case; to do this, we can use a switch statement:

```swift
func lookTowards(_ direction: CompassPoint) {
    switch direction {
    case .north:
        print("To the north lies a winding road")
    case .south:
        print("To the south is the Prancing Pony tavern")
    case .east:
        print("To the east is a blacksmith")
    case .west:
        print("The the west is the town square")
    }
}
```

At the top of the `switch` statement, we define the value that we want to switch on; then we define what we want to be done when that value matches each of the defined cases using the `case` keyword and then the matching pattern:

```
switch <#value#> {
case <#pattern#>:
    <#code#>
case <#pattern#>:
    <#code#>
//...
}
```

Each `case` statement is evaluated in turn, and if the pattern matches the value, the subsequent code is executed.

If you are familiar with switch statements from Objective-C, you may remember that you needed to add `break;` at the end of each case statement to stop the execution falling through to the next case statement. This is not needed in Swift; the break in execution is implied by the beginning of the next case statement. The only time this isn't the case, it is because your `case` statement is intentionally empty; in these cases, you need to add `break` to tell the compiler that it is intentionally blank for this case. If you do not want execution to fall through to the next case statement, you can add `fallthrough` as the end of the case statement.

In our `combine` function, we have two values that we want to switch on, so we can provide multiple values to the switch statement in the form of a tuple:

```
func combine(_ firstItem: Item, with secondItem: Item) -> Item? {
    switch (firstItem, secondItem) {
    //....
    }
}
```

Then, for each case statement, we define the valid value for each part of the tuple:

```
case (.key, .lockedDoor):
print("You have unlocked the door!")
return .openDoor
```

A switch statement in Swift requires that every possible case possible is covered; however, you can cover all the remaining possibilities in one go using the `default` case:

```
switch (firstItem, secondItem) {
//...
default:
    print("\(firstItem) and \(secondItem) cannot be combined)")
    return nil
}
```

For our preceding combine function, you will notice that the player will only be able to combine the items if they provide them in the right order:

```
let door1 = combine(.key, with: .lockedDoor) // openDoor
let door2 = combine(.lockedDoor, with: .key) // nil
```

This is not the desired behavior as there is no way for the player to know the correct order. To solve this, we can add multiple patterns to each case statement. So, when the player provides the `key` and `lockedDoor` items, we can handle the order `key`, `lockedDoor`, and the order `lockedDoor`, `key` with the same case statement, using the following format:

```
switch <#value#> {
case <#pattern#>, <#pattern#>:
    <#code#>
default:
    <#code#>
}
```

So, when we add the opposite order to each case, we get the following:

```
func combine(_ firstItem: Item, with secondItem: Item) -> Item? {
    switch (firstItem, secondItem) {
    case (.key, .lockedDoor), (.lockedDoor, .key):
        print("You have unlocked the door!")
        return .openDoor
    case (.bluntKnife, .sharpeningStone), (.sharpeningStone, .bluntKnife):
        print("Your knife is now sharp")
        return .sharpKnife
    default:
        print("\(firstItem) and \(secondItem) cannot be combined)")
        return nil
    }
}
```

Now the items can be combined in any order:

```
let door1 = combine(.key, with: .lockedDoor) // openDoor
let door2 = combine(.lockedDoor, with: .key) // openDoor
```

For our `say` method, we again have two values that we want to switch on, the text that the player says, and the character they want to say it to, but the character value is optional. Therefore, we will need to unwrap the value to compare with non-optional values:

```
func say(_ textToSay: String, to character: Character? = nil) {
    switch (textToSay, character) {
    case ("abracadabra", .wizard?):
        print("The wizard says, "Hey, that's my line!"")
        //...
    }
}
```

In a switch statement, when the value is optional, you can compare it to a non-optional value by adding a `?` to wrap it as an optional, making the comparison valid, as we did earlier, by comparing the optional `character` value to `.wizard?`.

Where we have two values for a certain set of options, we may only care about one of the values, and the other value can be anything and the case will still be valid. In our example, once all the specific `textToSay` and character pairings have been handled, and the case where there is no character is handled, we want to unwrap and retrieve the character, but we don't care about the `textToSay` value, so we can use `_` to indicate that any value is acceptable:

```
func say(_ textToSay: String, to character: Character? = nil) {
    switch (textToSay, character) {
    //...
    case (_, let anyCharacter?):
        print("The \(anyCharacter) looks at you, blankly)")
    }
}
```

To retrieve the value of the character entered as part of this case statement rather than declaring a value to be matched, we define a constant that will receive the value, and since the value we are switching on is optional, we also add a `?`, which will unwrap the value if not `nil`, and assign it to the constant.

See also

Further information about tuples can be found in Apple's documentation of the Swift language at `https://developer.apple.com/library/ios/documentation/Swift/Conceptual/Swift_Programming_Language/ControlFlow.html#//apple_ref/doc/uid/TP40014097-CH9-ID129`.

For the love of loops

For loops allow you to execute code for each element in a collection or range.

How to do it...

Take a look at the following steps and code:

1. Let's imagine that we have an array of elements, and we want to do something with every item in the array:

   ```
   let theBeatles = ["John", "Paul", "George", "Ringo"]
   ```

2. We can use a `for` loop, which will extract each element of the array in turn, and will execute the given block of code for each element. The syntax of a `for` loop is as follows:

   ```
   for <#each element#> in <#collection or range#> {
       <#code to execute#>
   }
   ```

3. So, to print all the musicians in the Beatles, let's loop through our `theBeatles` array and print each String element that the `for` loop provides:

   ```
   for musician in theBeatles {
       print(musician)
   }
   ```

4. Perhaps you don't need to loop through an array, and just want to execute some code a set number of times. We can do this by providing a range instead of a collection:

   ```
   // 5 times table
   for value in 1...12 {
       print("5 x \(value) = \(value*5)")
   }
   ```

5. We've looped through an array, but what about dictionaries? Dictionaries contain pairings between a key and a value, so when looping through a dictionary, we will be provided with both the key and the value in the form of a tuple:

   ```
   let beatlesByInstrument = ["rhythm guitar": "John",
                              "bass guitar": "Paul",
                              "lead guitar": "George",
   ```

```
                                    "drums": "Ringo"]
          for (key, value) in beatlesByInstrument {
              print("\(value) plays \(key)")
          }
```

How it works...

Let's look at how we loop through our `theBeatles` array:

```
for musician in theBeatles {
    print(musician)
}
```

First, we specify the `for` keyword, and then we provide a name for the local variable that will be used for each element in the collection or range. Then, the `in` keyword is provided, followed by the collection or range that will be looped through.

The syntax is the same for range-based loops, but the value provided for each loop is the next integer in the range:

```
for value in 1...12 {
    print("5 x \(value) = \(value*5)")
}
```

As we have seen earlier, a range can be a *closed range*, where the range includes the start value and the end value, like the one specified earlier, or a *half-open range*, which goes up to, but doesn't include, the last value. Consider the following example:

```
for value in 1..<13 {
    print("5 x \(value) = \(value*5)")
}
```

When looping through a dictionary, we need to be provided with both the key and value; this is done by providing a tuple that will receive each key and value in the dictionary:

```
for (key, value) in beatlesByInstrument {
    print("\(value) plays \(key)")
}
```

As in the preceding code, we can define the tuple and name each of the values, which can then be used in an execution block. Let's change the tuple values to better describe the values:

```
for (instrument, musician) in beatlesByInstrument {
    print("\(musician) plays \(instrument)")
}
```

See also

Further information about For-In loops can be found in Apple's documentation of the Swift language at `https://developer.apple.com/library/content/documentation/Swift/ Conceptual/Swift_Programming_Language/ControlFlow.html#//apple_ref/doc/uid/ TP40014097-CH9-ID121`.

While loops

For loops are great when you know how many times you intend to loop, but if you want to loop until a certain condition is met, you need a **while loop**.

A while loop has the following syntax:

```
while <#boolean expression#> {
    <#code to execute#>
}
```

The code block will execute over and over until the Boolean expression returns `false`. Therefore, it's a common pattern to change the current state in the code block that may cause the Boolean expression to change to `false`.

 If there is no chance that the Boolean expression can become true, the code will loop forever, which can lock up your app.

Getting ready

Let's work out how many times in a row we can flip a coin and get heads.

To flip our coin, we will need to randomly pick either heads or tails, so we will need to use a random number generator from the Foundation framework. We will discuss Foundation further in Chapter 5, *Beyond the Standard Library*, but for now, we just need to import the Foundation framework:

```
import Foundation
```

How to do it...

We'll write the code for counting our coin flip to heads, and then we'll look at how we did it, so let's get started:

1. Let's create an enum to represent a coin flip, and use the random number generator to randomly choose heads or tails:

```
enum CoinFlip: Int {
    case heads
    case tails
    static func flipCoin() -> CoinFlip {
        return CoinFlip(rawValue: Int(arc4random_uniform(2)))!
    }
}
```

2. Now, let's create a function that will return the number of heads in a row from coin flips. The function will flip the coin within a while loop and continue to loop while the coin flip results in heads:

```
func howManyHeadsInARow() -> Int {
    var numberOfHeadsInARow = 0
    var currentCoinFlip = CoinFlip.flipCoin()
    while currentCoinFlip == .heads {
        numberOfHeadsInARow = numberOfHeadsInARow + 1
        currentCoinFlip = CoinFlip.flipCoin()
    }
    return numberOfHeadsInARow
}

let noOfHeads = howManyHeadsInARow()
```

How it works...

In our function, we start by keeping track of how many coin flips in a row are heads and keep a reference to the current coin flip, which will form the condition for the while loop:

```
func howManyHeadsInARow() -> Int {
    var numberOfHeadsInARow = 0
    var currentCoinFlip = CoinFlip.flipCoin()
    //...
}
```

In our while loop, we will continue to loop while the current coin flip is heads; while that is true, the code in the following block is executed:

```
while currentCoinFlip == .heads {
    numberOfHeadsInARow = numberOfHeadsInARow + 1
    currentCoinFlip = CoinFlip.flipCoin()
}
```

Within the code block, we add one to our running total and we reflip the coin. Since we are flipping the coin and assigning it to `currentCoinFlip`, it will get rechecked on the next loop, which meets our requirement of changing the state to ensure that we don't loop forever.

As soon as the coin flip is tails, the while loop condition will be false, and so the execution will move on and return the running total we have been keeping:

```
return numberOfHeadsInARow
```

Now, every time you call the function, the coin will be randomly flipped and the number of heads in a row will be returned, so each time it's called, you may get a different value returned. Try it as follows:

```
let noOfHeads = howManyHeadsInARow()
```

There's more...

We can actually simplify our while loop by doing the coin flip as part of the loop continuation checking:

```
func howManyHeadsInARow() -> Int {
    var numberOfHeadsInARow = 0
    while CoinFlip.flipCoin() == .heads {
        numberOfHeadsInARow = numberOfHeadsInARow + 1
    }
    return numberOfHeadsInARow
}
```

Each time through the loop, the while condition is evaluated, which involves reflipping the coin and checking the outcome.

This is more concise and removes the need to track the `currentCoinFlip`.

See also

Further information about while loops can be found in Apple's documentation of the Swift language at `https://developer.apple.com/library/content/documentation/Swift/` `Conceptual/Swift_Programming_Language/ControlFlow.html#//apple_ref/doc/uid/` `TP40014097-CH9-ID124`.

Try, throw, do and, catch - Swift error handling

Errors happen; during programming, these errors may be due to your own code behaving in unexpected ways, or due to unexpected information or behavior from external systems. When these errors happen, it's important to handle them appropriately; indeed, good error handling can separate a good app from a great app.

Swift provides a deliberate and flexible pattern for handling errors, helpfully allowing specific errors to be cascaded through a complex system.

How to do it...

To examine error handling, we will model a process that can go wrong, and that, for me, is cooking a meal:

1. First, let's define the steps involved in cooking a meal as states that the meal will transition through:

```
enum MealState {
    case initial
    case buyIngredients
    case prepareIngredients
    case cook
    case plateUp
    case serve
}
```

2. Next, we will create an object to represent the meal we will be cooking, which will hold the state of the meal as it moves through the process. While we want to allow the meal to transition between states, not all state transitions should be possible; for instance, you can't move from buying ingredients to serving the meal; the meal should move sequentially from one state to the next. We can provide these restrictions by only allowing the state to be set internally, using access controls that we explored in the previous chapter.

3. Changing the state externally can happen through a function that will throw an error if the state transition isn't possible:

```
class Meal {
    private(set) var state: MealState = .initial
    func change(to newState: MealState) throws {
        switch (state, newState) {
        case (.initial, .buyIngredients),
            (.buyIngredients, .prepareIngredients),
            (.prepareIngredients, .cook),
            (.cook, .plateUp),
            (.plateUp, .serve):
            state = newState
        default:
            throw MealError.canOnlyMoveToAppropriateState
        }
    }
}
```

4. In Objective-C, errors took the form of a dedicated object, NSError; however, in keeping with Swift's protocol-orientated approach, errors in Swift are defined as a protocol--Error. This approach allows you to construct your own type to represent errors within your code, and just have it conform to the Error protocol.

5. A common approach is to define errors as enum, with the enum cases representing the different types of errors that can occur. Let's define the error thrown in the preceding Meal class:

```
enum MealError: Error {
    case canOnlyMoveToAppropriateState
}
```

6. We now have a method that can throw an error, so when using the method, we need to try to execute it in a do block and catch any error that may occur:

```
let dinner = Meal()
do {
    try dinner.change(to: .buyIngredients)
```

```
        try dinner.change(to: .prepareIngredients)
        try dinner.change(to: .cook)
        try dinner.change(to: .plateUp)
        try dinner.change(to: .serve)
        print("Dinner is served!")
    } catch let error {
        print(error)
    }
```

How it works...

The metaphor used in Swift error handling (as well as other languages) is *throwing* and *catching*. A method can *throw* an error if a problem occurs during its execution, at which point nothing further in the method will be executed, and the error is passed back to where the method was called from.

In order to receive this error (perhaps to provide the details of the error to the user), you must *catch* the error at the place the method is called.

To throw an error, you have to declare that the method has the potential to throw an error. Declaring that a method `throws` allows the compiler to expect potential errors from the method and ensure that you don't forget to catch these errors.

Methods can be declared as potentially throwing an error using the `throws` keyword:

```
func change(to newState: MealState) throws {
    //...
}
```

Within our change state method, we only change the state if we are moving to the next sequential state; anything else isn't allowed and should throw an error. We can do this using the `throw` keyword, followed by a value that conforms to the `Error` protocol:

```
func change(to newState: MealState) throws {
    //...
    default:
        throw MealError.canOnlyMoveToAppropriateState
    }
}
```

When we create the `Meal` object and move through the states of preparing the meal, each change of the state can throw an error. When we call a method that is marked as possibly throwing an error, we have to do it a certain way; we define a `do` block, within which we may call methods that can throw, and we then define a `catch` block that will be executed if any of these methods do throw an error. Each call to a throwing method must be prefixed with the `try` keyword:

```
let dinner = Meal()
do {
    try dinner.change(to: .buyIngredients)
    try dinner.change(to: .prepareIngredients)
    try dinner.change(to: .cook)
    try dinner.change(to: .plateUp)
    try dinner.change(to: .serve)
    print("Dinner is served!")
} catch let error {
    print(error)
}
```

If any of these methods does throw an error, execution will immediately move to the `catch` block; therefore, by placing code after the `try` methods are called, we are guaranteeing that it will only be executed if the method does not throw an error. By printing `Dinner is served!` after all the state transitions are called, we know this will only print if we have successfully moved through all the states. Try changing the order of these state change calls, and you'll see that the error is printed, and `Dinner is served!` is not.

In our catch block, after the `catch` keyword, we can define the local constant that we want the caught error to be assigned to. However, if we don't specify a local constant here, Swift will implicitly create one for us called `error`, so we can actually omit the constant declaration in the catch block and still print the value of the error:

```
do {
    //...
} catch {
    print(error)
}
```

There's more...

We have seen how we can throw and catch errors, but we mentioned in the introduction that we can cascade errors through a system, so let's look at how we can do this.

In our meal preparation example, we allow the meal state to be changed externally through a `change` method that can throw an error. Let's make that method private and instead, create some specific methods for moving to each state:

```swift
class Meal {
    private(set) var state: MealState = .initial
    private func change(to newState: MealState) throws {
        switch (state, newState) {
        case (.initial, .buyIngredients),
             (.buyIngredients, .prepareIngredients),
             (.prepareIngredients, .cook),
             (.cook, .plateUp),
             (.plateUp, .serve):
            state = newState
        default:
            throw MealError.canOnlyMoveToAppropriateState
        }
    }
    func buyIngredients() throws {
        try change(to: .buyIngredients)
    }
    func prepareIngredients() throws {
        try change(to: .prepareIngredients)
    }
    func cook() throws {
        try change(to: .cook)
    }
    func plateUp() throws {
        try change(to: .plateUp)
    }
    func serve() throws {
        try change(to: .serve)
    }
}
```

You'll notice that when we call the `change` method from within each of the new methods, we don't need to do it in a do block, and we don't need a `catch` block to catch the error. This is because we have defined each of the new methods as potentially throwing an error, so if the call to the `change` method throws an error, this error will be passed to the caller of our new method as though it were throwing an error.

This mechanism allows errors that may occur many levels deep in your code to be surfaced and handled appropriately.

We now need to amend our meal preparation code to use these new methods:

```
let dinner = Meal()
do {
    try dinner.buyIngredients()
    try dinner.prepareIngredients()
    try dinner.cook()
    try dinner.plateUp()
    try dinner.serve()
    print("Dinner is served!")
} catch let error {
    print(error)
}
```

Let's add the ability to actually affect our meal; we'll add a method to add salt to the meal and a property to allow us to track how much salt is added. Add these to the end of the Meal class:

```
class Meal {
    //...
    private(set) var saltAdded = 0
    func addSalt() throws {
        if saltAdded >= 5 {
            throw MealError.tooMuchSalt
        } else if case .initial = state, case .buyIngredients = state {
            throw MealError.wrongStateToAddSalt
        } else {
            saltAdded = saltAdded + 1
        }
    }
}
```

There are two ways in which adding salt can throw an error, either because we are in the wrong state to add salt (we can't add salt until after we have bought the ingredients), or because it would be too much salt. Let's add these two new errors to our MealError enum:

```
enum MealError: Error {
    case canOnlyMoveToAppropriateState
    case tooMuchSalt
    case wrongStateToAddSalt
}
```

So now, we have three possible errors that can occur during the preparation of a meal, and we may want to handle those errors differently. We can use multiple catch blocks to filter just specific errors that we want to catch, so we can handle each error separately:

```
let dinner = Meal()
do {
    try dinner.buyIngredients()
    try dinner.prepareIngredients()
    try dinner.cook()
    try dinner.plateUp()
    try dinner.serve()
    print("Dinner is served!")
} catch MealError.canOnlyMoveToAppropriateState {
    print("It's not possible to move to this state")
} catch MealError.tooMuchSalt {
    print("Too much salt!")
} catch MealError.wrongStateToAddSalt {
    print("Can't add salt at this stage")
} catch {
    print("Some other error: \(error)")
}
```

 It is important to ensure that all the possible errors are handled by the catch blocks, as an unhandled error will result in a crash. It is, therefore, safest to add an unfiltered catch block at the end to catch any errors not caught by the previous blocks.

Since functions can throw an error, and closures are a type of function that can be passed as a parameter; we can have a function that takes a throwing closure where it can also throw an error. It may be that the only errors our function will throw are errors produced by the throwing closure that was passed as a parameter.

When that is true, a function can be defined as rethrowing, using the rethrows keyword.

The situation described here is confusing, so let's look at an example:

```
func makeMeal(using block: (Meal) throws -> ()) rethrows -> Meal {
    let newMeal = Meal()
    try block(newMeal)
    return newMeal
}
```

This makeMeal function takes a closure as a parameter; that closure takes a Meal object as a parameter and doesn't return anything, but may throw an error.

The purpose of this function is to handle the creation of the meal object for you, just leaving you to do any meal preparation within the block; it then returns the meal that was created and prepared. Let's see it in use:

```
do {
    let dinner = try makeMeal { meal in
        try meal.buyIngredients()
        try meal.prepareIngredients()
        try meal.cook()
        try meal.addSalt()
        try meal.plateUp()
        try meal.serve()
    }
    if dinner.state == .serve {
        print("Dinner is served!")
    }
} catch MealError.canOnlyMoveToAppropriateState {
    print("It's not possible to move to this state")
} catch MealError.tooMuchSalt {
    print("Too much salt!")
} catch MealError.wrongStateToAddSalt {
    print("Can't add salt at this stage")
}
```

The `makeMeal` function only throws errors thrown by the closure parameter, so it can be declared as rethrowing. Declaring a function of this type with the `rethrows` keyword isn't required as it can be declared with `throws` instead; however, the compiler can make additional optimizations for a rethrowing function.

See also

Further information about error handling can be found in Apple's documentation of the Swift language at
https://developer.apple.com/library/content/documentation/Swift/Conceptual/Swift_Programming_Language/ErrorHandling.html.

Checking up front with guard

We have seen in previous recipes how we can use `if` statements to check Boolean expressions and unwrap optional values. It's a common use case to want to do some checks and conditional unwrapping at the beginning of a block of code, and then, only execute the subsequent code if everything is as expected. Often, this results in wrapping the whole block of code in an `if` statement:

```
if <#boolean check and unwrapping#> {
    <#a block of code#>
    <#that could be quite long#>
}
```

Swift has a better solution expressly for this purpose--the `guard` statement.

How to do it...

Let's imagine that we have some data that came from an external source, and we want to turn it into model objects that our code can understand and perhaps display it to the user:

1. First, for the purpose of this example, let's create the data that can be from an external source; in this example, it is data on the planets of the solar system in the form of an array of dictionaries:

```
// From
http://idahoptv.org/ntti/nttilessons/lessons2000/lau1.html
let inputData: [[String: Any]] = [
    ["name": "Mercury", "positionFromSun": 1, "diameterInKMs":
4800, "distanceFromSunInAUs": 0.387, "hasRings": false],
    ["name": "Venus", "positionFromSun": 2, "diameterInKMs":
12100, "distanceFromSunInAUs": 0.723, "hasRings": false],
    ["name": "Earth", "positionFromSun": 3, "diameterInKMs":
12750, "distanceFromSunInAUs": 1.0, "hasRings": false],
    ["name": "Mars", "positionFromSun": 4, "diameterInKMs":
6800, "distanceFromSunInAUs": 1.524, "hasRings": false],
    ["name": "Jupiter", "positionFromSun": 5, "diameterInKMs":
142800, "distanceFromSunInAUs": 5.203, "hasRings": false],
    ["name": "Saturn", "positionFromSun": 6, "diameterInKMs":
120660, "distanceFromSunInAUs": 9.523, "hasRings": true],
    ["name": "Uranus", "positionFromSun": 7, "diameterInKMs":
51800, "distanceFromSunInAUs": 19.208, "hasRings": false],
    ["name": "Neptune", "positionFromSun": 8, "diameterInKMs":
49500, "distanceFromSunInAUs": 30.087, "hasRings": false]
]
```

2. We want to take that data and create an array of `Planet` model structs, so we'll define the `Planet` structs we will be creating:

```
struct Planet {
    let name: String
    let positionFromSun: Int
    let diameterInKMs: Float
    let distanceFromSunInKMs: Float
    let hasRings: Bool
}
```

3. Taking this one step at a time, let's create a function that will take one of the planet dictionaries and make a `Planet` struct, if it can. We'll use a guard statement to ensure that the dictionary has all the values we expect:

```
func makePlanet(fromInput input: [String: Any]) -> Planet? {
    guard
        let name = input["name"] as? String,
        let positionFromSun = input["positionFromSun"] as? Int,
        let diameterInKMs = input["diameterInKMs"] as? Float,
        let distanceFromSunInKMs =
input["distanceFromSunInAUs"] as? Float,
        let hasRings = input["hasRings"] as? Bool
        else {
            return nil
    }
    return Planet(name: name,
                  positionFromSun: positionFromSun,
                  diameterInKMs: diameterInKMs,
                  distanceFromSunInKMs: distanceFromSunInKMs,
                  hasRings: hasRings)
}
```

4. Now that we can handle individual planet data, let's create a function that will take an array of planet dictionaries and make an array of `Planet` structs, using a guard statement to ensure that we successfully create a `Planet` struct:

```
func makePlanets(fromInput input: [[String: Any]]) -> [Planet]
{
    guard input.count > 0 else { return [] }
    var planets = [Planet]()
    for inputItem in input {
        guard let planet = makePlanet(fromInput: inputItem)
else { continue }
        planets.append(planet)
    }
    return planets
```

```
    }
```

How it works...

The `guard` statement works in a very similar way to an `if` statement, as optional values can be unwrapped and chained together in the same way. Since our planet data contains strings, ints, floats, and booleans, the dictionary is of the `[String: Any]` type. So, to create our `Planet` struct, we will need to check if the expected values exist for given keys and cast them to the correct type.

In our `makePlanet` function, we use the `guard` keyword and then access and conditionally cast all the values we require from the planet data dictionary. If any of these conditional casts fail, the `else` block, which is defined after the guard statement, is executed. Since we have defined our function to return an optional `Planet` if we don't have the information expected, then the `guard` will fail, and we'll return `nil`:

```swift
func makePlanet(fromInput input: [String: Any]) -> Planet? {
    guard
        let name = input["name"] as? String,
        let positionFromSun = input["positionFromSun"] as? Int,
        let diameterInKMs = input["diameterInKMs"] as? Float,
        let distanceFromSunInKMs = input["distanceFromSunInAUs"] as? Float,
        let hasRings = input["hasRings"] as? Bool
        else {
            return nil
    }
    return Planet(name: name,
                  positionFromSun: positionFromSun,
                  diameterInKMs: diameterInKMs,
                  distanceFromSunInKMs: distanceFromSunInKMs,
                  hasRings: hasRings)
}
```

Any value unwrapped by the `guard` statement is made available to any code below the guard statement in the same scope; this makes the guard statement perfect for ensuring that input values are as expected before continuing on to use those input values. This removes the need to nest our code within an `if` block. The unwrapped values are then used to initialize the `Planet` struct.

The makePlanets function accepts an array of planet data dictionaries and returns an array of Planet structs. If, however, the array provided is empty, we know that we will be returning an empty array as we have no data to process. So, we have made our function more efficient by checking that we don't have an empty input array, and returning an empty array if we do:

```
func makePlanets(fromInput input: [[String: Any]]) -> [Planet] {
    guard input.count > 0 else { return [] }
    //...
}
```

Our guard statement is that the input array count should be greater than 0; if it is, the rest of the function is executed; if the input array count is 0, the guard condition fails and the else block is executed, returning an empty array.

As we have seen, a guard statement is for breaking execution when the guard condition fails, and therefore, the compiler ensures that the execution breaking statement is placed in the else block; this can be, for example, return, break, or continue.

In the makePlanets function, we use a for loop to iterate through the dictionaries and try to create a Planet struct from each one. If our makePlanet call returns nil, we call continue to skip this iteration of the for loop and jump to the next iteration:

```
func makePlanets(fromInput input: [[String: Any]]) -> [Planet] {
    //...
    for inputItem in input {
        guard let planet = makePlanet(fromInput: inputItem) else { continue
}
        planets.append(planet)
    }
    //...
}
```

See also

Further information about guard statements can be found in Apple's documentation of the Swift language at
https://developer.apple.com/library/content/documentation/Swift/Conceptual/Swift_Programming_Language/Statements.html#//apple_ref/doc/uid/TP40014097-CH33-ID524.

Doing it later with defer

Typically, when we call a function, control passes from the call site to the function, and then the statements within the function are executed sequentially until either the end of the function or until a return statement, as shown in the following diagram:

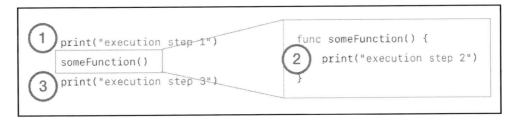

Sometimes, it can be useful to execute some code after the function has returned, but before control has been returned to the call site. This is where Swift's defer statement can be useful:

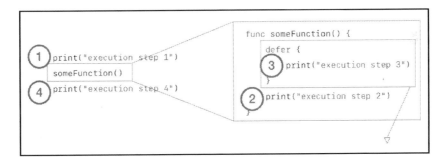

Getting ready

A **defer** statement can be useful to change state once a function's execution is complete, or to clean up values that are no longer needed. Let's look at an example of updating state with a defer statement.

Imagine that we have movie reviews with star ratings, and we want to classify them based on their star rating.

How to do it...

Let's get started:

1. First, let's define the options that a movie review may be classified into:

```
enum MovieReviewClass {
    case bad
    case average
    case good
    case brilliant
}
```

2. Let's create an object to do the classification:

```
class MovieReviewClassifier {
    func classify(forStarsOutOf10 stars: Int) ->
MovieReviewClass {
        if stars > 8 {
            return .brilliant // 9 or 10
        } else if stars > 6 {
            return .good // 7 or 8
        } else if stars > 3 {
            return .average // 4, 5 or 6
        } else {
            return .bad // 1, 2 or 3
        }
    }
}
```

3. We can use the classifier to classify the review:

```
let classifier = MovieReviewClassifier()
let review1 = classifier.classify(forStarsOutOf10: 9)
print(review1) // brilliant
```

4. This works great, but for the purpose of this example, let's imagine that this classification was a long-running process, and we wanted to keep track of the state of the classifier, so we can externally check if the classifier was in the middle of classifying or was completed. So, we'll define the possible classification states:

```
enum ClassificationState {
    case initial
    case classifying
    case complete
}
```

5. Now, let's update our classifier class to hold and update the state using a defer statement to move to the complete state:

```swift
class MovieReviewClassifier {
    var state: ClassificationState = .initial
    func classify(forStarsOutOf10 stars: Int) ->
MovieReviewClass {
        state = .classifying
        defer {
            state = .complete
        }
        if stars > 8 {
            return .brilliant // 9 or 10
        } else if stars > 6 {
            return .good // 7 or 8
        } else if stars > 3 {
            return .average // 4, 5 or 6
        } else {
            return .bad // 1, 2 or 3
        }
    }
}
```

6. We can use the classifier to classify the review and check the state:

```swift
let classifier = MovieReviewClassifier()
let review1 = classifier.classify(forStarsOutOf10: 9)
print(review1) // brilliant
print(classifier.state) // complete
```

How it works...

In the `classify` method without the defer statement, we have to transition to the `complete` state within each branch of the if statement before returning a value, as nothing after this will be executed. The end of that method will look as follows:

```swift
if stars > 8 {
    state = .complete
    return .brilliant // 9 or 10
} else if stars > 6 {
    state = .complete
    return .good // 7 or 8
} else if stars > 3 {
    state = .complete
    return .average // 4, 5 or 6
} else {
```

```
        state = .complete
        return .bad // 1, 2 or 3
    }
```

This repetition of updating the state can be avoided when we use the `defer` statement:

```
defer {
    state = .complete
}
```

Simply use the `defer` keyword; then, the code within the curly brackets will be run after the method has returned, but before control flow is returned to the caller.

There's more...

You can define multiple `defer` statements within a method, and they are executed in the reverse order that they were defined, so the last defer statement defined is the first one executed after the method returns.

To demonstrate, let's add a new state that we'll switch to when completing classifications subsequent to the first:

```
enum ClassificationState {
    case initial
    case classifying
    case complete
    case completeAgain
}
```

Now, let's amend our classifier to keep track of the number of classifications it makes and the changes to the `completeAgain` state if one or more classifications have been completed:

```
class MovieReviewClassifier {
    var state: ClassificationState = .initial
    var numberOfClassifications = 0
    func classify(forStarsOutOf10 stars: Int) -> MovieReviewClass {
        state = .classifying
        defer {
            numberOfClassifications += 1
        }
        defer {
            if numberOfClassifications > 0 {
                state = .completeAgain
            } else {
                state = .complete
            }
```

```
        }
        if stars > 8 {
            return .brilliant // 9 or 10
        } else if stars > 6 {
            return .good // 7 or 8
        } else if stars > 3 {
            return .average // 4, 5 or 6
        } else {
            return .bad // 1, 2 or 3
        }
    }
}
```

Finally, let's change how we use the classifier; the second time we use it, it will complete with a different state:

```
let classifier = MovieReviewClassifier()
let review1 = classifier.classify(forStarsOutOf10: 9)
print(review1) // brilliant
print(classifier.state) // complete
print(classifier.numberOfClassifications) // 1

let review2 = classifier.classify(forStarsOutOf10: 2)
print(review2) // bad
print(classifier.state) // completeAgain
print(classifier.numberOfClassifications) // 2
```

Since we have now defined two defer statements, let's take another look to understand the order in which they are executed:

```
defer {
    numberOfClassifications += 1
}
defer {
    if numberOfClassifications > 0 {
        state = .completeAgain
    } else {
        state = .complete
    }
}
```

As discussed earlier, the last defined `defer` statement is executed first, so on the first classification, once the method returns, the last defer statement is executed and the state is changed to `complete`, because `numberOfClassifications` will be 0. Next, the first defer statement is executed, which adds 1 to the `numberOfClassifications` variable, which will now be 1.

On the second classification, once the method returns, the last defer statement will execute and change the state to `completeAgain` since `numberOfClassifications` is greater than 0. Finally, the first defer statement will execute, incrementing `numberOfClassifications` and making it 2.

If the defer statements had been the other way around, the state would always be changed to `completeAgain`, as `numberOfClassifications` would have incremented to 1 before the state was set.

See also

Further information about defer statements can be found in Apple's documentation of the Swift language at `https://developer.apple.com/library/content/documentation/Swift/Conceptual/Swift_Programming_Language/Statements.html#//apple_ref/doc/uid/TP40014097-CH33-ID532`.

Bailing out with fatalError and precondition

It's comforting to think that, in the code you write, everything will always happen as expected, and your program can handle any eventuality. However, sometimes things can go wrong, really wrong; a situation can arise that you know is possible, but don't expect to ever happen, and the programs should terminate if it does. Swift has a way to define these situations, and in this recipe, we will look at two of them: `fatalError` and `precondition`.

Getting ready

Let's reuse our example from the previous recipe; we have an object that can be used to classify movie reviews based on how many stars out of ten the review gave the movie. However, let's simplify its use, and say that we only intend for a classifier object to classify one, and only one, movie review.

How to do it...

Let's look at some code that uses `fatalError` and `precondition`, and then we will look at how it works:

1. First, we'll define the classification state and the movie review class:

```
enum ClassificationState {
    case initial
    case classifying
    case complete
}

enum MovieReviewClass {
    case bad
    case average
    case good
    case brilliant
}
```

2. Next, we will redefine our classifier object, but we will use `precondition` and `fatalError` to indicate situations that are not expected to occur and would cause a problem:

```
class MovieReviewClassifier {
    var state: ClassificationState = .initial
    func classify(forStarsOutOf10 stars: Int) -> MovieReviewClass {
        precondition(state == .initial, "Classifier state must be initial
before
        classifying")
        state = .classifying
        defer {
            state = .complete
        }
        if stars > 8 && stars <= 10 {
            return .brilliant // 9 or 10
        } else if stars > 6 {
            return .good // 7 or 8
        } else if stars > 3 {
            return .average // 4, 5 or 6
        } else if stars > 0 {
            return .bad // 1, 2 or 3
        } else {
            fatalError("Star rating must be between 1 and 10")
        }
    }
}
```

```
let classifier = MovieReviewClassifier()
let review1 = classifier.classify(forStarsOutOf10: 9)
print(review1) // brilliant
print(classifier.state) // complete
```

How it works...

As we stated earlier, we only want to use the classifier once; therefore, when we begin to classify a movie review, the current state should be `initial` as this object has never been classified before and shouldn't be in the middle of classifying. If that is not the case, the classifier is being used incorrectly, and we should terminate the execution of the code:

```
func classify(forStarsOutOf10 stars: Int) -> MovieReviewClass {
    precondition(state == .initial, "Classifier state must be initial
before classifying")
    //...
}
```

We state a precondition using the `precondition` keyword, provide a Boolean statement that we expect to be true, and an optional message. If this Boolean statement is not true, the execution of the code will terminate and the message will be displayed in the console.

In our example, we are making it a precondition that the state must be `initial` when calling this method.

When our classifier performs the classification, it expects a number of stars between 1 and 10. However, the method accepts an `Int` as a parameter; so, any integer value can be provided, positive or negative. If the value provided is not between 1 and 10 and the classifier cannot provide a valid `MovieReviewClass`, the classifier is being used incorrectly, and we should terminate the execution of the code:

```
func classify(forStarsOutOf10 stars: Int) -> MovieReviewClass {
    //...
    if stars > 8 && stars <= 10 {
        return .brilliant // 9 or 10
    } else if stars > 6 {
        return .good // 7 or 8
    } else if stars > 3 {
        return .average // 4, 5 or 6
    } else if stars > 0 {
        return .bad // 1, 2 or 3
    } else {
        fatalError("Star rating must be between 1 and 10")
    }
}
```

The if-else statement covers all the valid `MovieReviewClass` options for the provided stars, so if none of these are triggered, we use a fatal error to indicate incorrect usage. This is done using the `fatalError` keyword, providing an optional message.

See also

Further information about `fatalError` can be found in Apple's documentation of the Swift language at `https://developer.apple.com/reference/swift/1538698-fatalerror`.

4

Generics, Operators, and Nested Types

In this chapter, we will cover the following recipes:

- Using generics with types
- Using generics with functions
- Using generics with protocols
- Advanced operators
- OptionSet
- Create custom operators
- Nesting types and namespacing

Introduction

Swift provides a number of advanced features for building a functionality that is flexible, but well defined, so that it feels like you are extending the language itself. In this chapter, we will examine two of these features: **generics** and **operators**. We will also see how nested types allow logical grouping, access, and namespacing for your constructs.

All the code for this chapter can be found in the following GitHub repository, `http://swiftbook.link/code/chapter4`

Using generics with types

When we build constructs that interact with other types, we often specify the type we are interacting with directly. This is helpful because it means we know the capabilities that the type has; we can put those capabilities to use and ensure that the outputs have the correct type. However, we now have a construct that can only interact with the specified type; it can't be reused with other types, even if the concepts are the same.

Generics give us the advantage of having a defined type while being generically applicable to other types. It is, perhaps, best illustrated with an example.

Let's create a custom collection object that will store the last five strings as copies so that the user can paste not just the last string copied, but any of the last five. You can add strings to the list and then ask it for all the strings in the list, and it will return all the added strings from the newest to the oldest:

```
class RecentList {
    var slot1: String?
    var slot2: String?
    var slot3: String?
    var slot4: String?
    var slot5: String?
    func add(recent: String) {
        // Move each slot down 1
        slot5 = slot4
        slot4 = slot3
        slot3 = slot2
        slot2 = slot1
        slot1 = recent
    }
    func getAll() -> [String] {
        var recent = [String]()
        if let slot1 = slot1 {
            recent.append(slot1)
        }
        if let slot2 = slot2 {
            recent.append(slot2)
        }
        if let slot3 = slot3 {
            recent.append(slot3)
        }
        if let slot4 = slot4 {
            recent.append(slot4)
        }
        if let slot5 = slot5 {
            recent.append(slot5)
```

```
        }
        return recent
    }
}
let recentlyCopiedList = RecentList()
recentlyCopiedList.add(recent: "First")
recentlyCopiedList.add(recent: "Next")
recentlyCopiedList.add(recent: "Last")
var recentlyCopied = recentlyCopiedList.getAll()
print(recentlyCopied) // Last, Next, First
```

This is great; it does just what we want. Now, let's say that we want to add a list of five recent contacts to a contacts app. The concept is exactly the same as the list of copied strings; I want to add something to a list, and then I want to get all the things on the list so that I can present them to the user. However, because I specified that the RecentList object can only work with strings, it can't work with my custom Person object. We can use generics to make this more useful.

The following recipe will show you how to do this.

How to do it...

Let's add generics to our RecentList object so that it can be used in these situations and many more. Then we will break down how we did it.

1. Let's amend our RecentList object to define a generic type, ListItemType, that we use in place of String:

```
class RecentList<ListItemType> {
    var slot1: ListItemType?
    var slot2: ListItemType?
    var slot3: ListItemType?
    var slot4: ListItemType?
    var slot5: ListItemType?
    func add(recent: ListItemType) {
        // Move each slot down 1
        slot5 = slot4
        slot4 = slot3
        slot3 = slot2
        slot2 = slot1
        slot1 = recent
    }
    func getAll() -> [ListItemType] {
        var recent = [ListItemType]()
        if let slot1 = slot1 {
```

```
            recent.append(slot1)
    }
    if let slot2 = slot2 {
        recent.append(slot2)
    }
    if let slot3 = slot3 {
        recent.append(slot3)
    }
    if let slot4 = slot4 {
        recent.append(slot4)
    }
    if let slot5 = slot5 {
        recent.append(slot5)
    }
    return recent
    }
}
```

2. We can continue to use our RecentList as we have previously; we just need to provide a specific type, String in this case, that will replace the generic type for this RecentList instance:

```
let recentlyUsedWordList = RecentList<String>()
recentlyUsedWordList.add(recent: "First")
recentlyUsedWordList.add(recent: "Next")
recentlyUsedWordList.add(recent: "Last")
var recentlyUsedWords = recentlyUsedWordList.getAll()
print(recentlyUsedWords) // Last, Next, First
```

3. We could have replaced the String type references in our original implementation with Any; this would have satisfied the requirement of allowing RecentList to work with Strings and a custom Person object, as the add method would look like this:

```
func add(recent: Any) {
    //...
}
```

4. However, this would have lost a key feature of RecentList. Each item in the list is of the same type; you can't have a recent list containing a string, an integer, a Person, and a Boolean, as this wouldn't be useful, but by specifying the input type as Any, it will be entirely possible. By contrast, our generic version of RecentList retains the type safety of the original implementation, ensuring that all items in the list have the same type. If you try to pass something other than a string to the add method, the compiler won't allow it.

5. Let's examine how our newly genericised `RecentList` can be used for the other example we discussed earlier, the list of recent contacts.

6. First, we'll create a simple `Person` object:

```
class Person {

    let name: String
    init(name: String) {
        self.name = name
    }
}
```

7. Next, we'll create some people to add to our recent contact list:

```
let rod = Person(name: "Rod")
let jane = Person(name: "Jane")
let freddy = Person(name: "Freddy")
```

8. By providing the specific `Person` type, `RecentList` works just as before, but now taking a `Person` object as an input parameter to the `add` method, and providing an array of `Person` objects as an output to the `getAll` method:

```
let lastCalledList = RecentList<Person>()
lastCalledList.add(recent: freddy)
lastCalledList.add(recent: jane)
lastCalledList.add(recent: rod)
let lastCalled = lastCalledList.getAll()
for person in lastCalled {
    print(person.name)
}
// Rod
// Jane
// Freddy
```

How it works...

To add generics to a `class` or `struct`, the generic type is defined in angle brackets after the class or struct name, and can be given any type name, although it should begin with a *capital letter* like other type names:

```
class RecentList<ListItemType> {
    //...
}
```

This generic type now becomes a stand-in for the specific type that will be specified when it is used, and we can used this stand-in wherever we would use the specific type.

Consider the following example as a property type:

```
var slot1: ListItemType?
```

Now, consider it as a parameter value:

```
func add(recent: ListItemType)
```

Alternatively, we can consider it as a return type:

```
func getAll() -> [ListItemType]
```

In many other programming languages that have a generics system, the generic type is often given a one-letter type name, usually T. Swift aims to be concise, but not at the expense of clarity, so I suggest using a more descriptive type name.

A descriptive type name becomes especially important if you have multiple generic types, which you can have as a comma-separated list within the angle brackets:

```
class RecentList<ListItemType, SomeOtherType> {
    //...
}
```

There's more...

While being extremely generic has its advantages, you may want to constrain which types can be used as your generic type, especially if you need to use some features of that constrained type.

Let's say that in addition to returning an array of items from our RecentList, we want to be able to print out the list directly. To do this, we need to ensure that the type of item used in our RecentList is something that can be converted into a *string* to be printed. There is already a CustomStringConvertible protocol that defines this behavior, so we want to ensure that any specific type used with RecentList has to conform to CustomStringConvertible:

```
class RecentList<ListItemType: CustomStringConvertible> {
    //...
}
```

We add the constraint after the generic type name, separated by a colon, similar to how we specify protocol conformance and class inheritance. Indeed, while this example constrains the generic type to implement a protocol, we can instead specify a class that the specific type must be, or inherit from.

Now that we have this constraint, we can be sure that any specific type given will conform to `CustomStringConvertible`, and therefore we can print the value, so let's create a method to do that:

```
class RecentList<ListItemType: CustomStringConvertible> {
    //...
    func printRecentList() {
        for item in getAll() {
            let printableItem = String(describing: item)
            print(printableItem)
        }
    }
}
```

The only thing left to do is to make our `Person` class conform to `CustomStringConvertible` so that it can continue to be used as a specific type in `RecentList`:

```
extension Person: CustomStringConvertible {
    public var description: String {
        return name
    }
}
```

Now we can use this functionality with our `String` type's `RecentlyList` and our `Person` type's `RecentList`:

```
// Using Strings type
let recentlyUsedWordList = RecentList<String>()
recentlyUsedWordList.add(recent: "First")
recentlyUsedWordList.add(recent: "Next")
recentlyUsedWordList.add(recent: "Last")
recentlyUsedWordList.printRecentList()
// Last
// Next
// First

// Using Person type
let rod = Person(name: "Rod")
let jane = Person(name: "Jane")
let freddy = Person(name: "Freddy")
let lastCalledList = RecentList<Person>()
```

```
lastCalledList.add(recent: freddy)
lastCalledList.add(recent: jane)
lastCalledList.add(recent: rod)
lastCalledList.printRecentList()
// Rod
// Jane
// Freddy
```

See also

Further information about generic types can be found in Apple's documentation of the Swift language at: http://swiftbook.link/docs/generics

Using generics with functions

In addition to being able to specific generic types, as we saw in the previous recipe, you can use generics to build functions that are both widely applicable and strongly typed.

How to do it...

Let's use generics to build functions, and then we'll look at how they work:

1. Let's imagine that we want to create a dictionary where the same value is inserted for multiple keys; we can use a generic function to create that functionality:

```
func makeDuplicates<ItemType>(of item: ItemType,
                              withKeys keys: Set<String>) ->
[String: ItemType] {
    var duplicates = [String: ItemType]()
    for key in keys {
        duplicates[key] = item
    }
    return duplicates
}
```

2. To use this function, we pass in a single value and multiple keys, and the value is stored against each of the given keys:

```
let awards: Set<String> = ["Director",
                           "Cinematography",
                           "Film Editing",
                           "Visual Effects",
                           "Original Music Score",
                           "Sound Editing",
                           "Sound Mixing"]
let oscars2014 = makeDuplicates(of: "Gravity", withKeys:
awards)
print(oscars2014["Director"]) // Gravity
print(oscars2014["Visual Effects"]) // Gravity
```

How it works...

Just like generics for types, the generic type for a function is specified within angle brackets:

```
func makeDuplicates<ItemType>(of item: ItemType,
                              withKeys keys: Set<String>) -> [String:
ItemType] {
    //...
}
```

The defined generic type name can then be used as a type definition within the rest of the method definition; in our example, we want to define the type of our input item to be duplicated, and we also want the values that are held in the dictionary to be returned to be of the same type.

Instead of using generics, we could have used the Any type in place of the generic type:

```
func makeDuplicates(of item: Any, withKeys keys: Set<String>) -> [String:
Any] {
    //...
}
```

This approach has a few problems for anyone using this function:

- They will get back a dictionary containing values of the Any type, which will need to be cast to a more useful type.
- Without seeing the implementation, they can't be sure that the dictionary contains values of the same type. One key may have a String stored against it, and another may have an Int.

- Without seeing the implementation, they can't be sure that the values of the returned dictionary are of the same type as the item provided.

By using a generic type, we allow the functionality to be widely applicable while enforcing our type logic at compile time.

You'll notice that unlike instantiating a type with generics, we don't need to explicitly state the specific type to use when executing the function:

```
let oscars2014 = makeDuplicates(of: "Gravity", withKeys: awards)
```

This is because the compiler is able to infer it from the type of the first parameter provided. Since `Gravity` is a string, and the compiler knows that the parameter has the `ItemType` generic type, the compiler infers that for this use of the method, the `ItemType` generic type becomes the specific type of `String`.

There's more...

We can increase the usability of our function by providing a generic type for the set of keys we provide as the second parameter:

```
func makeDuplicates<ItemType, KeyType>(of item: ItemType, withKeys keys:
Set<KeyType>) -> [KeyType: ItemType] {
    var duplicates = [KeyType: ItemType]()
    for key in keys {
        duplicates[key] = item
    }
    return duplicates
}
```

Multiple generic types are defined just as they were in the previous recipe--as a comma-separated list within the angle brackets.

All the collection types in Swift (array, dictionary, set, and so on) use generics, and in the preceding function, we are passing in the generic type from our function into the set; therefore, `KeyType` must have the same constraints that are imposed by the set, which means the type must conform to `Hashable`.

If we wanted to make this constraint explicit, or constrain the generic type for some other reason, this is defined after a colon:

```
func makeDuplicates<ItemType, KeyType: Hashable>(of item: ItemType,
withKeys keys: Set<KeyType>) -> [KeyType: ItemType] {
    var duplicates = [KeyType: ItemType]()
    for key in keys {
        duplicates[key] = item
    }
    return duplicates
}
```

Just as before, since we provide a parameter with specific types when using our method, the generic type is given a specific type:

```
let awards: Set<String> = ["Director",
                           "Cinematography",
                           "Film Editing",
                           "Visual Effects",
                           "Original Music Score",
                           "Sound Editing",
                           "Sound Mixing"]
let oscars2014 = makeDuplicates(of: "Gravity", withKeys: awards)
print(oscars2014["Director"]) // Gravity
print(oscars2014["Visual Effects"]) // Gravity
```

See also

Further information about generic functions can be found in Apple's documentation of the Swift language at: http://swiftbook.link/docs/generic-functions

Using generics with protocols

In the previous recipes, we investigated how we can use generics within types and functions. Now we will round off our journey through generics in Swift by looking at how Swift can be used in protocols to produce abstract interfaces, while maintaining strongly typed requirements that allow for a more descriptive model.

Getting ready

In this recipe, we will build a model for a transport app in the UK with the goal of providing the distance that a journey may take over different methods of transport.

How to do it...

At the outset, it may not be clear as to what is the best structure to use for defining a transport method; indeed, there might be different structures appropriate for different methods. Therefore, we will define a transport method as a protocol that appropriate types can conform to:

```
protocol TransportMethod {
    associatedtype CollectionPoint
    var defaultCollectionPoint: CollectionPoint { get }
    var averageSpeedInKPH: Double { get }
}
```

We define an associated generic type that we name `CollectionPoint`, which will represent the type of location that someone can be collected from when using this `TransportMethod`. By using generics, we have ultimate flexibility in how a transport method chooses to define what can serve as a collection point.

Having defined an associated type, it can then be used as a placeholder for the specific type that will be defined in properties and methods. We use it to define a default collection point that each transport method should provide.

Each transport method also provides an average speed, which will be used later in calculating the travel time.

Let's look at a concrete example of a transport method to help define the model further:

```
struct Train: TransportMethod {
    typealias CollectionPoint = TrainStation
    // User's home or nearest station
    var defaultCollectionPoint: CollectionPoint {
        return TrainStation.BMS
    }
    var averageSpeedInKPH: Double {
        return 100
    }
}
```

To implement the transport method for `Train` and conform to the `TransportMethod` protocol, we must provide a specific version of the `CollectionPoint` generic type that is required by the protocol. In the case of travelling by train, the collection point will be a `TrainStation`, so we now have to define the `TrainStation` type:

```
enum TrainStation: String {
    case BMS = "Bromley South"
    case VIC = "London Victoria"
    case RAI = "Rainham (Kent)"
    case BTN = "Brighton (East Sussex)"
    // Full list of UK train stations codes can be found at
    //
http://www.nationalrail.co.uk/static/documents/content/station_codes.csv
}
```

Since there are a finite number of train stations that are discretely definable, an `enum` is a good way to represent them, although I've only listed a small number here, for brevity.

Our goal is to model a journey and calculate the duration of the journey over specific transport methods, so let's create our `Journey` object:

```
class Journey<TransportType: TransportMethod> {
    let start: TransportType.CollectionPoint
    let end: TransportType.CollectionPoint
    init(start: TransportType.CollectionPoint,
        end: TransportType.CollectionPoint) {
        self.start = start
        self.end = end
    }
}
```

A journey takes place from one point to another, so we take the journey's start and end as input parameters. We need to have the flexibility to provide any type as the start and end, but we need them to be types connected to a transport method, with the same type for the start and end values. To accomplish this, we can have a generic type constrained to conform to the `TransportMethod` protocol; we can then define our start and end property types by referencing the `CollectionPoint` associated type of the generic type.

Our goal is to calculate the duration of a journey. To do this, we will need the speed of travel during the journey and the distance from start to end. Our `TransportMethod` protocol defines that it will provide an average speed, so let's also take the transport method as an input to our journey:

```
class Journey<TransportType: TransportMethod> {
    let start: TransportType.CollectionPoint
    let end: TransportType.CollectionPoint
```

```
        let method: TransportType
        init(method: TransportType,
            start: TransportType.CollectionPoint,
            end: TransportType.CollectionPoint) {
            self.start = start
            self.end = end
            self.method = method
        }
    }
```

To get the distance of the journey, we need to calculate the distance between the start and end, but the type of both the start and end of the journey is the generic CollectionPoint type, which could be any type, and so does not have any location information that we can use to calculate distance.

To solve this, let's constrain CollectionPoint so that it must conform to a new protocol, TransportLocation:

```
    protocol TransportLocation {
        var location: CLLocation { get }
    }
```

Anything conforming to TransportLocation must provide a location in the form of a CLLocation object. The CLLocation object is part of the CoreLocation framework on iOS. Further investigation of the CoreLocation framework is outside the scope of this book, but it's enough to know that it provides ways to calculate the distance between two CLLocation objects, and we need to include the following at the top of this playground to use it:

```
    import CoreLocation
```

With our TransportLocation protocol defined, we can constrain the CollectionPoint associated type on the TransportMethod protocol:

```
    protocol TransportMethod {
        associatedtype CollectionPoint: TransportLocation
        var defaultCollectionPoint: CollectionPoint { get }
        var averageSpeedInKPH: Double { get }
    }
```

Since our CollectionPoint will now conform to TransportLocation, and therefore must have a location property, we can go back to our Journey object and use this to calculate the distance of the journey and the duration:

```
    class Journey<TransportType: TransportMethod> {
        var start: TransportType.CollectionPoint
```

```
    var end: TransportType.CollectionPoint
    let method: TransportType
    var distanceInKMs: Double
    var durationInHours: Double
    init(method: TransportType,
        start: TransportType.CollectionPoint,
        end: TransportType.CollectionPoint) {
        self.start = start
        self.end = end
        self.method = method
        // CoreLocation provides the distance in meters,
        // so we divide by 1000 to get kilometers
        distanceInKMs = end.location.distance(from: start.location) / 1000
        durationInHours = distanceInKMs / method.averageSpeedInKPH
    }
}
```

The last thing we need to do is to ensure that our `TrainStation` enum conforms to
`TransportLocation` as this is now a requirement; we just need to declare conformance
and add a location property:

```
enum TrainStation: String, TransportLocation {
    case BMS = "Bromley South"
    case VIC = "London Victoria"
    case RAI = "Rainham (Kent)"
    case BTN = "Brighton (East Sussex)"
    // Full list of UK train stations codes can be found at
    // http://www.nationalrail.co.uk/static/documents/content/station_
codes.csv
    var location: CLLocation {
        switch self {
        case .BMS: return CLLocation(latitude: 51.4000504, longitude:
0.0174237)
        case .VIC: return CLLocation(latitude: 51.4952103, longitude:
-0.1438979)
        case .RAI: return CLLocation(latitude: 51.3663, longitude: 0.61137)
        case .BTN: return CLLocation(latitude: 50.829, longitude: -0.14125)
        }
    }
}
```

Let's see how we would use our travel model to create a journey with specific types:

```
let trainJourney = Journey(method: Train(), start: TrainStation.BMS, end:
TrainStation.VIC)
let distanceByTrain = trainJourney.distanceInKMs
let durationByTrain = trainJourney.durationInHours
print("Journey distance: \(distanceByTrain) km")
print("Journey duration: \(durationByTrain) hours")
```

There's more...

Our first conformance to `TransportMethod`, as we defined earlier, is our `Train` struct. Let's look at another tool to see how tackling things in a protocol-oriented way allows flexibility in implementation.

The next `TransportMethod` we will implement is `Road`, but there are a number of different vehicle types that we can use to travel by road, and they may have different average speeds. Since we have a finite list of options for travel by road, let's define it using an `enum`:

```
enum Road: TransportMethod {
    typealias CollectionPoint = CLLocation
    case car
    case motobike
    case van
    case hgv
    // The users home or current location
    var defaultCollectionPoint: CLLocation {
        return CLLocation(latitude: 51.1, longitude: 0.1)
    }
    var averageSpeedInKPH: Double {
        switch self {
        case .car: return 60
        case .motobike: return 70
        case .van: return 55
        case .hgv: return 50
        }
    }
}
```

A journey by train has a finite list of collection points, the train stations, but almost anywhere can be a collection point when travelling by road. Therefore, for Road, we can define the collection point to be any CLLocation; the only problem is that CLLocation doesn't conform to TransportLocation. No problem--we can extend CLLocation to add conformance:

```
extension CLLocation: TransportLocation {
    var location: CLLocation {
        return self
    }
}
```

Now, we can define a journey by road and calculate the duration:

```
let start = CLLocation(latitude: 51.476853, longitude: -0.0005002)
let end = CLLocation(latitude: 51.4218504, longitude: -0.0723853)
let roadJourney = Journey(method: Road.car, start: start, end: end)
let distanceByRoad = roadJourney.distanceInKMs
let durationByRoad = roadJourney.durationInHours
print("Journey distance: \(distanceByTrain) km")
print("Journey duration: \(durationByTrain) hours")
```

By taking a protocol-orientated approach to tackling the task of calculating a journey's duration, and by using protocol generics, we were able to use completely different, but appropriate, implementations for two transport methods while providing an interface so that they can be handled in a common way.

For a train journey, we used an enum to model the train stations and a struct to model the transport method, and for road, we implemented an enum for the transport method and used the CLLocation object for the transport location.

See also

Further information about associated types can be found in Apple's documentation of the Swift language at: http://swiftbook.link/docs/associated-types

Advanced operators

Swift is a programming language that takes a relatively small number of well-defined principles and builds on them to create expressive and powerful language features. The concept of mathematical operators, such as +, -, *, and / for addition, subtraction, multiplication, and division, respectively, seems so fundamental as to not warrant a mention. However, in Swift, this common mathematical functionality is built on top of an underlying operator system that is extensible and powerful.

Getting ready

In this recipe, we will look at some of the more advanced operators provided by the Swift standard library, and in the next recipe, we will create our own custom operators.

How to do it...

The operators we will explore are known as bitwise operators, and are used to manipulate numerical bit representations, so let's get started.

An integer value in Swift can be represented in its binary form by prefixing the integer literal with 0b:

```
let zero: Int   = 0b000
let one: Int    = 0b001
let two: Int    = 0b010
let three: Int  = 0b011
let four: Int   = 0b100
let five: Int   = 0b101
let six: Int    = 0b110
let seven: Int  = 0b111
```

A bit is the smallest value in a computer system, consisting of either a 1 or 0. The integers mentioned here can be represented by three bits, which are clearly visible when it's represented in binary form, as illustrated in the preceding snippet. The integer 6 can be represented by the three bits 1, 1, and 0.

These binary representations are really useful when you need to represent multiple options in one value. For example, let's say that we want to indicate which devices are supported for a specific feature of an app. The available devices are as listed:

- Phone
- Tablet
- Watch
- Laptop
- Desktop
- TV
- Brain implant

Certain features may be appropriate for all the devices, or you may still be working on a feature, and so it isn't currently appropriate for any device, or it may be a combination of different devices. We can have Boolean values for each of the devices to indicate whether the feature is supported for that device, but this is not the best solution as there is nothing intrinsically tying the properties to each other, and you can forget to update some of the values as circumstances change.

Instead, we can represent all the supported devices with one integer value, and use each bit of the integer to represent a different device:

```
let phone: Int        = 0b0000001
let tablet: Int       = 0b0000010
let watch: Int        = 0b0000100
let laptop: Int       = 0b0001000
let desktop: Int      = 0b0010000
let tv: Int           = 0b0100000
let brainImplant: Int = 0b1000000

var supportedDevices: Int
```

To see how this enables us to store multiple devices in one value, let's look at an example:

```
phone  = 0b0000001  +
tablet = 0b0000010  +
tv     = 0b0100000
-------------------
phone
tablet = 0b0100011
tv
```

As each device is represented by a different bit, the device values are combined by adding the values, and they don't overlap.

To test whether a particular device or combination of devices is supported, we can use a bitwise **AND** operation. A bitwise AND operation will compare the corresponding bits for two different binary values, and will set that bit to 1 in a new binary value if both the values for that bit input value are 1. As an example, let's test whether phones are supported in the combined value we created earlier:

```
Supported Devices      = 0b 0 1 0 0 0 1 1
Phone                  = 0b 0 0 0 0 0 0 1
AND Operation Result   = 0b 0 0 0 0 0 0 1
```

The result only has a 1 bit value for the right-most bit because this is the only bit that was set to 1 in both the supported devices value and the phone value.

Once we have that result, we can directly compare it to the value for phone, and if they are equal, then we know that the value of the supported devices included the phone value:

```
AND Operation Result = 0b 0 0 0 0 0 0 1
Phone                = 0b 0 0 0 0 0 0 1
```

We now have a way to combine the possible options into one value, and a way to compare those values to see whether one is contained in another, using bitwise operations. The Swift standard library contains bitwise operators that allow us to perform these operations as easily as other mathematical operations, such as +, -, *, and /.

Typically, an operator will be in the following form:

```
<#left hand side value#> <#operator#> <#right hand side value#>
```

Consider the following example:

```
2 + 3
```

In the preceding example, we have these:

- 2: This is the left-hand side value
- +: This is the operator
- 3: This is the right-hand side value

The **bit shift operator** (<<) will take an integer value on the left-hand side and shift it by the number of bit positions to the right-hand side. Therefore, we can use this to express our intention better when declaring the device values:

```
let phone: Int     = 1 << 0 // 0b0000001
let tablet: Int    = 1 << 1 // 0b0000010
let watch: Int     = 1 << 2 // 0b0000100
let laptop: Int    = 1 << 3 // 0b0001000
```

```
let desktop: Int      = 1 << 4 // 0b0010000
let tv: Int           = 1 << 5 // 0b0100000
let brainImplant: Int = 1 << 6 // 0b1000000
```

The bitwise **AND operator** (&) will perform the same bit comparison that was previously described manually, and we can use this to create a function to determine whether a particular device exists within the value for the supported devices:

```
supportedDevices = phone + tablet + tv

func isSupported(device: Int) -> Bool {
    let bitWiseANDResult = supportedDevices & device
    let containsDevice = bitWiseANDResult == device
    return containsDevice
}

let phoneSupported = isSupported(device: phone)
print(phoneSupported) // true

let brainImplantSupported = isSupported(device: brainImplant)
print(brainImplantSupported) // false
```

The Swift standard library also provides operators for the following logical operations:

- **OR**: The OR operation, denoted by |, compares bits and sets the corresponding bit to 1 if either value has the bit set to 1. For our devices, this will mean creating a union between two device combinations:

  ```
  let deviceThatSupportUIKit = phone + tablet + tv
  let stationaryDevices = desktop + tv
  let stationaryOrUIKitDevices = deviceThatSupportUIKit |
  stationaryDevices
  let orIsUnion = stationaryOrUIKitDevices == (phone + tablet +
  tv + desktop)
  print(orIsUnion) // true
  ```

- **XOR (exclusive or)**: The XOR operation, denoted by ^, will only set the bit to 1 if either value has the bit set to 1, but not if they both do:

  ```
  let onlyStationaryOrUIKitDevices = deviceThatSupportUIKit ^
  stationaryDevices
  let xorIsUnionMinusIntersection = stationaryOrUIKitDevices ==
  (phone + tablet + desktop)
  print(xorIsUnionMinusIntersection) // true
  ```

See also

- Further information about advanced operators can be found in Apple's documentation of the Swift language at:
  - `http://swiftbook.link/docs/advanced-operators`

Option set

The use of bitwise operations to hold multiple options in one value is a common pattern, and is used throughout the **Cocoa Touch framework**, with one example being `UIDeviceOrientation`. In Swift, there is a protocol, `OptionSet`, that formalizes this pattern and provides additional convenience.

How to do it...

Let's rewrite our supported device values to be an `OptionSet`:

```
struct Devices: OptionSet {
    let rawValue: Int
    static let phone        = Devices(rawValue: 1 << 0)
    static let tablet       = Devices(rawValue: 1 << 1)
    static let watch        = Devices(rawValue: 1 << 2)
    static let laptop       = Devices(rawValue: 1 << 3)
    static let desktop      = Devices(rawValue: 1 << 4)
    static let tv           = Devices(rawValue: 1 << 5)
    static let brainImplant = Devices(rawValue: 1 << 6)
    static let none: Devices = []
    static let all: Devices = [.phone, .tablet, .watch, .laptop, .desktop,
.tv, .brainImplant]
    static let stationary: Devices = [.desktop, .tv]
    static let supportsUIKit: Devices = [.phone, .tablet, .tv]
}

let supportedDevices: Devices = [.phone, .tablet, .watch, .tv]
```

How it works...

The `OptionSet` protocol requires a `rawValue` property, and the convention is to define static constants for each of the options. Additionally, convenient combinations of options can also be defined as static constants, and an array of options can be provided through a convenience initializer, where the options will be combined and stored as one value.

The `OptionSet` protocol provides set-like manipulation and comparison methods that perform the same bitwise operations that we covered in the last recipe:

```
// Contains / AND and comparison
let phoneIsSupported = supportedDevices.contains(.phone)

// Union / OR
let stationaryOrUIKitDevices =
Devices.supportsUIKit.union(Devices.stationary)

// Intersection / AND
let stationaryAndUIKitDevices =
Devices.supportsUIKit.intersection(Devices.stationary)
```

Many of the set methods that we examined in Chapter 2, *Building on the Building Blocks,* are also provided.

See also

Further information about the `OptionSet` protocol can be found in Apple's documentation of the Swift language at: http://swiftbook.link/docs/optionset

Create custom operators

In an earlier recipe, we looked at some of the advanced operators that Swift offers on top of the common mathematical operators. In this recipe, we will look at how we can create our own operators, enabling very concisely expressed behaviors that feel like part of the language.

Getting ready

The custom operator we will create will be used to append the information in one value to the information in another value, producing a new value that contains the second value, followed by the first. The functionality we are looking to achieve is similar to the >> Unix command.

How to do it...

Let's see how this works:

1. Open up the **Terminal** application on your Mac:

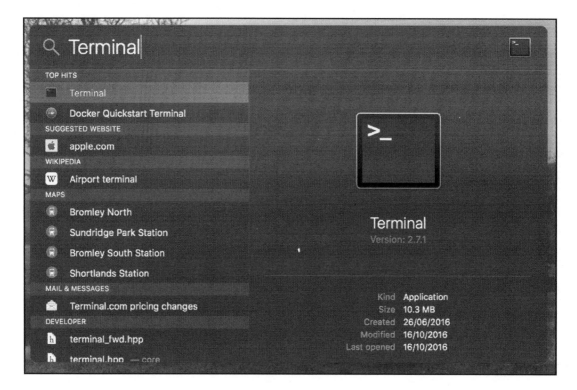

2. Since macOS is Unix based, we can provide Unix commands within **Terminal**. Type `cd ~/Desktop` and press *Enter*; this takes you to the folder containing all the files and folders on your desktop. Type `touch Tasks.txt` and then press *Enter*; this will create a black text file on your desktop, called `Tasks.txt`. We now want to add tasks to our tasks text file.

3. Enter the following command, followed by *Enter*:

```
echo "buy milk" >> Tasks.txt
```

Now open the text file on your desktop, and you'll see that it has added **buy milk** on the first line.

4. Now, enter another task in the same way:

```
echo "mow the lawn" >> Tasks.txt
```

5. Reopen the `Tasks.txt` file, and you will see that "`mow the lawn`" has been added on the second line:

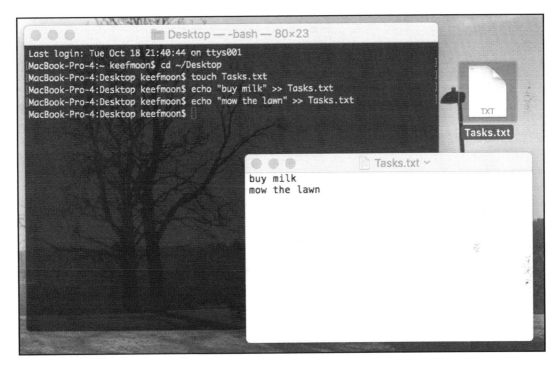

6. Add a few more tasks in the same way, and you'll see that each task is appended to the text file on the next line.
The command we issue in Terminal takes the following form:

```
<#What to append#> >> <#Where to append it#>
```

7. Let's create similar behavior in Swift; however, we can't use the same command string, >>, as this already defines as bit shifting to the right, so let's make it >>>.

8. We'll declare an infix operator--infix operator >>>. Operators can come in three types:

    1. prefix: Operates on one value and is placed before the value. The example for the NOT operator is let trueValue = !falseValue.

    2. postfix: Operates on one value and is placed after the value. The example for the force unwrap operator is let unwrapped = optional!.

    3. infix: Operates on two values and is placed between them. The example for the addition operator is let five = 2 + 3.

9. We can now define how this operator will work with different input types. First, we'll append one string to another:

```
func >>> (lhs: String, rhs: String) -> String {
    var combined = rhs
    combined.append(lhs)
    return combined
}
```

10. Next, let's implement appending a String to an array of strings:

```
func >>> (lhs: String, rhs: [String]) -> [String] {
    var combined = rhs
    combined.append(lhs)
    return combined
}
```

11. Finally, let's implement appending the elements in an array of strings to another array of strings:

```
func >>> (lhs: [String], rhs: [String]) -> [String] {
    var combined = rhs
    combined.append(contentsOf: lhs)
    return combined
}
```

 We can implement our appending operator on every type of array that we think might be useful, but instead, we can implement it as a generic function and have it work for all arrays.

12. Let's refactor the preceding two array implementations to use a generic element type:

```
func >>> <Element>(lhs: Element, rhs: Array<Element>) ->
Array<Element> {
    var combined = rhs
    combined.append(lhs)
    return combined
}

func >>> <Element>(lhs: Array<Element>, rhs: Array<Element>) ->
Array<Element> {
    var combined = rhs
    combined.append(contentsOf: lhs)
    return combined
}
```

13. With these implementations in place, let's look at how we can use our new operator:

```
let appendedString = "Two" >>> "One"
print(appendedString)

let appendedStringToArray = "three" >>> ["one", "two"]
print(appendedStringToArray)

let appendedArray = ["three", "four"] >>> ["one", "two"]
print(appendedArray)
```

How it works...

Once we have defined the operator, we can write top-level functions that implement the behavior for each pair of types: one on the **left-hand side (LHS)** and one on the **right-hand side (RHS)**. Method parameter overloading allows us to specify the operator implementation for multiple-type pairings.

We can also implement it for our own custom types. Let's create `Task` and `TaskList`, which might benefit from using the operator:

```
struct Task {
    let name: String
}

class TaskList: CustomStringConvertible {
    private var tasks: [Task] = []
```

```
func append(task: Task) {
    tasks.append(task)
}
var description: String {
    return tasks.map { $0.name }.joined(separator: "\n")
}
}
```

We'll add `CustomStringConvertible` conformance so that we can easily print out the result.

An alternative to implementing the use of an operator as a top-level function is to declare it within the relevant type as a static function. We'll declare it within an extension on our `TaskList` object, but we can just as easily declare it within the main `TaskList` class declaration:

```
extension TaskList {
    static func >>> (lhs: Task, rhs: TaskList) {
        rhs.append(task: lhs)
    }
}
```

Implementing this within a type has a few advantages: The implementation code is right next to the type itself, making it easier to find, and taking advantage of any values or types that might have a private, or otherwise restricted, access control, which will prevent them from being visible to a top-level function.

Now we can use our >>> operator to append `Task` to a `TaskList`:

```
let shoppingList = TaskList()
print(shoppingList)
Task(name: "get milk") >>> shoppingList
print(shoppingList)
Task(name: "get teabags") >>> shoppingList
print(shoppingList)
```

There's more...

Operators don't just work individually--they are often used within the same expression as other operators; the mathematical operators are a helpful example of this. Let's take a look at this mathematical expression:

```
let result = 6 + 8 / 2 / 4
```

The order that each of these operations is performed in will affect the result. To understand the order in which the operations are performed, we can add brackets that will perform the same function:

```
let result = 6 + ((8 / 2) / 4)
```

In Swift, the decision of how to order the operations is made using two components, precedence and associativity.

- **Precedence**: This defines how important the operation type is. Therefore the operations with the highest precedence are performed first; for example, multiplication (*) has a higher precedence than addition (+), and is therefore always performed first.
- **Associativity**: This defines which side, left or right, a value should associate itself with for evaluation when it has an operation with the same precedence on either side. This has the effect of defining the order that operations of the same precedence should be evaluated in: left to right or right to left.

Let's use this information to understand the operation ordering of the preceding mathematical operation. We have an expression comprising of one addition and two division operations. Division operations have a higher precedence than addition; therefore, the division operations are evaluated first:

```
let result = 6 + (8 / 2 / 4)
```

We now have two division operations that need to be evaluated before the addition operation. Since both are division operators, they have the same precedence, so we have to look at associativity to know in which order to evaluate them. The division operation has an associativity of `left`, so they should be evaluated from left to right. Therefore, 8 / 2 is evaluated first and 4 / 4 is evaluated next. This gives us the following:

```
let result = 6 + ((8 / 2) / 4)
```

We need to define precedence and associativity for our custom operator, as the compiler does not currently know how it should be ordered within an expression containing multiple operations. Because of this, the following expression will not compile:

```
let multiOperationArray = [5,6] >>> [3,4] >>> [1,2] + [9,10] >>> [7,8]
print(multiOperationArray)
```

Precedence and associativity are defined within a precedence group, and an operator can either conform to an existing group or one that has been newly defined.

Let's define a new precedence group for our appending operator:

```
precedencegroup AppendingPrecedence {
    associativity: left
    higherThan: AdditionPrecedence
    lowerThan: MultiplicationPrecedence
}
```

Here, we give it the name `AppendingPrecedence` and define its values within curly brackets. We'll set its associativity to left to match mathematical operations, and to establish a precedence, we define that this precedence group is higher than another precedence group and lower than some other precedence groups. For the appending operator, we'll set the precedence to be higher than addition, so it will be evaluated before the addition operators but after the multiplication operators. Both the `AddictionPrecendence` and `MultiplicationPrecedence` groups are defined by the *standard library*.

Now that we have a precedence group defined, we can ensure that our custom operator conforms to it:

```
infix operator >>> : AppendingPrecedence
```

With precedence and associativity declared, the composite expression previously created will now compile:

```
let multiOperationArray = [5,6] >>> [3,4] >>> [1,2] + [9,10] >>> [7,8]
  print(multiOperationArray) // [1,2,3,4,5,6,7,8,9,10]
```

See also

Further information about custom operators can be found in Apple's documentation of the Swift language at: http://swiftbook.link/docs/custom-operators

Nested types

In Objective-C, all objects are at the **top level**, and given global scope, they can be said to be in the same **namespace**. This is one reason for the convention among Objective-C developers, including Apple, to prefix their class names with two-or-three letter identifiers.

These prefix characters allow similarly named classes from different frameworks to be differentiated, for example, *UIView* from *UIKit* and *SKView* from *SpriteKit*. Swift solves this problem by allowing types to be nested within other types, providing namespacing with nested types and modules.

Getting ready

Any type can be defined as being nested within another type. This allows us to tightly associate one type with another, in addition to providing namespacing, which helps differentiate types with the same name.

In Swift 3, only types that didn't use generics could be nested within another type, or have a nested type within it. This limitation was removed with Swift 4.

How to do it...

Let's build a system to monitor a physical device and the user interface that it displays. Both the device and the user interface have the concept of orientation, although these concepts have differing definitions for each.

First, we'll define a class to represent the device:

```
class Device {
    enum Category {
        case watch
        case phone
        case tablet
    }
    enum Orientation {
        case portrait
        case portraitUpsideDown
        case landscapeLeft
        case landscapeRight
    }
    let category: Category
    var currentOrientation: Orientation = .portrait
    init(category: Category) {
        self.category = category
    }
}
```

Within this class, we have defined two enums, which only have value when used in relation to the `Device` class. Nesting the type also allows us to simplify the names of these types. It would be customary to name them `DeviceCategory` and `DeviceOrientation` to avoid confusion, but since they are nested, we can remove the `Device` prefix.

Any use of the nested types, within the type that contains it, can be used without any qualifiers; however, this is not the case for use outside of the containing type:

```
let phone = Device(category: .phone)
let desiredOrientation: Device.Orientation = .portrait
let phoneHasDesiredOrientation = phone.currentOrientation ==
desiredOrientation
```

To reference a nested type, we must first specify the containing type, so the `Orientation` enum, within the `Device` class, becomes `Device.Orientation`.

Next, let's define a struct to represent a user interface:

```
struct UserInterface {
    struct Version {
        let major: Int
        let minor: Int
        let patch: Int
    }
    enum Orientation {
        case portrait
        case landscape
    }
    let version: Version
    var orientation: Orientation
}
```

Our `UserInterface` struct also includes a nested `Orientation` enum, but as these two enums lie in different namespaces, there is no naming conflict. As before, the nested types can be used within without any qualifiers in the containing type.

Let's create a function to convert from device orientation to user interface orientation, to see how these two nested types can be used in conjunction with one another:

```
func uiOrientation(for deviceOrientation: Device.Orientation) ->
UserInterface.Orientation {
    switch deviceOrientation {
    case Device.Orientation.portrait,
Device.Orientation.portraitUpsideDown:
        return UserInterface.Orientation.portrait
    case Device.Orientation.landscapeLeft,
Device.Orientation.landscapeRight:
```

```
            return UserInterface.Orientation.landscape
    }
}
let phoneUIOrientation = uiOrientation(for: phone.currentOrientation)
print(phoneUIOrientation) // UserInterface.Orientation.portrait
```

How it works...

Our orientation conversion function specifies the full enum case for the switch statement and the return statements. For example:

```
Device.Orientation.portrait
UserInterface.Orientation.portrait
```

However, as we've seen previously, when the compiler knows the type of the enum, only the case needs to be specified--the enum type can be removed. For our function, the input parameter type is `Device.Orientation` and the return type is `UserInterface.Orientation`, so the compiler does know enum types, and therefore we can remove the types:

```
    */
func uiOrientation(for deviceOrientation: Device.Orientation) ->
UserInterface.Orientation {
    switch deviceOrientation {
    case .portrait, .portraitUpsideDown:
        return .portrait
    case .landscapeLeft, .landscapeRight:
        return .landscape
    }
}
```

Note that the switch case contains `.portrait` and returns a `.portrait`, but these are cases from different enums, and the compiler knows the difference.

There's more...

We've seen how namespacing separates types nested within different containing types, but types within modules are also namespaced. This allows you to name your types without fear of collision with types in other modules.

Let's imagine that we are building an app for hospitals to keep track of their events and resources. As part of this, we create a class to represent surgical operations that we intend to track:

```
class Operation {
    let doctorsName: String
    let patientsName: String
    init(doctorsName: String, patientsName: String) {
        self.doctorsName = doctorsName
        self.patientsName = patientsName
    }
}
```

There is another class called `Operation`, provided by the **Foundation** framework, that can be used to execute and manage a long-running task. We can use both types of `Operation` side by side, because the `Foundation` framework is exposed as a module, and so the long-running `Operation` class can be used by referencing the `Foundation` module:

```
import Foundation

let medicalOperation = Operation(doctorsName: "Dr. Crusher", patientsName:
"Commander Riker")
let longRunningOperation = Foundation.Operation()
```

See also

Further information about nested types can be found in Apple's documentation of the Swift language at: http://swiftbook.link/docs/nested-types

5

Beyond the Standard Library

In this chapter, we will cover the following recipes:

- Foundation
- Networking
- JSON
- XML
- Cocoa Touch

Introduction

Apple's intention when open sourcing Swift was to provide a cross-platform, general purpose programming language that is ready to use. The Swift standard library provides the core language features and common collection types; however, this does not provide everything needed to get up and running.

In this chapter, we will explore functionalities outside of the standard library, provided by frameworks such as `Foundation` and `UIKit`, which provide additional functionalities to help you make full use of Swift.

All the code for this chapter can be found in a GitHub repository available at `http://swiftbook.link/code/chapter5`.

Foundation

Since the inception of the platforms, macOS and iOS developers have had access to the Foundation framework, a collection of classes and utilities that provide a foundational set of functionality that will be needed to perform common programming tasks, including networking, date manipulation and formatting, and localization.

It was, therefore, necessary to provide the functionality of Foundation as part of the open sourcing efforts, especially for non-Apple platforms, where the existing Foundation framework is not available due to its reliance on the Objective-C runtime. To this end, Apple has released an open source, Swift-based version of Foundation as a core library, which can be found at `https://github.com/apple/swift-corelibs-foundation`.

In addition to providing the Foundation functionality to non-Apple platforms, the version of Foundation included with Swift also provides more Swift-friendly implementations for a number of common types. The types, previously implemented as Objective-C class objects, have been reimplemented as Swift structs, giving them more appropriate semantics (we will cover the difference between reference and value semantics in more detail in `Chapter 8`, *Performance and Responsiveness in Swift*).

With this reimplementation, Swift Foundation also drops the "NS" prefix from many types. We discussed in the previous chapter that modules and namespacing make this prefixing unnecessary.

There is a huge amount of functionalities within Foundation, so in this recipe, let's focus on one area that is very widely used date and time manipulation and formatting.

Getting ready

We will create a function that determines how long there is until Christmas and returns this information as a string that can be displayed to a user.

Let's break this problem down into its component parts:

- Get the current date and time
- Get a date and time for the next "Christmas" (midnight, or 00:00, at the beginning of the next December 25)
- Compare the preceding two dates to find the difference
- Prepare a string that displays this information for the user

How to do it...

First, let's look at this implementation, then we can pick it apart in more detail:

```swift
import Foundation

func howLongUntilChristmas() -> String {

    let calendar = Calendar.current
    let timeZone = TimeZone.current

    let now = Date()
    let yearOfNextChristmas = calendar.component(.year, from: now)

    var christmasComponents = DateComponents(calendar: calendar,
    timeZone: timeZone,
    era: nil,
    year: yearOfNextChristmas,
    month: 12,
    day: 25,
    hour: 0,
    minute: 0,
    second: 0,
    nanosecond: 0,
    weekday: nil,
    weekdayOrdinal: nil,
    quarter: nil,
    weekOfMonth: nil,
    weekOfYear: nil,
    yearForWeekOfYear: nil)

    var christmas = christmasComponents.date!
    // If we have already had Christmas this year,
    // then we need to use Christmas next year.
    if christmas < now {
      christmasComponents.year = yearOfNextChristmas + 1
      christmas = christmasComponents.date!
    }

    let componentFormatter = DateComponentsFormatter()
    componentFormatter.unitsStyle = .full
    componentFormatter.allowedUnits = [.month, .day, .hour, .minute, .second]

    return componentFormatter.string(from: now, to: christmas)!
}

let timeUntilChristmas = howLongUntilChristmas()
print("Time until Christmas: \(timeUntilChristmas)")
```

How it works...

To create our `howLongUntilChristmas` function, let's first get the currently set calendar and time zone as they will be needed for the date calculations to come:

```
let calendar = Calendar.current
let timeZone = TimeZone.current
```

While retrieving the current time zone is self-explanatory, it is not immediately obvious what the `Calendar` type represents and why we need to retrieve it.

How dates are represented is not as universally agreed as you might believe. Certain time components are mostly universal, such as the length of years and days, as they are connected to astronomical events, such as the time it takes for the earth to perform one revolution of the sun, and for the earth to complete one revolution on its axis, respectively. However, other time components such as months and weeks, and how the years are numbered, are rooted in the culture that created them.

 The calendar used through Europe, and most of the world, is known as the Gregorian calendar, introduced in 1582 by Pope Gregory XIII, replacing the Julian calendar. There are seven calendars currently in use around the world: Gregorian, Chinese, Hebrew, Islamic, Persian, Ethiopian, and Balinese Pawukon.

The way in which we present how long there is until Christmas will depend on the calendar that is relevant to the user. This is why we ask for the current calendar, which the user can change if they want a different representation.

Our first task is to get the current date and time:

```
let now = Date()
```

The default initializer for the `Date` value type uses the current date and time as its value. Note that this date value is set at the point of creation, it does not continually update with the current date and time.

Our next step is to get a date and time for the next Christmas. We know the time, day, and month of Christmas, so to construct a date for Christmas, we just need to know the year. There is a method on `Calendar` that allows us to retrieve specific components from a `Date`:

```
let yearOfNextChristmas = calendar.component(.year, from: now)
```

We now have the current year, within the user's current calendar, which we can use to create the Christmas date.

Next, we'll need to create a date for the next Christmas, so we use `DateComponents`, passing in the calendar, time zone, and the fact that we are defining December 25 at midnight, for the current year:

```
var christmasComponents = DateComponents(calendar: calendar,
                                        timeZone: timeZone,
                                        era: nil,
                                        year: yearOfNextChristmas,
                                        month: 12,
                                        day: 25,
                                        hour: 0,
                                        minute: 0,
                                        second: 0,
                                        nanosecond: 0,
                                        weekday: nil,
                                        weekdayOrdinal: nil,
                                        quarter: nil,
                                        weekOfMonth: nil,
                                        weekOfYear: nil,
                                        yearForWeekOfYear: nil)

var christmas = christmasComponents.date!
```

We can then create a `Date` from the `DateComponents`. This is optional as we may not have provided enough information to the components to generate a day; however, since we know that we have, we can force unwrap the optional.

Next, we need to handle an edge case--what if we have already had Christmas this year? For example, let's imagine that the current date is December 27, 2017; we are trying to find the date of the next Christmas, but if we use the current year, we will get December 25, 2017, which is the Christmas just gone. So, we need to add one to the current year, to get next Christmas, December 25, 2018:

```
if christmas < now {
    christmasComponents.year = yearOfNextChristmas + 1
    christmas = christmasComponents.date!
}
```

To account for this, we check whether the Christmas for this year is before now; if it is, we bump the year component to next year and recreate the Christmas date from the `DateComponent`.

We now have the current date and the next Christmas date, and `Foundation` provides functionality to both calculate the time difference between two dates, and format that for display to a user, through the use of `DateComponentsFormatter`:

```
let componentFormatter = DateComponentsFormatter()
componentFormatter.unitsStyle = .full
componentFormatter.allowedUnits = [.month, .day, .hour, .minute, .second]
return componentFormatter.string(from: now, to: christmas)!
```

After creating the `DateComponentsFormatter`, we set the `unitStyle` to `full`, which will provide a string using the full unit name, without abbreviation. Next, we can configure how we want time divided for display.

Finally, we can retrieve a string from the formatter that describes the time between the two dates given, with the settings provided to the formatter. This returns an optional string, so it is unwrapped and returned.

See also

There is a lot more to discover in Foundation, so check the documentation for further functionality:

- Swift 3 Documentation for Foundation--`http://swiftbook.link/docs/foundation`
- Open Source Repository for Foundation--`https://github.com/apple/swift-corelibs-foundation`

Networking

Every app worth building will need to send or receive information from the internet at some point and therefore networking support is a critical part of any development platform. In Swift, this support for networking is provided by the Foundation framework.

When we need to retrieve information from the internet, we send out a request to a server on the internet, and that server sends a response that hopefully contains the information we requested.

The main networking components that Foundation provides are as listed:

- URL: The address of a resource on a remote server. It contains information about the server and where the resource can be found on the server.

- `URLRequest`: Represents the request that will be made to the remote server. Defines the URL of the resource, how the request should be sent, metadata in the form of headers, and data that should be sent with it.
- `URLSession`: Manages the communication with remote servers, holds configuration for that communication, creates and optimizes the underlying connections.
- `URLSessionDataTask`: Object that manages the state of the request and delivers the response.
- `URLResponse`: Holds the metadata of the response from the remote server.

How to do it...

Let's use these networking tools to retrieve an image from a remote server:

1. First, we'll import Foundation and create our `URLSession`:

   ```
   import Foundation
   let config = URLSessionConfiguration.default
   let session = URLSession(configuration: config)
   ```

2. When creating a `URLSession`, we pass in a `URLSessionConfiguration` object, which allows configuring how long it takes for a request to timeout and how to cache responses, among other things. For our purposes, we will just use the default configuration.

3. Next, we will construct a request for the remote image:

   ```
   let urlString = "https://imgs.xkcd.com/comics/api.png"
   let url = URL(string: urlString)!
   let request = URLRequest(url: url)
   ```

4. We will be requesting the image from the excellent web comic XKCD (http://xkcd.com). We can create the URL from a string, and then create a `URLRequest` from the URL.

5. Now that we have our `URLRequest`, we can create a data task to retrieve the image from the remote server:

   ```
   let task = session.dataTask(with: request, completionHandler: {
   (data, response, error) in

   })
   ```

6. You shouldn't create a data task directly; instead, we ask our `URLSession` instance to create the data task, and we pass in a `URLRequest` and a completion handler. The completion handler will be fired once a response has been received from the remote server, or some error has occurred.

The completion handler has three inputs, all optional:

- `data: Data`: The data returned in the body of the response; if our request was successful, this will contain our image data.
- `response: URLResponse`: The response metadata, including response headers. If the request was over HTTP/HTTPS, then this will be an `HTTPURLResponse`, which will contain the HTTP status code.
- `error: Error`: If the request was unsuccessful, due to a network issue, for example, this value will have the error, and the data and response value will be `nil`. If the request was successful, this error value will be `nil`.

7. With that in mind, let's check for response data, and turn it into an image. To do this, we will need to construct a `UIImage` from the data. `UIImage` is a class that represents an image on iOS and can be found in the `UIKit` framework. So first, let's import `UIKit` at the top of the playground:

```
import UIKit
```

8. Now, we will check for image data in the completion handler and create a `UIImage`:

```
let task = session.dataTask(with: request) { (data, response,
error) in
    guard let imageData = data else {
        return // No Image, handle error
    }
    let image = UIImage(data: imageData)
}
```

9. We have now created the data task to retrieve the image, but we need to actually start the task to make the request; to do that, we call `resume` on the task:

```
task.resume()
```

How it works...

If you run the playground now, you will find that the `completion handler` is never executed and the image is never created; this is because of the way playgrounds execute the code they contain.

Playgrounds execute the code they contain from top to bottom. When the end of the playground page is reached, the playground stops executing. In our example, the task is created and started, but then the playground reaches the end of the page and stops executing. This happens before the response is received, so the `completion handler` is never executed. This isn't a problem in a normal app, which is continually running while it is in use; it is just specific to how Swift playgrounds work.

To solve this, we need to tell the playground that we don't want it to stop executing when it reaches the end of the page and, instead, it should run indefinitely, while we wait for the response to be received.

We'll need to import the `PlaygroundSupport` framework, which will allow users to configure the playground, so add this import to the top of the playground:

```
import PlaygroundSupport
```

Next, we get the current page and set that it needs indefinite execution:

```
PlaygroundPage.current.needsIndefiniteExecution = true
```

Now, we have the completed playground that retrieves an image from a remote server:

```
import Foundation
import PlaygroundSupport
import UIKit

PlaygroundPage.current.needsIndefiniteExecution = true

let config = URLSessionConfiguration.default
let session = URLSession(configuration: config)

let urlString = "https://imgs.xkcd.com/comics/api.png"
let url = URL(string: urlString)!
let request = URLRequest(url: url)

let task = session.dataTask(with: request) { (data, response, error) in

  guard let imageData = data else {
  return // No Image, handle error
  }
```

```
    let image = UIImage(data: imageData)
}
task.resume()
```

We can now run the playground, and eventually, you will see that the image value has been populated in the playground right sidebar, and you can click on the preview icon to see the image that has been downloaded:

See also

- Further information about networking can be found in Apple's networking overview at http://swiftbook.link/docs/networking

- It can also be found in Apple's URL Session Programming Guide at `http://swiftbook.link/docs/urlsession-guide`

JSON

As discussed in the last recipe, almost every app will need to exchange information with the internet at some point and, in that recipe, we retrieved an image from a remote server. Very often your app will need to retrieve more varied data, perhaps relating to the result of a search, or information about shared state held on the server.

This information can be represented in any number of ways, but one of the most common ways is as **JSON (JavaScript Object Notation)**, which is a text-based structure for representing information. A JSON object contains key-value pairs, where the keys are strings, and the values can be strings, numbers, booleans, null, other objects, or arrays.

Consider this example of a JSON objects:

```
{
  "name": {
    "givenName": "Keith",
    "middleName": "David",
    "familyName": "Moon"
  },
  "age": 36,
  "heightInMetres": 1.778,
  "isMale": true,
  "favouriteFootballTeam": null
}
```

The next is an example of an array of JSON objects:

```
[
  {
    "name": {
      "givenName": "Keith",
      "middleName": "David",
      "familyName": "Moon"
    },
    "age": 36,
    "heightInMetres": 1.778,
    "isMale": true,
    "favouriteFootballTeam": null
  },
  {
    "name": {
```

```
            "givenName": "Alissa",
            "middleName": "May",
            "familyName": "Moon"
        },
        "age": 32,
        "heightInMetres": 1.765,
        "isMale": false,
        "favouriteFootballTeam": null
    }
]
```

Foundation provides tools for reading information from, and writing information as, JSON data. In this recipe, we will interact with a JSON-based **API (Application Programming Interface)**, to both send and receive information.

Getting ready

Our goal is to interact with the GitHub API and create an issue for this book's repository. A full explanation of Git and GitHub is beyond the scope of this book, suffice to say that it's a service that stores versioned copies of your source code. Resources relevant to this book are stored in repositories on GitHub, and a GitHub user can create "issues" that serve as bug reports or feature requests.

If you don't already have one, you will need to sign up for a GitHub account:

1. Go to https://github.com.
2. Fill in your details and press **Sign up for GitHub**.

Once you have created a GitHub account, you will need to create a personal access token, which we will use to authenticate some of the requests to the GitHub API.

To create a personal access token, go to the settings page--https://github.com/settings/tokens--and click on **Generate new token**.

Give the token a name and check the box next to **repo**:

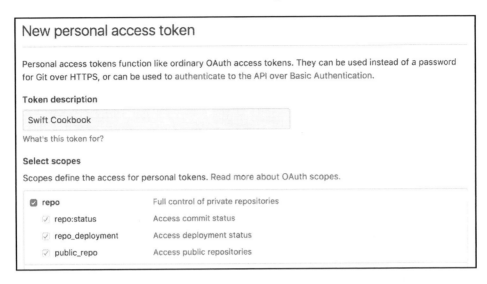

Click on **Generate token** at the bottom of the page.

You will now see your newly generate personal access token. Copy this token and paste it somewhere, as we will need it later:

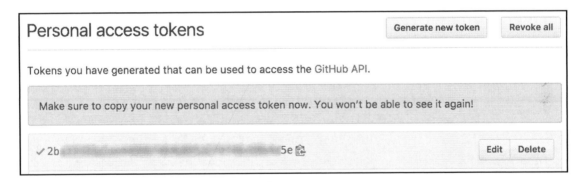

How to do it...

To create our issue, we will first retrieve all the public repositories created for this book, then find the relevant repository for this chapter and, finally, create a new issue.

As in the preceding recipe, we will need a `URLSession` to perform our requests, and we need to tell the playground not to finish executing when it reaches the end of the playground:

```
import Foundation
import PlaygroundSupport

PlaygroundPage.current.needsIndefiniteExecution = true

let config = URLSessionConfiguration.default
let session = URLSession(configuration: config)
```

Our first step is to fetch all the public repositories for a given user, so let's create a function to do that:

```
func fetchRepos(forUsername username: String) {

  let urlString = "https://api.github.com/users/\(username)/repos"
  let url = URL(string: urlString)!
  var request = URLRequest(url: url)
  request.setValue("application/vnd.github.v3+json", forHTTPHeaderField:
"Accept")

  let task = session.dataTask(with: request) { (data, response, error) in

  }
  task.resume()
}
```

- You will note that after creating the `URLRequest`, we set an HTTP header; this particular header ensures that we will always get back version 3 of the GitHub API.

We know from the GitHub API documentation--`https://developer.github.com/v3/`--that this response data is in JSON format We need to parse the JSON data to turn it into something that we can use; enter `JSONSerialization`. `JSONSerialization` is part of the `Foundation` framework and provides class methods for turning Swift dictionaries and arrays into JSON data (known as **serialization**), and back again (known as **deserialization**).

- Let's use `JSONSerialization` to turn our JSON response data into something more useful:

```
func fetchRepos(forUsername username: String) {

    let urlString = "https://api.github.com/users/\(username)/repos"
    let url = URL(string: urlString)!
    var request = URLRequest(url: url)
    request.setValue("application/vnd.github.v3+json",
forHTTPHeaderField: "Accept")
    let task = session.dataTask(with: request) { (data, response,
error) in

        // Once we have handled this response, the Playground
        // can finish executing.
        defer {
            PlaygroundPage.current.finishExecution()
        }

        // First unwrap the optional data
        guard let jsonData = data else {
            // If it is nil, there was probably a network error
            print(error ?? "Network Error")
            return
        }

        do {
            // Deserialisation can throw an error, so we have to `try`
and catch errors
            let deserialised = try JSONSerialization.jsonObject(with:
jsonData, options: [])
            print(deserialised)

        } catch {
            print(error)
        }
    }
    task.resume()
}
```

- Now, let's fetch the repositories that I have made public by executing our function and passing `SwiftProgrammingCookbook` in my GitHub username:

```
fetchRepos(forUsername: "SwiftProgrammingCookbook")
```

- Once run, the print output should look like this:

```
(
    {
    "archive_url" = "https://<GitHub API URL>/{archive_format}{/ref}";
    "assignees_url" = "https://<GitHub API URL>/assignees{/user}";
    // ..Truncated..
    description = "Code relating to Chapter 5 of Swift 4 Programming
                                                    Cookbook";
    "downloads_url" = "https://<GitHub API URL>/downloads";
    "events_url" = "https://<GitHub API URL>/events";
    fork = 0;
    forks = 0;
    "forks_count" = 0;
    "forks_url" = "https://<GitHub API URL>/forks";
    "full_name" = "SwiftProgrammingCookbook/BeyondTheStandardLibrary";
    // ..Truncated..
    "issue_comment_url" = "https://<GitHub API
                                URL>/issues/comments{/number}";
    "issue_events_url" = "https://<GitHub API
                                URL>/issues/events{/number}";
    "issues_url" = "https://<GitHub API URL>/issues{/number}";
    "keys_url" = "https://<GitHub API URL>/keys{/key_id}";
    "labels_url" = "https://<GitHub API URL>/labels{/name}";
    language = Swift;
    "languages_url" = "https://<GitHub API URL>/languages";
    "merges_url" = "https://<GitHub API URL>/merges";
    "milestones_url" = "https://<GitHub API URL>/milestones{/number}";
    "mirror_url" = "<null>";
    name = BeyondTheStandardLibrary;
    "notifications_url" = "https://<GitHub API URL>/notifications{?
     since,all,participating}";
    "open_issues" = 0;
    "open_issues_count" = 0;
    owner = {
        "avatar_url" =
            "https://avatars1.githubusercontent.com/u/28363559?v=4";
        "events_url" = "https://<GitHub API URL>/events{/privacy}";
        "followers_url" = "https://<GitHub API URL>/followers";
        "following_url" = "https://<GitHub API
            URL>/following{/other_user}";
        "gists_url" = "https://<GitHub API URL>/gists{/gist_id}";
        "gravatar_id" = "";
        "html_url" = "https://<GitHub URL>";
        id = 28363559;
        login = SwiftProgrammingCookbook;
        "organizations_url" = "https://<GitHub API URL>/orgs";
        "received_events_url" = "https://<GitHub API
```

```
                                         URL>/received_events";
            "repos_url" = "https://<GitHub API URL>/repos";
            "site_admin" = 0;
            "starred_url" = "https://<GitHub API
                               URL>/starred{/owner}{/repo}";
            "subscriptions_url" = "https://<GitHub API URL>/subscriptions";
            type = Organization;
            url = "https://<GitHub API URL>";
        };
        private = 0;
        // ..Truncated..
        url = "https://<GitHub API URL>";
        watchers = 0;
        "watchers_count" = 0;
    },
    // More Repos...
)
```

JSONSerializer has turned our JSON data into familiar arrays and dictionaries that can be used to retrieve the information we need in the normal way. The JSON data is deserialized with the Any type, as the JSON can have a JSON object or an array at its root.

Since, from the preceding output, we know that the response has an array of JSON objects at its root, we need to turn the value from type Any to an array of dictionaries of the [String: Any] type. This is referred to as **casting** from one type to another, which we can do using the as keyword and then specifying the new type. This keyword can be used in three different ways:

- as will perform a trivial cast. This is possible if the existing type is synonymous with the intended type; for instance, casting from a subclass to a superclass.
- as? will conditionally perform a cast, returning an optional value. If it is not possible to represent the value as the intended type, the value will be nil.
- as! will perform a forced cast. If it is not possible to represent the value as the intended type, you will get a crash.

So, let's cast the deserialized data to an array of dictionaries with string keys, with the [[String: Any]] type:

```
func fetchRepos(forUsername username: String) {
    //...
    let task = session.dataTask(with: request) { (data, response, error) in
        //...
        do {
            // Deserialisation can throw an error, so we have to `try` and catch
errors
```

```
        let deserialised = try JSONSerialization.jsonObject(with: jsonData,
                                                            options: [])
      print(deserialised)
      // As `deserialised` has type `Any` we need to cast
      guard let repos = deserialised as? [[String: Any]] else {
        print("Unexpected Response")
        return
      }
      print(repos)
    } catch {
      print(error)
    }
  }
}
```

Now, we have an array of dictionaries for the repositories in the API response, which we need to provide as an input for this function. A common pattern for providing results for asynchronous work is to provide a completion handler as a parameter. A completion handler is a closure that can be executed once the asynchronous work is completed.

Since the output we want to provide is the array of repository dictionaries, we will define this as an input for the closure if the request was successful, and an error if it wasn't:

```
func fetchRepos(forUsername username: String,
                completionHandler: @escaping ([[String: Any]]?, Error?) ->
Void) {

  let urlString = "https://api.github.com/users/\(username)/repos"
  let url = URL(string: urlString)!
  var request = URLRequest(url: url)
  request.setValue("application/vnd.github.v3+json", forHTTPHeaderField:
"Accept")
  let task = session.dataTask(with: request) { (data, response, error) in

    // Once we have handled this response, the Playground
    // can finish executing.
    defer {
      PlaygroundPage.current.finishExecution()
    }

    // First unwrap the optional data
    guard let jsonData = data else {
      // If it is nil, there was probably a network error
      completionHandler(nil, ResponseError.requestUnsucessful)
      return
    }

    do {
```

```
            // Deserialisation can throw an error, so we have to `try` and catch
    errors
        let deserialised = try JSONSerialization.jsonObject(with: jsonData,
                                                             options: [])
            // As `deserialised` has type `Any` we need to cast
        guard let repos = deserialised as? [[String: Any]] else {
           completionHandler(nil, ResponseError.unexpectedResponseStructure)
           return
        }

        completionHandler(repos, nil)

    } catch {
      completionHandler(nil, error)
    }
  }
  task.resume()
}
```

Now, whenever an error is generated, we execute the `completionHandler`, passing in the error and a `nil` for the results value; also, when we have the repository results, we execute the completion handler, passing in the parsed JSON and `nil` for the error.

We passed in a few new errors in the preceding code, so let's define those errors:

```
enum ResponseError: Error {
  case requestUnsucessful
  case unexpectedResponseStructure
}
```

This changes how we call this `fetchRepos` function:

```
fetchRepos(forUsername: "keefmoon") { (repos, error) in

  if let repos = repos {
    print(repos)
  } else if let error = error {
    print(error)
  }
}
```

Now that we have retrieved the details of the public repositories, we will submit an issue to the repository for this chapter. This issue can be any feedback you would like to give on this book, it can be a review, a suggestion for new content, or you can tell me about a Swift project you are currently working on.

This request to the GitHub API will be authenticated against your user account and therefore we will need to include details of the personal access token that we created at the beginning of this recipe. There are a number of ways to authenticate requests to the GitHub API, but the simplest is basic authentication, which involves adding an authorization string to the request header. Let's create a method to format the personal access token correctly for authentication:

```
func authHeaderValue(for token: String) -> String {
   let authorisationValue = Data("\(token):x-oauth-
basic".utf8).base64EncodedString()
   return "Basic \(authorisationValue)"
}
```

Next, let's create our function to submit our issue. From the API documentation at `https://developer.github.com/v3/issues/#create-an-issue`, we can see that unless you have push access, you can only create an issue with the following components:

- `title` (required)
- `body` (optional)

So, our function will take this information as an input, along with the repository name and username:

```
func createIssue(inRepo repo: String,
                 forUser user: String,
                 title: String,
                 body: String?) {

}
```

Creating an issue is achieved by sending a `POST` request, and information about the issue is provided as JSON data in the request body. To create our request, we can use `JSONSerialization`, but we will take our intended JSON structure and serialize it into `Data` this time:

```
func createIssue(inRepo repo: String,
                 forUser user: String,
                 title: String,
                 body: String?) {
    // Create the URL and Request
    let urlString = "https://api.github.com/repos/\(user)/\(repo)/issues"
    let url = URL(string: urlString)!
    var request = URLRequest(url: url)
    request.httpMethod = "POST"
    request.setValue("application/vnd.github.v3+json",
                forHTTPHeaderField: "Accept")
```

```
    let authorisationValue = authHeaderValue(for: <#your personal access
token#>)
    request.setValue(authorisationValue, forHTTPHeaderField:
"Authorization")
    // Put the issue information into the JSON structure required
    var json = ["title": title]
    if let body = body {
        json["body"] = body
    }
    // Serialise the json into Data. We can use try! as we know it is valid
JSON, the try will fail
    // if the provided JSON object contains elements that aren't valid
JSON.
    let jsonData = try! JSONSerialization.data(withJSONObject: json,
options: .prettyPrinted)
    request.httpBody = jsonData
    session.dataTask(with: request) { (data, response, error) in
        // TO FINISH
    }
}
```

As with the previous API request, we need a way to provide the result of creating the issue, so let's add a `completionHandler`:

```
func createIssue(inRepo repo: String,
                 forUser user: String,
                 title: String,
                 body: String?,
                 completionHandler: @escaping ([String: Any]?, Error?) ->
                                                           Void) {
    // Create the URL and Request
    let urlString = "https://api.github.com/repos/\(user)/\(repo)/issues"
    let url = URL(string: urlString)!
    var request = URLRequest(url: url)
    request.httpMethod = "POST"
    request.setValue("application/vnd.github.v3+json",
                     forHTTPHeaderField: "Accept")
    let authorisationValue = authHeaderValue(for: <#your personal access
                                                       token#>)
    request.setValue(authorisationValue, forHTTPHeaderField:
                                                 "Authorization")
    // Put the issue information into the JSON structure required
    var json = ["title": title]
    if let body = body {
        json["body"] = body
    }
    // Serialise the json into Data. We can use try! as we know
    // it is valid JSON, the try will fail if the provided
```

```
            // JSON object contains elements that aren't valid JSON.
            let jsonData = try! JSONSerialization.data(withJSONObject: json,
                                                        options:
            .prettyPrinted)
            request.httpBody = jsonData
            session.dataTask(with: request) { (data, response, error) in
                guard let jsonData = data else {
                    completionHandler(nil, ResponseError.requestUnsucessful)
                    return
                }
                do {
                    // Deserialisation can throw an error, so we have to `try`
                    // and catch errors
                    let deserialised = try JSONSerialization.jsonObject(with:
                            jsonData, options: [])
                    // As `deserialised` has type `Any` we need to cast
                    guard let createdIssue = deserialised as? [String: Any] else {
                        completionHandler(nil,
    ResponseError.unexpectedResponseStructure)
                        return
                    }
                    completionHandler(createdIssue, nil)
                } catch {
                    completionHandler(nil, error)
                }
            }
        }
    }
```

The API response to a successfully created issue provides a JSON representation of that issue. Our function will return this representation if it was successful, or an error if it was not.

Now that we have a function to create issues in a repository, it's time to use it to create an issue:

```
createIssue(inRepo: </span>"BeyondTheStandardLibrary",
            forUser: "SwiftProgrammingCookbook",
            title: <#The title of your feedback#>,
            body: <#Extra detail#>) { (issue, error) in
                if let issue = issue {
                    print(issue)
                } else if let error = error {
                    print(error)
                }
    }
```

I will check these created issues, so provide genuine feedback on this book. How have you found the content? Too detailed? Not detailed enough? Anything I've missed or not fully explained? Any questions that you have? This is your opportunity to let me know.

There's more...

When we created our completion handlers, we gave them two inputs: the successful result (either the repository information or the created issue), or an error if there is a failure. Both these values are optional; one or the other will be nil, and the other has a value. However, this convention is not enforced by the language, and a user of this function will have to consider the possibility that it may not be the case. What should the user of this function do if the fetchRepos function fires the completion handler with non-nil values for both the repository and the error? What if both are nil?

The user of this function, without viewing the function's internal code, can't be sure that this won't happen, which means they may need to write functionality and tests to account for this possibility, even though it may never happen.

It would be better if we can more accurately represent the intended behavior of our function, providing the user with a clear indication of the possible outcomes and leaving no room for ambiguity. We know that there are two possible outcomes from calling the function: it will either succeed and return the relevant value, or it will fail and return an error to indicate the reason for the failure.

Instead of optional values, we can use an enum to represent these possibilities. Let's create an enum to be used as a response to the fetchRepos function:

```
enum FetchReposResult {
    case success([[String: Any]])
    case failure(Error)
}
```

We can now define the success and failure states, and use associated values to hold the value that is relevant for each state, which is the repository information for the success state and the error for the failure state.

Now, let's amend our `fetchRepos` function to provide a `FetchReposResult` in the `completionHandler`:

```
func fetchRepos(forUsername username: String,
    completionHandler: @escaping (FetchReposResult) -> Void) {

    let urlString = "https://api.github.com/users/\(username)/repos"
    let url = URL(string: urlString)!
    var request = URLRequest(url: url)
    request.setValue("application/vnd.github.v3+json",
                     forHTTPHeaderField: "Accept")
    let task = session.dataTask(with: request) { (data, response, error) in

        // Once we have handled this response, the Playground
        // can finish executing.
        defer {
            PlaygroundPage.current.finishExecution()
        }

        // First unwrap the optional data
        guard let jsonData = data else {
            // If it is nil, there was probably a network error
            completionHandler(.failure(ResponseError.requestUnsucessful))
            return
        }

        do {
            // Deserialisation can throw an error,
            // so we have to `try` and catch errors
            let deserialised = try JSONSerialization.jsonObject(with:
                                        jsonData, options: [] )
            // As `deserialised` has type `Any` we need to cast
            guard let repos = deserialised as? [[String: Any]] else {
                let error = ResponseError.unexpectedResponseStructure
                completionHandler(.failure(error))
                return
            }

            completionHandler(.success(repos))

        } catch {
            completionHandler(.failure(error))
        }
    }
    task.resume()
}
```

We need to update how we call the `fetchRepos` function:

```
fetchRepos(forUsername: "SwiftProgrammingCookbook", completionHandler:{
result in
    switch result {
        case .success(let repos):
            print(repos)

        case .failure(let error):
            print(error)
    }
})
```

We now use a `switch` statement instead of `if/else`, and we get the added benefit that the compiler will ensure that we have covered all possible outcomes.

Having made this improvement to the `fetchRepos` function, we can similarly improve the `createIssue` function. We can create another `enum` to represent the result of this function; however, we can, instead, use generics to make this a common pattern that we can use for all tasks that attempt to retrieve information with either a success or failure:

```
enum Result<SuccessType> {
    case success(SuccessType)
    case failure(Error)
}
```

Now, by just specifying the generic type, this `enum` can be used in any scenario; situations with multiple returned values can also be handled by specifying a tuple as the generic type:

```
let result = Result<(Data, HTTPURLResponse)>.success((someData,
someHTTPURLResponse))
```

We can use this new `Result` in our `fetchRepos` function by just changing the definition of the completion handler:

```
func fetchRepos(forUsername username: String,
                completionHandler: @escaping (Result<[[String: Any]]>) ->
Void) {
    //...
}
```

Lastly, let's rewrite the `createIssue` function, and how we call it, to also use our `Result` enum:

```
func createIssue(inRepo repo: String,
                 forUser user: String,
                 title: String,
                 body: String?,
                 completionHandler: @escaping (Result<[String: Any]>) ->
Void) {

    // Create the URL and Request

    let urlString = "https://api.github.com/repos/\(user)/\(repo)/issues"
    let url = URL(string: urlString)!
    var request = URLRequest(url: url)
    request.httpMethod = "POST"
    let authorisationValue = authHeaderValue(for: <#your personal access
token#>)
    request.setValue(authorisationValue, forHTTPHeaderField:
"Authorization")
    request.setValue("application/vnd.github.v3+json", forHTTPHeaderField:
"Accept")

    // Put the issue information into the JSON structure required
    var json = ["title": title]

    if let body = body {
        json["body"] = body
    }

    // Serialise the json into Data. We can use try! as we know it is valid
JSON,
    // the try will fail if the provided JSON object contains elements that
    // aren't valid JSON.
    let jsonData = try! JSONSerialization.data(withJSONObject: json,
                                               options: .prettyPrinted)
    request.httpBody = jsonData

    let task = session.dataTask(with: request) { (data, response, error) in

        guard let jsonData = data else {
            completionHandler(.failure(ResponseError.requestUnsucessful))
            return
        }

        do {
            // Deserialisation can throw an error,
            // so we have to `try` and catch errors
```

```
            let deserialised = try JSONSerialization.jsonObject(with:
jsonData,
                                                        options:
[])

            // As `deserialised` has type `Any` we need to cast
            guard let createdIssue = deserialised as? [String: Any] else {
                let error = ResponseError.unexpectedResponseStructure
                completionHandler(.failure(error))
                return
            }

            completionHandler(.success(createdIssue))

        } catch {
            completionHandler(.failure(error))
        }
    }
    task.resume()
}

createIssue(inRepo: "BeyondTheStandardLibrary",
            forUser: "SwiftProgrammingCookbook",
            title: <#The title of your feedback#>,
            body: <#Extra detail#>) { result in

    switch result {
        case .success(let issue):
            print(issue)

        case .failure(let error):
            print(error)
    }
}
```

See also

Working with JSON data and extracting relevant information from it can be frustrating. Consider the JSON response for our fetchRepos function:

```
[
    {
        "id": 68144965,
        "name": "JSONNode",
        "full_name": "keefmoon/JSONNode",
        "owner": {
```

```
            "login": "keefmoon",
            "id": 271298,
            "avatar_url":
    "https://avatars.githubusercontent.com/u/271298?v=3",
            "gravatar_id": "",
            "url": "https://api.github.com/users/keefmoon",
            "html_url": "https://github.com/keefmoon",
            "followers_url":
    "https://api.github.com/users/keefmoon/followers",
            //... Some more URLs
            "received_events_url":
            "https://api.github.com/users/keefmoon/received_events",
            "type": "User",
            "site_admin": false
        },
        "private": false,
        //... more values
    }
    //... more repositories
]
```

If we want to get the username for the owner of the first repository, we need to do the following:

```
let jsonData = //... returned from the network

guard
    let deserialised = try? JSONSerialization.jsonObject(with: jsonData,
options: []),
    let repoArray = deserialised as? [[String: Any]],
    let firstRepo = repoArray.first,
    let ownerDictionary = firstRepo["owner"] as? [String: Any],
    let username = ownerDictionary["login"] as? String
    else {
        return
}
print(username)
```

That's a lot of optional unwrapping and casting, just to get one value! Swift's strongly typed nature doesn't work well with JSON's loosely defined schema, which is why you have to do a lot of work to turn loosely-typed information into strongly-typed values.

To help with these problems, a number of open source frameworks are available, which make working with JSON in Swift easier. SwiftyJSON is a popular framework that can be found on GitHub at https://github.com/SwiftyJSON/SwiftyJSON.

I have also built a lightweight JSON helper called JSONNode, which can also be found on GitHub at https://github.com/keefmoon/JSONnode.

With JSONNode, you can perform the same task of retrieving the owner's username for the first repository, with the following code:

```
let jsonData = //... returned from the network
guard
    let jsonNode = try? JSONNode(data: jsonData),
    let username = jsonNode[0]["owner"]["username"].string
    else {
        return
}

print(username)
```

Information within JSON, of any depth, can be retrieved in one line using subscripts.

If you find JSONNode useful, let me know.

XML

XML stands for **eXtensible Markup Language** and is a popular way of representing data for storage and transfer across a network. XML is a very flexible format and is used to represent many types of data. The current specification of HTML, which powers most of the web, is an implementation of XML.

The version of XML that we will concern ourselves with is **RSS**, which stands for **Really Simple Syndication**. RSS is used to define a collection of time-ordered pieces of digestible content; these RSS feeds can then be used to aggregate content from a number of different sources. RSS is typically used as a distribution mechanism for news articles and podcasts.

Getting ready

In this recipe, we will investigate how to read and write XML data using functionalities within the Foundation framework. However, while the classes that help with reading XML data are available on all of Apple's platforms, the classes that assist with writing XML data are only available on the macOS platform.

This is an unfortunate oversight and means that if you need to write XML data within an iOS app, you will likely need to look for a third-party helper or build your own. We will investigate third-party helpers at the end of this recipe.

To investigate both reading and writing XML using the `Foundation` framework, we need to create a new macOS-based playground instead of an iOS-based playground, which we created earlier.

Create a new Swift playground, as usual, but choose a blank template from the macOS tab:

 The RSS feed that we will retrieve and read is from the front page of the BBC News website, which is accessible at
`http://feeds.bbci.co.uk/news/rss.xml`.

Our first step is to retrieve the data at this URL so that we can start making sense of it. Since we previously covered retrieving information over the network, I'll add the code without further comment; check out the *Networking* recipe in this chapter for more information:

```
import Foundation
import PlaygroundSupport

PlaygroundPage.current.needsIndefiniteExecution = true

func fetchBBCNewsRSSFeed() {

    let session = URLSession.shared
    let url = URL(string: "http://feeds.bbci.co.uk/news/rss.xml")!
    let dataTask = session.dataTask(with: url) { (data, response, error) in

        guard let data = data, error == nil else {
            print(error ?? "Unexpected response")
            return
        }

        let dataAsString = String(data: data, encoding: .utf8)!
        print(dataAsString)
    }
    dataTask.resume()
}

fetchBBCNewsRSSFeed()
```

When you run the playground, you will get an output that looks like the following:

```
<?xml version="1.0" encoding="UTF-8"?>
<?xml-stylesheet title="XSL_formatting" type="text/xsl"
href="/shared/bsp/xsl/rss/nolsol.xsl"?>
<rss xmlns:dc="http://purl.org/dc/elements/1.1/"
    xmlns:content="http://purl.org/rss/1.0/modules/content/"
    xmlns:atom="http://www.w3.org/2005/Atom" version="2.0"
    xmlns:media="http://search.yahoo.com/mrss/">
    <channel>
        <title><![CDATA[BBC News - Home]]></title>
        <description><![CDATA[BBC News - Home]]></description>
        <link>http://www.bbc.co.uk/news/</link>
        <image>
<url>http://news.bbcimg.co.uk/nol/shared/img/bbc_news_120x60.gif</url>
            <title>BBC News - Home</title>
            <link>http://www.bbc.co.uk/news/</link>
        </image>
        <generator>RSS for Node</generator>
        <lastBuildDate>Sun, 27 Nov 2016 00:10:08 GMT</lastBuildDate>
```

```
        <copyright>
            <![CDATA[Copyright: (C) British Broadcasting Corporation, see
            http://news.bbc.co.uk/2/hi/help/rss/4498287.stm for terms and
conditions of
            reuse.]]>
        </copyright>
        <language><![CDATA[en-gb]]></language>
        <ttl>15</ttl>
        <item>
            <title><![CDATA[Donald Trump calls Fidel Castro 'brutal
dictator']]>
            </title>
            <description><![CDATA[Cuba's former leader Fidel Castro was a
"brutal
            dictator", US President-elect Donald Trump
says.]]></description>
<link>http://www.bbc.co.uk/news/world-latin-america-38118739</link>
            <guid
isPermaLink="true">http://www.bbc.co.uk/news/world-latin-america-
            38118739</guid>
            <pubDate>Sat, 26 Nov 2016 18:13:09 GMT</pubDate>
            <media:thumbnail width="976" height="549"
url="http://c.files.bbci.co.uk/12789/production/_92675657_mediaitem92675656
.jpg"/>
        </item>
        <item>
            <title><![CDATA[Fidel Castro: Jeremy Corbyn praises 'huge
figure']]>
            </title>
            <description><![CDATA[Fidel Castro, who has died aged 90, was a
"huge
            figure in our lives", Labour leader Jeremy Corbyn
says.]]></description>
            <link>http://www.bbc.co.uk/news/uk-38117068</link>
            <guid
isPermaLink="true">http://www.bbc.co.uk/news/uk-38117068</guid>
            <pubDate>Sat, 26 Nov 2016 18:26:19 GMT</pubDate>
            <media:thumbnail width="976" height="549"
url="http://c.files.bbci.co.uk/160EB/production/_92674309_hi036585895.jpg"/
>
        </item>
        //... More items
    </channel>
</rss>
```

How to do it...

The overall structure should be familiar to anyone who has seen HTML. Apart from the first two lines, which define the version and formatting of the XML, the information is structured with opening and closing **tags**; consider the following example:

```
<link>http://www.bbc.co.uk/news/world-latin-america-38118739</link>
```

The name of the opening tag defines the contents of this element of XML; in this case, it is a link. Then follows the content of the element, and the end of the content is defined by a closing tag that has a / before its name.

In addition to this simple example, an XML element can have attributes that describe extra information about the content of the element:

```
<guid
isPermaLink="true">http://www.bbc.co.uk/news/world-latin-
america-38118739</guid>
```

These are defined as key/value pairs within the opening tag.

The contents of the XML element may be a string, as in the preceding examples, or can be nested child XML elements:

```
<image>
    <url>http://news.bbcimg.co.uk/nol/shared/img/bbc_news_120x60.gif</url>
    <title>BBC News - Home</title>
    <link>http://www.bbc.co.uk/news/</link>
</image>
```

Lastly, the contents of an XML element can be data. This data might be represented as a string, especially if the string is likely to be longer and may include line breaks, special characters, and other components that may be confused for being part of the enclosing XML formatting:

```
<title><![CDATA[Donald Trump calls Fidel Castro 'brutal
dictator']]></title>
```

Now that we have retrieved the XML, we want to parse it into something useful. The parser we will be using is provided by the Foundation framework, and available on iOS and macOS, it is called XMLParser. XMLParser is a **SAX** parser, which stands for **Simple API for XML**; the features of a SAX parser are as follows:

- Event driven
- Low memory overhead

- Only retains relevant information
- One pass

The parser takes a delegate object that it will deliver event information to as it parses the document. It is the delegate object's responsibility to take and retain the relevant information from these delegate callbacks as the XML data is parsed, as the parser will not retain the parsed data.

We will step through a simple example to see how the parser reports events to the delegate. Here's the simple XML that we intend to parse:

```
<?xml version="1.0" encoding="UTF-8"?>
<quotes>
    <quote attribution="Homer Simpson">
        Press any key to continue, where's the any key?
    </quote>
    <quote attribution="Unknown">
        Why do nerds confuse Halloween and Christmas? Because OCT31=DEC25
    </quote>
</quotes>
```

The parser will start parsing the XML, character by character, and as an event is triggered, the delegate will be informed. The first event will be the start of the document, where the parser will call this:

```
func parserDidStartDocument(_ parser: XMLParser)
```

Here, we can do any setup or resetting of the state that is required. Then, the parser will move through the document until it reaches this point:

```
<?xml version="1.0" encoding="UTF-8"?>
<quotes>
** Parser is here **
    <quote attribution="Homer Simpson">
        Press any key to continue, where's the any key?
    </quote>
    <quote attribution="Unknown">
        Why do nerds confuse Halloween and Christmas? Because OCT31=DEC25
    </quote>
</quotes>
```

The parser has finished parsing the opening tag for the first element and so, it fires the delegate callback:

```swift
func parser(_ parser: XMLParser,
            didStartElement elementName: String,
            namespaceURI: String?,
            qualifiedName qName: String?,
            attributes attributeDict: [String : String] = [:]) {
    /*
    elementName = quotes
    namespaceURI = nil
    qName = nil
    attributeDict = [:]
    */
}
```

The parser then continues until it reaches this point:

```
<?xml version="1.0" encoding="UTF-8"?>
<quotes>
    <quote attribution="Homer Simpson">
** Parser is here **
        Press any key to continue, where's the any key?
    </quote>
    <quote attribution="Unknown">
        Why do nerds confuse Halloween and Christmas? Because OCT31=DEC25
    </quote>
</quotes>
```

Since the parser has seen another starting tag, it fires the same delegate callback with information about this new element:

```swift
func parser(_ parser: XMLParser,
            didStartElement elementName: String,
            namespaceURI: String?,
            qualifiedName qName: String?,
            attributes attributeDict: [String : String] = [:]) {
    /*
    elementName = quote
    namespaceURI = nil
    qName = nil
    attributeDict = ["attribution": "Homer Simpson"]
    */
}
```

This time, as the element has attribute information, it is provided by the delegate callback in the `attributeDict` dictionary.

The parse now moves through the content of the first `quote` element; at some point, it fires the delegate callback with the content it has collected up to that point:

```xml
<?xml version="1.0" encoding="UTF-8"?>
<quotes>
    <quote attribution="Homer Simpson">
        Press any key to continue, ** Parser is here **where's the any key?
    </quote>
    <quote attribution="Unknown">
        Why do nerds confuse Halloween and Christmas? Because OCT31=DEC25
    </quote>
</quotes>
```

It then provides this content collected so far to the delegate:

```swift
func parser(_ parser: XMLParser, foundCharacters string: String) {
    /*
    string = "Press any key to continue, "
    */
}
```

The reason the parser stops halfway through the content to fire the delegate callback is to make the most efficient use of memory. All the data that the parser processes must be kept in memory by the parser until it can be delivered to the delegate; therefore, if the parser determines that memory usage is getting high, it will take the content it has collected so far, and deliver it to the delegate. Once it has done this, it can free up the memory and start collecting further content afresh.

In this simple example, it is very unlikely that the parser will not provide all the content of the element in one delegate callback. It is, however, useful to see an example of this, as we have to account for the possibility, and it will affect how we implement the delegate later.

The parser will fire the same `foundCharacters` delegate callback until all of the content of an element has been delivered to the delegate:

```xml
<?xml version="1.0" encoding="UTF-8"?>
<quotes>
    <quote attribution="Homer Simpson">
        Press any key to continue, where's the any key?** Parser is here **
    </quote>
    <quote attribution="Unknown">
        Why do nerds confuse Halloween and Christmas? Because OCT31=DEC25
    </quote>
</quotes>
```

It then provides the new content, since the last call, to the delegate:

```
func parser(_ parser: XMLParser, foundCharacters string: String) {
    /*
    string = "where's the any key?"
    */
}
```

The parse now processes the closing tag for the first quote element:

```
<?xml version="1.0" encoding="UTF-8"?>
<quotes>
    <quote attribution="Homer Simpson">
        Press any key to continue, where's the any key?
    </quote>
** Parser is here **
    <quote attribution="Unknown">
        Why do nerds confuse Halloween and Christmas? Because OCT31=DEC25
    </quote>
</quotes>
```

Then, it fires the delegate callback, signalling the end of the element:

```
func parser(_ parser: XMLParser,
            didEndElement elementName: String,
            namespaceURI: String?,
            qualifiedName qName: String?) {
    /*
    elementName = "quote"
    namespaceURI = nil
    qName = nil
    */
}
```

The parser will then continue to process the next quote element in the same way, firing the same sequence of didStartElement, followed by a number of foundCharacters callbacks, and finishing with a call to didEndElement.

Having finished processing the last quote element, the parser will process the closing tag of the quotes element:

```
<?xml version="1.0" encoding="UTF-8"?>
<quotes>
    <quote attribution="Homer Simpson">
        Press any key to continue, where's the any key?
    </quote>
    <quote attribution="Unknown">
        Why do nerds confuse Halloween and Christmas? Because OCT31=DEC25
```

```
    </quote>
  </quotes>
** Parser is here **
```

It will fire another `didEndElement` callback for the `quotes` element:

```swift
func parser(_ parser: XMLParser,
            didEndElement elementName: String,
            namespaceURI: String?,
            qualifiedName qName: String?) {
  /*
  elementName = "quotes"
  namespaceURI = nil
  qName = nil
  */
}
```

And finally, the parser will fire a delegate callback to indicate that the parsing of the document is complete:

```swift
func parserDidEndDocument(_ parser: XMLParser) {

}
```

Now that you understand how the parser passes information to the delegate, we can return to our RSS example.

How it works...

You will remember that we retrieved XML data that looks like this:

```xml
<?xml version="1.0" encoding="UTF-8"?>
<?xml-stylesheet title="XSL_formatting" type="text/xsl"
href="/shared/bsp/xsl/rss/nolsol.xsl"?>
<rss xmlns:dc="http://purl.org/dc/elements/1.1/"
    xmlns:content="http://purl.org/rss/1.0/modules/content/"
    xmlns:atom="http://www.w3.org/2005/Atom" version="2.0"
    xmlns:media="http://search.yahoo.com/mrss/">
  <channel>
      <title><![CDATA[BBC News - Home]]></title>
      <description><![CDATA[BBC News - Home]]></description>
      <link>http://www.bbc.co.uk/news/</link>
      <image>
<url>http://news.bbcimg.co.uk/nol/shared/img/bbc_news_120x60.gif</url>
        <title>BBC News - Home</title>
        <link>http://www.bbc.co.uk/news/</link>
```

```
        </image>
        <generator>RSS for Node</generator>
        <lastBuildDate>Sun, 27 Nov 2016 00:10:08 GMT</lastBuildDate>
        <copyright><![CDATA[Copyright: (C) British Broadcasting
Corporation, see
         http://news.bbc.co.uk/2/hi/help/rss/4498287.stm for terms and
conditions of
         reuse.]]></copyright>
        <language><![CDATA[en-gb]]></language>
        <ttl>15</ttl>
        <item>
            <title><![CDATA[Donald Trump calls Fidel Castro 'brutal
dictator']]>
            </title>
            <description><![CDATA[Cuba's former leader Fidel Castro was a
"brutal
             dictator", US President-elect Donald Trump
says.]]></description>
<link>http://www.bbc.co.uk/news/world-latin-america-38118739</link>
            <guid
isPermaLink="true">http://www.bbc.co.uk/news/world-latin-america-
            38118739</guid>
            <pubDate>Sat, 26 Nov 2016 18:13:09 GMT</pubDate>
            <media:thumbnail width="976" height="549"
url="http://c.files.bbci.co.uk/12789/production/_92675657_mediaitem92675656
.jpg"/>
        </item>
        <item>
            <title><![CDATA[Fidel Castro: Jeremy Corbyn praises 'huge
figure']]>
             </title>
            <description><![CDATA[Fidel Castro, who has died aged 90, was a
"huge
            figure in our lives", Labour leader Jeremy Corbyn
says.]]></description>
            <link>http://www.bbc.co.uk/news/uk-38117068</link>
            <guid
isPermaLink="true">http://www.bbc.co.uk/news/uk-38117068</guid>
            <pubDate>Sat, 26 Nov 2016 18:26:19 GMT</pubDate>
            <media:thumbnail width="976" height="549"
url="http://c.files.bbci.co.uk/160EB/production/_92674309_hi036585895.jpg"/
>
        </item>
        //... More items
    </channel>
</rss>
```

From this, we want to extract the news articles in a usable form, so let's define a `NewsArticle` model containing some useful information and place it near the top of the playground:

```
struct NewsArticle {
    let title: String
    let url: URL
}
```

Since the information we require will be spread over multiple delegate callbacks, our delegate will need to keep track of the information it has received, so it can be pieced together at the appropriate time.

Let's create a class object to be the delegate for the parser and have it conform to `XMLParserDelegate`:

```
class RSSNewsArticleBuilder: NSObject, XMLParserDelegate {

}
```

In the preceding XML, each news article is contained in an `item` element, so our delegate will need to keep track of when the parser is delivering content for the `item` element so that it can ignore content from other elements:

```
class RSSNewsArticleBuilder: NSObject, XMLParserDelegate {

    var inItem = false

    func parser(_ parser: XMLParser,
                didStartElement elementName: String,
                namespaceURI: String?,
                qualifiedName qName: String?,
                attributes attributeDict: [String : String] = [:]) {

        switch elementName {

        case "item":
            inItem = true

        default:
            break

        }
    }

    func parser(_ parser: XMLParser,
                didEndElement elementName: String,
```

```
                        namespaceURI: String?,
                        qualifiedName qName: String?) {

            switch elementName {

            case "item":
                inItem = false

            default:
                break
            }
        }
    }
}
```

The two parts we want to extract from the `item` element to create our `NewsArticle` are the title and the URL. As we can see from the XML, the title is contained in a CDATA wrapper within a `title` element, and the URL is within a `link` element:

```
<item>
    <title><![CDATA[Donald Trump calls Fidel Castro 'brutal
dictator']]></title>
    <description><![CDATA[Cuba's former leader Fidel Castro was a "brutal
dictator", US
    President-elect Donald Trump says.]]></description>
    <link>http://www.bbc.co.uk/news/world-latin-america-38118739</link>
    <guid isPermaLink="true">http://www.bbc.co.uk/news/world-latin-america-
    38118739</guid>
    <pubDate>Sat, 26 Nov 2016 18:13:09 GMT</pubDate>
    <media:thumbnail width="976" height="549"
url="http://c.files.bbci.co.uk/12789/production/_92675657_mediaitem92675656
.jpg"/>
</item>
```

We will, therefore, also need to keep track of when the parser is in the `link` element, and when it is, append the received content to a string property so that we can hold on to the received link content. Similarly, we need to keep track of when the parser is in the `title` element, and when it is, append the received content to a data property so that we can hold on to the received title content.

We must also remember to reset the link and title properties as we start the relevant element. This way, we don't continue to append content meant for the next item element onto content from the previous one:

```
class RSSNewsArticleBuilder: NSObject, XMLParserDelegate {
    var inItem = false
    var inTitle = false
    var inLink = false
```

```
var titleData: Data?
var linkString: String?
func parser(_ parser: XMLParser,
            didStartElement elementName: String,
            namespaceURI: String?,
            qualifiedName qName: String?,
            attributes attributeDict: [String : String] = [:]) {
    switch elementName {
    case "item":
        inItem = true
    case "title":
        inTitle = true
        titleData = Data()
    case "link":
        inLink = true
        linkString = ""
    default:
        break
    }
}
func parser(_ parser: XMLParser,
            didEndElement elementName: String,
            namespaceURI: String?,
            qualifiedName qName: String?) {
    switch elementName {
    case "item":
        inItem = false
        guard
            let titleData = titleData,
            let titleString = String(data: titleData, encoding: .utf8),
            let linkString = linkString,
            let link = URL(string: linkString)
            else { break }
        print(titleString)
        print(link)
    case "title":
        inTitle = false
    case "link":
        inLink = false
    default:
        break
    }
}
func parser(_ parser: XMLParser, foundCDATA CDATABlock: Data) {
    if inTitle {
        titleData?.append(CDATABlock)
    }
}
```

```
func parser(_ parser: XMLParser, foundCharacters string: String) {
    if inLink {
        linkString?.append(string)
    }
}
}
}
```

Now that we have extracted the title and URL of the news article, we can use this to create a NewsArticle model object. We can do this at the end of the item element as this is when we will have all the relevant content.

To hold these created news articles, we will place a news article array property on the delegate, and this can be used to retrieve all the articles extracted from the XML once the parser has finished:

```
class RSSNewsArticleBuilder: NSObject, XMLParserDelegate {
    var inItem = false
    var inTitle = false
    var inLink = false
    var titleData: Data?
    var linkString: String?
    var articles = [NewsArticle]()
    func parser(_ parser: XMLParser,
                didStartElement elementName: String,
                namespaceURI: String?,
                qualifiedName qName: String?,
                attributes attributeDict: [String : String] = [:]) {
        switch elementName {
        case "item":
            inItem = true
        case "title":
            inTitle = true
            titleData = Data()
        case "link":
            inLink = true
            linkString = ""
        default:
            break
        }
    }
    func parser(_ parser: XMLParser,
                didEndElement elementName: String,
                namespaceURI: String?,
                qualifiedName qName: String?) {
        switch elementName {
        case "item":
            inItem = false
```

```
        guard
            let titleData = titleData,
            let titleString = String(data: titleData, encoding: .utf8),
            let linkString = linkString,
            let link = URL(string: linkString)
            else { break }
        let article = NewsArticle(title: titleString, url: link)
        articles.append(article)
    case "title":
        inTitle = false
    case "link":
        inLink = false
    default:
        break
    }
}
func parser(_ parser: XMLParser, foundCDATA CDATABlock: Data) {
    if inTitle {
        titleData?.append(CDATABlock)
    }
}
func parser(_ parser: XMLParser, foundCharacters string: String) {
    if inLink {
        linkString?.append(string)
    }
}
}
}
```

Lastly, when the document starts, we should ensure that all the properties are reset:

```
class RSSNewsArticleBuilder: NSObject, XMLParserDelegate {
    //...
    func parserDidStartDocument(_ parser: XMLParser) {
        inItem = false
        inTitle = false
        inLink = false
        titleData = nil
        linkString = nil
        articles = [NewsArticle]()
    }
    //...
}
```

Now that we have completed parser delegate, let's go back to our `fetchBBCNewsRSSFeed` function:

```
func fetchBBCNewsRSSFeed() {
    let session = URLSession.shared
    let url = URL(string: "http://feeds.bbci.co.uk/news/rss.xml")!
    let dataTask = session.dataTask(with: url) { (data, response, error) in
        guard let data = data, error == nil else {
            print(error ?? "Unexpected response")
            return
        }
        let dataAsString = String(data: data, encoding: .utf8)!
        print(dataAsString)
    }
    dataTask.resume()
}
```

Once the XML data has been retrieved, we'll pass it to an `XMLParser`, set up the delegate, and tell the parser to parse the data:

```
func fetchBBCNewsRSSFeed() {
    let session = URLSession.shared
    let url = URL(string: "http://feeds.bbci.co.uk/news/rss.xml")!
    let dataTask = session.dataTask(with: url) { (data, response, error) in
        guard let data = data, error == nil else {
            print(error ?? "Unexpected response")
            return
        }
        let parser = XMLParser(data: data)
        let articleBuilder = RSSNewsArticleBuilder()
        parser.delegate = articleBuilder
        parser.parse()
        let articles = articleBuilder.articles
        print(articles)
    }
    dataTask.resume()
}
```

We want to provide the articles as an output from this function, so we can add a completion handler to provide an array of news articles or an error:

```
func fetchBBCNewsRSSFeed(completion: @escaping ([NewsArticle]?, Error?) ->
Void) {
    let session = URLSession.shared
    let url = URL(string: "http://feeds.bbci.co.uk/news/rss.xml")!
    let dataTask = session.dataTask(with: url) { (data, response, error) in
        guard let data = data, error == nil else {
            completion(nil, error)
```

```
            return
        }
        let parser = XMLParser(data: data)
        let articleBuilder = RSSNewsArticleBuilder()
        parser.delegate = articleBuilder
        parser.parse()
        let articles = articleBuilder.articles
        completion(articles, nil)
    }
    dataTask.resume()
}
```

Finally, we can call this function, which will retrieve the RSS feed, parse it, and return an array of news articles:

```
fetchBBCNewsRSSFeed() { (articles, error) in
    if let articles = articles {
        print(articles)
    } else if let error = error {
        print(error)
    }
}
```

There's more...

Foundation also provides the ability to write XML data although, currently, this functionality is only available on macOS.

Having retrieved the RSS feed and created our news articles, let's write this information to an XML data structure and save it to disk. This XML will take the following form:

```
<articles>
    <article>
        <title>Donald Trump calls Fidel Castro 'brutal dictator'</title>
        <url>http://www.bbc.co.uk/news/world-latin-america-38118739</url>
    </article>
    <article>
        <title>Fidel Castro: Jeremy Corbyn praises 'huge figure'</title>
        <url>http://www.bbc.co.uk/news/uk-38117068</url>
    </article>
</articls>
```

At the root of the XML structure is an `articles` element, this contains multiple `article` elements, which in turn contain a `title` element and a `url` element.

To write the XML data, we will recreate the preceding structure using the XMLDocument and XMLElement objects. Once constructed, the xmlData property of the XMLDocument object provides the document as Data.

Let's create a function to produce XML data from an array of NewsArticle:

```
func createXML(representing articles: [NewsArticle]) -> Data {
    let root = XMLElement(name: "articles")
    let document = XMLDocument(rootElement: root)
    for article in articles {
        let articleElement = XMLElement(name: "article")
        let titleElement = XMLElement(name: "title",
                                      stringValue: article.title)
        let urlElement = XMLElement(name: "url",
                                    stringValue:
article.url.absoluteString)
        articleElement.addChild(titleElement)
        articleElement.addChild(urlElement)
        root.addChild(articleElement)
    }
    print(document.xmlString)
    return document.xmlData
}
```

We create each XMLElement and add it as a child to the element that we want to nest it within.

If you are building this in a storyboard, ensure that you place this function after the RSSNewsArticleBuilder, and before the code that calls fetchBBCNewsRSSFeed, as this function will need to be available to the completion handler soon.

Our call to fetchBBCNewsRSSFeed will provide an array of NewsArticle, so we can pass this to our new function to write this information to XML data:

```
fetchBBCNewsRSSFeed() { (articles, error) in
    if let articles = articles {
        let articleXMLData = createXML(representing: articles)
        print(articleXMLData.length)
    } else if let error = error {
        print(error)
    }
}
```

Now that we have the data, we can obtain a URL for `documents` directory, append the name of the file we will create, and write it to disk:

```
fetchBBCNewsRSSFeed() { (articles, error) in
    if let articles = articles {
        let xmlData = createXML(representing: articles)
        let documentsURL = FileManager.default.urls(for:
.documentDirectory,
                                                    in:
.userDomainMask).first!
        let writeURL = documentsURL.appendingPathComponent("articles.xml")
        print("Writing data to: \(writeURL)")
        try! xmlData.write(to: writeURL)
    } else if let error = error {
        print(error)
    }
}
```

We have now retrieved an RSS feed, extracted useful information from it, written that information to a custom XML format, and saved that data to disk. Give yourself a pat on the back!

See also

Further information about XMLParser can be found in Apple's Foundation reference at `http://swiftbook.link/docs/xmlparser`.

Other XML parsers are available, which may have advantages over Apple's, including being able to write XML on iOS. They are as follows:

RaptureXML: `https://github.com/ZaBlanc/RaptureXML`

TBXML: `https://github.com/71squared/TBXML`

Cocoa Touch

The focus of this book is the Swift programming language itself, rather than the uses of the language to produce apps for Apple platforms or to build server-side services. That being said, it can't be ignored that the vast majority of the Swift code being written is to build, or build upon, iOS apps.

In this recipe, we will take a brief look at how we can interact with the Cocoa Touch frameworks using Swift.

Cocoa Touch is a name given to the collection of UI frameworks available as part of the iOS SDK. Its name derives from the Cocoa framework on macOS that provides UI elements for macOS apps. While Cocoa on macOS is a framework in its own right, Cocoa Touch is a collection of frameworks that collectively provide UI elements for iOS apps and handle the app life cycle; the core of these frameworks is **UIKit**.

Getting ready

First, we'll need to create a new iOS app project. From the Xcode menu, choose **file**, then **new**, and from the dialog box that opens, choose a **Single View App** from the iOS tab:

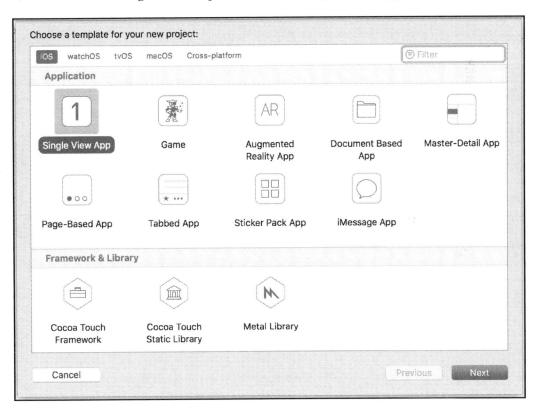

The next dialog box asks you to enter details about the app, pick a product name and organization name, and an organization identifier in reverse DNS style. Reverse DNS style means to take a website that you or your company owns, and reverse the order of the domain name components, so `http://maps.google.com` becomes `com.google.maps`:

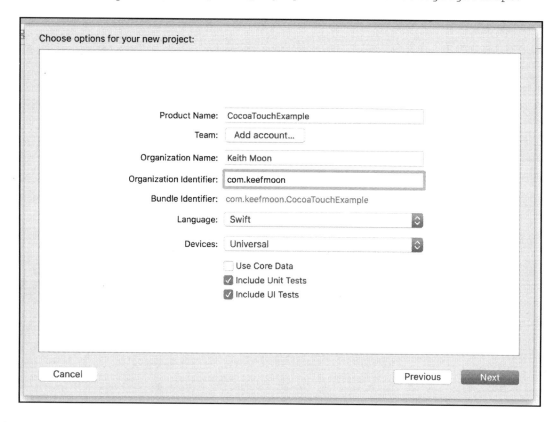

You may want to have **Include Unit Tests** and **Include UI Tests** ticked, as it will make it easier if you wish to add these testing strategies later.

Choose a place for your project to be saved, and you will be presented with the following Xcode configuration:

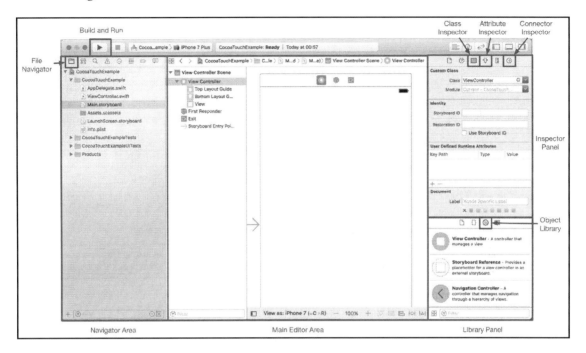

You now have a project that will be a blank, one view app. Press the **build and run** button, and Xcode will compile the code, launch the simulator, and run your built app in the simulator.

How to do it...

We will build a simple app based on our previous recipe that used the GitHub API. We will make an app that shows all the public repositories for a given GitHub user, and tapping on one will launch a WebView showing that repository on GitHub.

In the file explorer, click on **Main.storyboard**; the view you see now is a representation of how the app will look, and is called Interface Builder. At the moment, there is only one blank screen visible, which matches how the app looked when we ran it earlier. This screen represents a View Controller object; as the name suggests, this is an object that controls views.

Cocoa Touch implements the programming design pattern **MVC**, which stands for **Model View Controller**; it is a way of structuring your code to keep its elements reusable, with well-defined responsibilities. In the MVC pattern, all code related to displaying information falls broadly into three areas of responsibility:

- **Model** objects hold the data that will eventually be displayed on the screen; this might be data retrieved from the network or device, or generated during the running of the app. The objects may be used in multiple places in the app, where different view representations of the same data can be required.
- **View** objects represent the UI elements that are displayed on the screen; these may just display information that they are provided, or capture input from the user. View objects can be used in multiple places where the same visual element is needed, even if it is showing different data.
- **Controller** objects act as the bridge between the models and the views; they are responsible for obtaining the relevant model objects and for providing the data for display to the right view objects at the right time. Controller objects are also responsible for handling user input from the views and updating the model objects as needed:

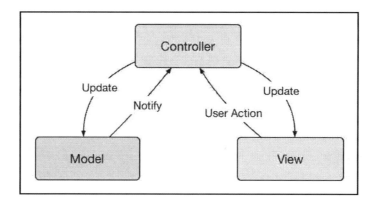

We will display our list of repositories in a table; we actually want to create a view controller class that is a subclass of `UITableViewController`. So from the menu, choose **File**, then **New**, and select a **Cocoa Touch Class** template:

We will be displaying repositories in this view controller, so let's call it
`ReposTableViewController`; specify that it's a subclass of `UITableViewController`
and ensure that the language is Swift:

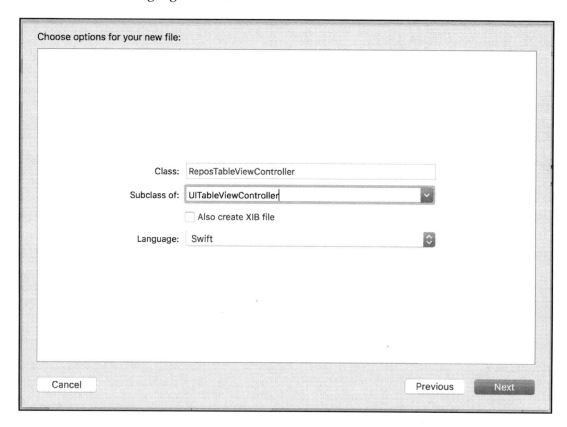

Now that we have created our view controller class, let's switch back the
`Main.storyboard` and delete the blank view controller that was created for us.

From the object library, find the **Table View Controller** and drag it into the Interface
Builder editor:

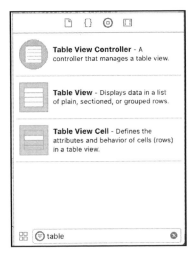

We now have a table view controller, but we want this controller to be of our custom
subclass, so select the controller, go into the class inspector, enter
`ReposTableViewController` as the class type, and press enter:

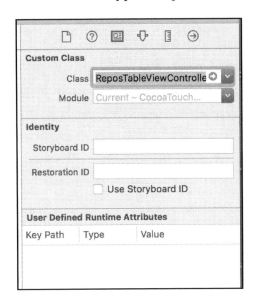

Although we have the view controller that will be displaying the repositories, when a user selects a repository, we want to present a new view controller that will show the repository's web page. We will cover what type of view controller that is, and how we present it later. However, we need a mechanism for navigating between view controllers.

If you have ever used an iOS app, you will be familiar with the standard push and pop way that you can use to navigate between views. The following screenshot shows an app in the middle of that transition:

The management of these view controllers, and the presentation and dismissal transitions, are handled by a navigation controller, which is provided by Cocoa Touch in the form of UINavigationController. To place our view controller inside a navigation controller, select the ReposTableViewController in Interface Builder, then on the Xcode menu, go to **Editor** and then **Embed In**, and choose **Navigation Controller**.

This will add a navigation controller to the storyboard and set the selected view controller as its root view controller.

Next, we need to define which view controller is initially on the screen when the app starts. Select the **Navigation Controller** on the left-hand side of the screen and within the property inspector, and select **Is Initial View Controller**. You will see that an entry arrow will point toward the navigation controller from the left, indicating that it will be shown initially.

With that setup, we can switch to working on our ReposTableViewController by selecting it from the file navigator.

When we created our view controller, the template gave us a bunch of code to start with, some of it commented out. The first method that the template provides is viewDidLoad. This is part of a set of methods that cover the life cycle of the root view that the view controller is managing; the full details about the view life cycle and the relevant method calls can be found at http://swiftbook.link/docs/vc-lifecycle.

viewDidLoad is fired quite early in the view controller life cycle, but before the view controller is visible to the user and therefore it is a good place to do any configuration of the view, and to retrieve any information that you want to present to the user.

Let's give the view controller a title:

```
class ReposTableViewController: UITableViewController {
    override func viewDidLoad() {
        super.viewDidLoad()
        self.title = "Repos"
    }
    //...
}
```

If you now run build and run the app, you will now see that the view has a navigation bar with the title we just added in the center.

We will fetch and display a list of GitHub repositories. You will remember that we have already implemented code that fetches GitHub repositories for a username; we created it as part of the recipe on JSON, so we can take our `fetchRepos` function and drop it into our view controller class as a method:

```
func fetchRepos(forUsername username: String,
                completionHandler: @escaping (FetchReposResult) -> Void) {
    let urlString = "https://api.github.com/users/\(username)/repos"
    let url = URL(string: urlString)!
    var request = URLRequest(url: url)
    request.setValue("application/vnd.github.v3+json",
                forHTTPHeaderField: "Accept")
    let task = session.dataTask(with: request) { (data, response, error) in
        // First unwrap the optional data
        guard let jsonData = data else {
            // If it is nil, there was probably a network error
            completionHandler(.failure(ResponseError.requestUnsucessful))
            return
        }
        do {
            // Deserialisation can throw an error,
            // so we have to `try` and catch errors
            let deserialised = try JSONSerialization.jsonObject(with:
            jsonData, options: [])
            // As `deserialised` has type `Any` we need to cast
            guard let jsonRepos = deserialised as? [[String: Any]] else {

                let error = ResponseError.unexpectedResponseStructure
                completionHandler(.failure(error))
                return
            }
            var reposToProvide = [Repo]()
            for jsonRepo in jsonRepos {
                guard let name = jsonRepo["name"] as? String,
                    let urlString = jsonRepo["html_url"] as? String,
                    let url = URL(string: urlString) else {
                        continue
                }
                let repo = Repo(name: name, url: url)
                reposToProvide.append(repo)
            }
            completionHandler(.success(reposToProvide))
        } catch {
            completionHandler(.failure(error))
        }
    }
    task.resume()
```

```
    }
```

This method relies on some other components from the recipes, so let's add these to the top of the file, before the start of the class definition. We will also add a session property to the view controller, which is needed for the network request:

```
import UIKit

struct Repo {
    let name: String
    let url: URL
}

enum FetchReposResult {
    case success([Repo])
    case failure(Error)
}

enum ResponseError: Error {
    case requestUnsucessful
    case unexpectedResponseStructure
}

class ReposTableViewController: UITableViewController {
    let session = URLSession.shared
    //...
}
```

In our table view, each row of the table view will display the name of one of the repositories that we retrieve from the GitHub API. We need a place to store the repositories that we retrieve from the API:

```
class ReposTableViewController: UITableViewController {
    let session = URLSession.shared
    var repos = [Repo]()
    //...
}
```

The repos array has an initially empty array value, but we will use this property to hold the fetched results from the API.

Let's leave aside the actual fetching of the repository data for the time being, and instead, examine how we provide data to be used in the table view. Let's create a couple of fake repositories to temporarily populate our table view:

```
class ReposTableViewController: UITableViewController {
    let session = URLSession.shared
    var repos = [Repo]()
    override func viewDidLoad() {
        super.viewDidLoad()
        let repo1 = Repo(name: "Test repo 1",
                         url: URL(string: "http://example.com/repo1")!)
        let repo2 = Repo(name: "Test repo 2",
                         url: URL(string: "http://example.com/repo2")!)
        repos.append(repo1)
        repos.append(repo2)
    }
    //...
}
```

The information in a table view is populated from the table view's data source, which can be any object that conforms to the UITableViewDataSource protocol. As the table view is displayed, and the user interacts and scrolls it, the table view will ask the data source for the information it needs to populate the table view. For simple table view implementations, it is often the view controller that controls the table view that acts as the data source. In fact, when you create a subclass of UITableViewController, as we have, the view controller already conforms to UITableViewDataSource and is assigned as the table view's data source.

Some of the methods defined in UITableViewDataSource were created as part of the UITableViewController template; the three we will take a look at are as follows:

```
// MARK: - Table view data source
override func numberOfSections(in tableView: UITableView) -> Int {
    // #warning Incomplete implementation, return the number of sections
    return 0
}

override func tableView(_ tableView: UITableView,
                        numberOfRowsInSection section: Int) -> Int {
    // #warning Incomplete implementation, return the number of rows
    return 0
}

/*
override func tableView(_ tableView: UITableView,
                        cellForRowAt indexPath: IndexPath) ->
```

```
UITableViewCell {
    let cell = tableView.dequeueReusableCell(withIdentifier:
"reuseIdentifier",
                                              for: indexPath)
    // Configure the cell...
    return cell
}
*/
```

Data in a table view can be divided into sections and information is presented in rows within those sections; information is referenced through an `IndexPath` that consists of a section integer value and a row integer value.

The first thing that the data source methods ask us to provide is the number of sections that the table view will have. Our app will only be displaying a simple list of repositories, and as such, we only need one section, so we will `return 1` from this method:

```
override func numberOfSections(in tableView: UITableView) -> Int {
    return 1
}
```

The next thing we have to provide is the number of rows the table view should have for a given section. If we had multiple sections, we could examine the provided section index and return the right number of rows, but since we only have one section, we can return the same number in all scenarios.

We are displaying all the repositories we have retrieved, so the number of rows is simply the number of repositories in the `repos` array:

```
override func tableView(_ tableView: UITableView,
                        numberOfRowsInSection section: Int) -> Int {
    return repos.count
}
```

Now that we have told the table view how many pieces of information to display, we have to provide the means for the display of that information. A table view displays information in a type of view called `UITableViewCell`, and this cell is what we have to provide next.

For each index path within the section and row bounds that we have provided, we will be asked to provide a cell that will be displayed by the table view.

A table view can be very large in size as it may need to represent a large amount of data. However, there are only a handful of cells that can be displayed to the user at any one time, as only a portion of the table view can be visible at any one time:

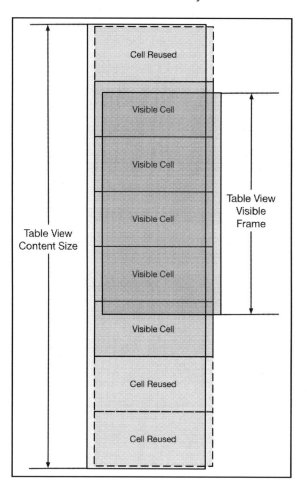

To be efficient, and prevent your app from slowing down as the user scrolls, the table view can reuse cells that have already been created, but have since moved off screen. Implementing cell reuse happens in two stages:

- Registering cell type with the table view with a reuse identifier
- Dequeuing a cell for a given reuse identifier; this will return a cell that has moved off screen or create a new cell if none are available for reuse

How a cell is registered will depend on how it has been created. If the cell has been created, and its subviews laid out, completely in code, then the cell's class is registered with the table view through this method on `UITableView`:

```
func register(_ cellClass: AnyClass?,
              forCellReuseIdentifier identifier: String)
```

If the cell has been laid out in `.xib` (usually called a "nib" for historical reasons), which is a visual layout file for views similar to a storyboard, then the cell's nib is registered with the table view through this method on `UITableView`:

```
func register(_ nib: UINib?, forCellReuseIdentifier identifier: String)
```

Lastly, cells can be defined and laid out within the table view in a storyboard. An advantage of this approach is that there is no need to manually register the cell, as with the previous two approaches; the registration with the table view comes for free. A disadvantage of this approach is that the cell layout is tied to table view, so it can't be reused in other table views, unlike the previous two implementations.

Let's lay out our cell in the Storyboard, as we will only be using it with one table view. Switch to our **Main.storyboard** file and select the table view in our `ReposTableViewController`. On the attributes inspector, change the number of prototype cells to 1; this will add a cell to the table view in the main window. This cell will define the layout of all the cells that will be displayed in our table view. You should create a prototype cell for each type of cell layout you will need; we are only displaying one type of information in our table view, so all our cells will be of the same type.

Select a cell in the storyboard and the attributes inspector will switch to showing the attributes for the cell. The cell style will be set to custom, and very often, this will be what you want. When you are displaying multiple pieces of information in a cell, you will usually want to create a subclass of `UITableViewCell`, set this to be the cell's class in the class inspector, and then lay out subviews in this custom cell type. However, for this example, we just want to show the name of the repository, so we can use a basic cell style that just has one text label, without needing a custom subclass, so choose **basic** from the style dropdown.

We need to set the reuse identifier that we will use to dequeue the cell later, so type an appropriate string, such as `RepoCell`, into the reuse identifier box of the attributes inspector:

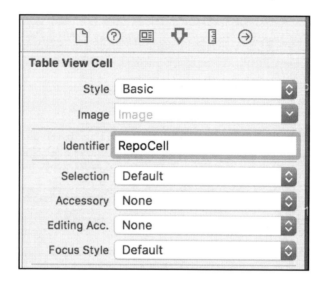

Now that we have a cell that is registered for reuse with the table view, we can go back to our view controller and complete our conformance to `UITableViewDataSource`.

Our `ReposTableViewController` has some commented code created as part of the template:

```
/*
override func tableView(_ tableView: UITableView,
                     cellForRowAt indexPath: IndexPath) ->
UITableViewCell {
    let cell = tableView.dequeueReusableCell(withIdentifier:
"reuseIdentifier",
                                            for: indexPath)
    // Configure the cell...
```

```
        return cell
    }
    */
```

Remove the /* */ comment signifiers as we are now ready to implement this method.

This data source method will be called every time the table view needs to place a cell on screen; this will happen the first time the table is displayed, as it needs cells to fill the visible part of the table view. It will also be called when the user scrolls the table view in a way that will reveal a new cell as visible.

You will see, from the method definition, that we are provided with the table view in question and the index path of the cell that is needed, and we are expected to return a UITableViewCell. The code provided by the template actually does most of the work for us; we just need to provide the reuse identifier that we set in the storyboard, and set the title label of the cell to have the name of the correct repository:

```
override func tableView(_ tableView: UITableView,
                        cellForRowAt indexPath: IndexPath) ->
UITableViewCell {
    let cell = tableView.dequeueReusableCell(withIdentifier: "RepoCell",
                                             for: indexPath)
    // Configure the cell...
    let repo = repos[indexPath.row]
    cell.textLabel?.text = repo.name
    return cell
}
```

The cell's textLabel property is optional because it only exists when the cell's style is not custom.

Since we've now provided everything the table view needs to display our repository information, let's click on build and run and take a look:

Great! We now have our two test repositories displaying in our table view, so let's replace our test data with real repositories from the GitHub API. We added our `fetchRepos` method earlier, so all we need to do is call this method, set the results to our `repos` property, and tell our table view that it needs to reload as the data has changed:

```
class ReposTableViewController: UITableViewController {
    let session = URLSession.shared
    var repos = [Repo]()
    override func viewDidLoad() {
        super.viewDidLoad()
```

```
            title = "Repos"
            fetchRepos(forUsername:"SwiftProgrammingCookbook"){ [weak self]
    result in
            switch result {
            case .success(let repos):
                self?.repos = repos
            case .failure(let error):
                self?.repos = []
                print("There was an error: \(error)")
            }
            self?.tableView.reloadData()
        }
    }
    //...
}
```

As we did in the previous recipes, we fetch the repositories from the GitHub API and receive a result enum informing us whether this was a success or a failure. If it was successful, we store the resulting repository array in our repos property. Once we have handled the response, we call the reloadData method on UITableView, which instructs the table view to re-query its source for cells to display.

Also, we provide a weak reference to self in our closure's capture list to prevent a retain cycle; you can see more about why this is important in the recipe on *Closures* in Chapter 1, *Swift Building Blocks*.

This is all that will be needed; however, there is an important consideration that needs to be addressed. The iOS platform is a multithreaded environment, which means that it is able to do more than one thing at once. This is critical to being able to maintain a responsive user interface, while also being able to process data and perform long running tasks. The iOS system uses queues to manage this work, and reserves the "main" queue for any work involving the user interface. Therefore, anytime you need to interact with the user interface, it is important that this work is done from the main queue.

Our fetchRepos method presents a situation where this might not be true. Our fetchRepos method performs networking, and we provide a closure to URLSession as part of creating a URLSessionDataTask, but there is no guarantee that this closure will be executed on the main thread. Therefore, when we receive a response from fetchRepos, we need to "dispatch" the work of handling that response to the main queue to ensure that our updates to the UI happen on the main queue. We do this using the Dispatch framework, so we need to import that at the top of the file:

```
import Dispatch

//...
```

```
class ReposTableViewController: UITableViewController {
    let session = URLSession.shared
    var repos = [Repo]()
    override func viewDidLoad() {
        super.viewDidLoad()
        title = "Repos"
        fetchRepos(forUsername:"SwiftProgrammingCookbook"){ [weak self]
result in
            DispatchQueue.main.async {
                switch result {
                case .success(let repos):
                    self?.repos = repos
                case .failure(let error):
                    self?.repos = []
                    print("There was an error: \(error)")
                }
                self?.tableView.reloadData()
            }
        }
    }
}
```

We will be discussing multithreading and the Dispatch framework in greater depth in Chapter 8, *Performance and Responsiveness in Swift*.

Click on build and run and after a few seconds, the table view will be filled with names of repositories from the GitHub API.

Now that we have repositories displayed to the user, the next piece of functionality for our app is to be able to tap on a cell and have it display the repository's GitHub page in a WebView.

Actions triggered by the table view, such as when a user taps on a cell, are provided to the table view's delegate, which can be anything that conforms to UITableViewDelegate. As was the case with the table view's data source, our ReposTableViewController already conforms to UITableViewDelegate because it is a subclass of UITableViewController.

Take a look at the documentation for the UITableViewDelegate protocol, and you will see a lot of optional methods; the documentation can be found at https://developer.apple.com/reference/uikit/uitableviewdelegate.

The one relevant for our purposes is this:

```
func tableView(_ tableView: UITableView, didSelectRowAt indexPath:
IndexPath)
```

This will be called on the table view's delegate whenever a cell is selected by the user, so let's implement this in our view controller:

```
override func tableView(_ tableView: UITableView, didSelectRowAt indexPath:
IndexPath) {
    let repo = repos[indexPath.row]
    let repoURL = repo.url
    // TODO: Present the repo's URL in a webview
}
```

Cocoa Touch provides a number of options for presenting web content:

- `UIWebView`, provided by the UIKit framework, is a view that will load and display web content. It is suitable for most uses, although it uses an older Javascript engine and can, therefore, be slower to load complex websites than Mobile Safari.
- `WKWebView`, provided by the WebKit framework, is a view that uses the latest rendering and Javascript engine for loading and displaying web content. While it is newer, it is less mature in some respects and has issues with caching content.
- `SFSafariViewController`, provided by the `SafariServices` framework, is a view controller that displays web content, and also provides many of the features that are available in Mobile Safari, including sharing and adding to reading list and bookmarks, and provides a convenient button for opening in Mobile Safari.

For the functionality it provides, we will use `SFSafariViewController`, passing it the repository's URL. Then, we will pass that view controller to the `show` method, which will present the view controller in the most appropriate way:

```
override func tableView(_ tableView: UITableView,
                        didSelectRowAt indexPath: IndexPath) {
    let repo = repos[indexPath.row]
    let repoURL = repo.url
    let webViewController = SFSafariViewController(url: repoURL)
    show(webViewController, sender: nil)
}
```

Don't forget to `import SafariServices` at the top of the file.

Click on **Build and Run**, and once the repositories are loaded, tap on one of the cells. A new view controller will be pushed on the screen, and the relevant repositories web page will load.

Congratulations! You just built your first app!

There's more...

Currently, our app fetches repositories from a specific, hardcoded GitHub username. It would be great, if, rather than hard coding the username, the user of the app can enter the GitHub username that the repositories will be retrieved for. So, let's add this functionality.

First, we need a way for the user to enter the GitHub username; the most appropriate way to allow a user to enter a small amount of text is through the use of UITextField.

In the main storyboard, find **Text Field** in the object library, drag it over to the main window, and drop it on the navigation bar of our ReposTableViewController:

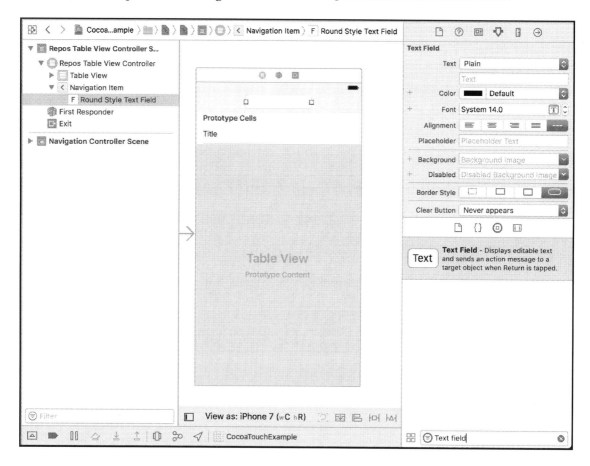

Like a table view, UITextField communicates user events through a delegate, which needs to conform to UITextFieldDelegate.

Let's switch back to `ReposTableViewController` and add conformance to `UITextFieldDelegate`; it is a common practice to add protocol conformance to an extension, so add the following at the bottom of `ReposTableViewController`:

```
extension ReposTableViewController: UITextFieldDelegate {
}
```

With this conformance in place, we need to set our view controller to be the delegate of `UITextField`. Head back to the main storyboard and select the text field, and then open the connections inspector. You will see that the text field has an outlet for its delegate property; now click on, hold, and drag from the circle **Next** to the **delegate** over to the symbol representing our **Repos Table View Controller**:

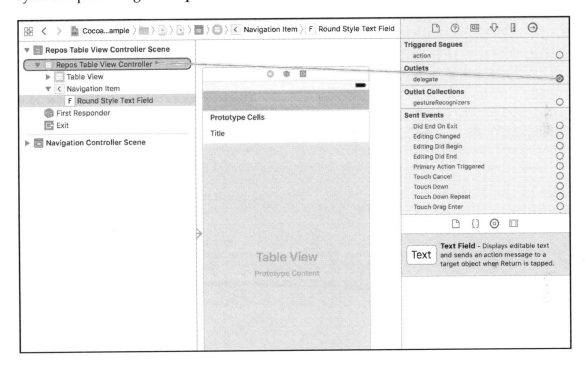

The delegate outlet should now have a value:

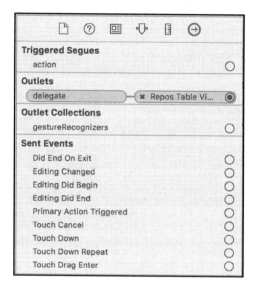

Taking a look at the documentation for `UITextFieldDelegate`, we can see that the `textFieldShouldReturn` method is called when the user presses the return button on the keyboard after entering text, so this is the method we will implement.

Let's switch back to the `ReposViewController` and implement that method in our extension:

```
extension ReposTableViewController: UITextFieldDelegate {
    public func textFieldShouldReturn(_ textField: UITextField) -> Bool {
        // TODO: Fetch repositories from username entered into text field
        // TODO: Dismiss keyboard
        // Returning true as we want the system to have the default
behaviour
        return true
    }
}
```

Since the fetching of repositories will now take place here instead of when the view is loaded, let's move the code from `viewDidLoad` to this method:

```
extension ReposTableViewController: UITextFieldDelegate {
    public func textFieldShouldReturn(_ textField: UITextField) -> Bool {
        // If no username, clear the data
        guard let enteredUsername = textField.text else {
            repos = []
```

```
            tableView.reloadData()
            return true
        }
        // Fetch repositories from username entered into text field
        fetchRepos(forUsername: enteredUsername) { [weak self] result in
            DispatchQueue.main.async {
                switch result {
                case .success(let repos):
                    self?.repos = repos
                case .failure(let error):
                    self?.repos = []
                    print("There was an error: \(error)")
                }
                self?.tableView.reloadData()
            }
        }
        // TODO: Dismiss keyboard
        // Returning true as we want the system to have the default
behaviour
        return true
    }
}
```

The last thing we need to do is dismiss the keyboard. Cocoa Touch refers to the object that is currently receiving user events as the first responder, which is, currently, the text field. It is the act of the text field becoming the first responder that caused the keyboard to be shown on screen. Therefore, to dismiss the keyboard, the text field just needs to resign its place as the first responder:

```
extension ReposTableViewController: UITextFieldDelegate {
    public func textFieldShouldReturn(_ textField: UITextField) -> Bool {
        //...
        // Dismiss keyboard
        textField.resignFirstResponder()
        // Returning true as we want the system to have the default
behaviour
        return true
    }
}
```

Now build and run, and you can enter any GitHub name into the text field to retrieve a list of their public repositories.

See also

Further discussion of multithreading and the Dispatch framework can be found in `Chapter 8`, *Performance and Responsiveness in Swift*.

Further information about the view hierarchy on iOS can be found in the Apple guide, View Controller Programming Guide for iOS at `http://swiftbook.link/docs/vc-guide`.

6

Swift Playgrounds

In this chapter, we will cover the following recipes:

- Using Swift Playgrounds for UI
- Import Resources into Playgrounds
- Import Code into Playgrounds
- Multi-Page Playgrounds

Introduction

Throughout this book, we have used Swift Playgrounds predominantly to work through code examples as we have explored the Swift language. Playgrounds are great for this use case as they allow you to explore code and framework APIs without needing the infrastructure of an iOS, macOS, or tvOS app to execute the code.

Their features go beyond how we have used them so far in this book, and in this chapter, we will explore some of those features, from using additional code and resources to creating fully interactive experiences.

Using Swift Playgrounds for UI

Playgrounds are great for exploring the Swift language and the APIs available on Apple platforms, but they can also be very useful for experimenting with UI and testing custom views and interfaces. Let's build a very simple bar chart view that we can use to display numerical data in chart form, and use a playground to test it.

All the code for this chapter can be found in a GitHub repository at `http://swiftbook.link/code/chapter6`.

Getting ready

First, we'll create an iOS-based playground to build our bar chart. In `Chapter 1`, *Swift Building Blocks*, we went through creating a new playground, so go back there if you need a refresher.

We will create a custom view that will display information in bar chart form, and use that to test some features of playgrounds. You can either enter the following code into a new iOS-based playground or download the playground named `Simple_iOS.playground` in the GitHub repository for this chapter:

```
import UIKit

struct Color {
    let red: Float
    let green: Float
    let blue: Float
    let alpha: Float = 1.0
    var displayColor: UIColor {
        return UIColor(red: CGFloat(red),
                      green: CGFloat(green),
                      blue: CGFloat(blue),
                      alpha: CGFloat(alpha))
    }
}

struct Bar {
    var value: Float
    var color: Color
}

class BarView: UIView {
    init(frame: CGRect, color: UIColor) {
        super.init(frame: frame)
```

```
                backgroundColor = color
        }
        required init?(coder: NSCoder) {
            super.init(coder: coder)
            backgroundColor = UIColor.red
        }
}

class BarChart: UIView {
    var bars: [Bar] = [] {
        didSet {
            self.barViews.forEach { $0.removeFromSuperview() }
            var barViews = [BarView]()
            let barCount: Int = bars.count
            // Calculate the max value before calculating size
            for bar in bars {
                maxValue = max(maxValue, bar.value)
            }
            var xOrigin: CGFloat = interBarMargin
            for bar in bars {
                let width = (frame.width-(interBarMargin*(barCount+1))) /
barCount
                let height = barHeight(forValue: bar.value)
                let rect = CGRect(x: xOrigin, y: bounds.height - height,
                                   width: width, height: height)
                let view = BarView(frame: rect, color:
bar.color.displayColor)
                barViews.append(view)
                addSubview(view)
                xOrigin = view.frame.maxX + interBarMargin
            }
            self.barViews = barViews
        }
    }
    var interBarMargin: CGFloat = 5.0
    private var barViews: [BarView] = []
    private var maxValue: Float = 0.0
    private func barHeight(forValue value: Float) -> CGFloat {
        return (frame.size.height / CGFloat(maxValue)) * CGFloat(value)
    }
}
```

How to do it...

The preceding bar chart code is pretty straightforward; once the view is created with a frame and a background color, you add bars that take the form of a `Bar` struct containing a value and a color. The `BarChart` view uses these to create subviews of the correct relative size and scale to represent the values of the bars.

Now, let's write some code to make use of our `BarChart` view:

1. Enter the following into the playground at the bottom:

```
let barView = BarChart(frame: CGRect(x: 0, y: 0, width: 300,
height: 300))
barView.backgroundColor = .white
let bar1 = Bar(value: 20, color: Color(red: 1, green: 0, blue: 0))
let bar2 = Bar(value: 40, color: Color(red: 0, green: 1, blue: 0))
let bar3 = Bar(value: 25, color: Color(red: 0, green: 0, blue: 1))
barView.bars = [bar1, bar2, bar3]
```

2. Now, press the blue play button at the bottom-left of the playground window to execute the code. As your code executes, you will see that the playground sidebar fills up with information.

3. In `Chapter 1`, *Swift Building Blocks*, we saw that playgrounds have a timeline that provides information about each line of execution; as you pass your cursor over the line, you see an eye-shaped icon that will display a preview of the result of that line of execution. Where the line involves a UI element such as a `view`, the playground will render that view and display it in a preview box:

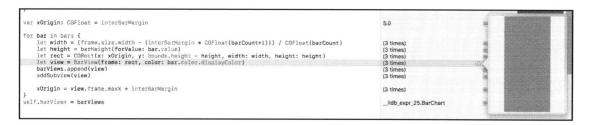

4. The same is true for the pinned in-line preview that you can get by pressing the square button in the timeline:

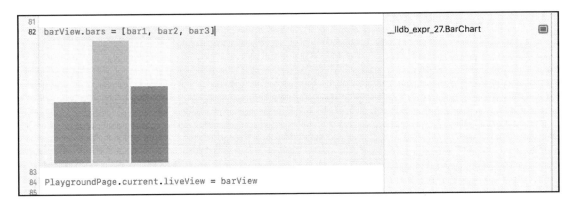

```
81
82  barView.bars = [bar1, bar2, bar3]                      __lldb_expr_27.BarChart

83
84  PlaygroundPage.current.liveView = barView
85
```

These features can be great for testing and tweaking view code.

5. If the purpose of the playground is to demo or experiment with a custom view component and you'd like a more prominent view output, you can use playground's live view feature.

6. First, we'll need to import the PlaygroundSupport framework at the top of the playground:

```
import PlaygroundSupport
```

7. The PlaygroundSupport framework provides a number of features for accessing various features of the playground. In this case, we will use it to set our BarChart view to be the playground's live view:

```
PlaygroundPage.current.liveView = barView
```

8. To view the playground's live view, we need to open the **Assistant Editor**. To view this, from the menu, go to **View | Assistant Editor | Show Assistant Editor**:

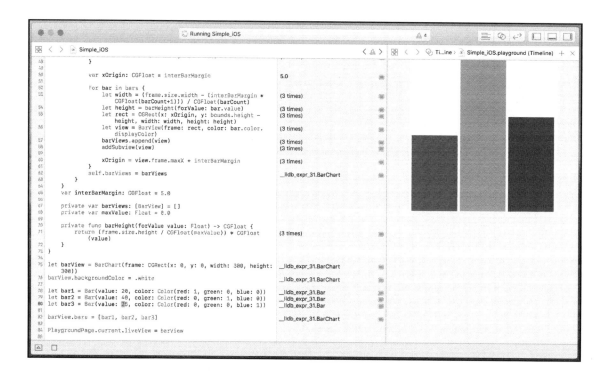

This view will be updated as the code in the playground changes; try changing the value of the bars and see the view change.

How it works...

A playground's live view can be anything that conforms to `PlaygroundLiveViewable`. On iOS, both `UIView` and `UIViewController` conform to `PlaygroundLiveViewable`, as do their equivalents on macOS: `NSView` and `NSViewController`.

These live views respond to touch events just as they would in a macOS app or in the iOS simulator; therefore, you can use them to test interactive views and controls.

Unfortunately, playgrounds do not currently support interface builder layout files, which are .xibs and .storyboard files; therefore, you will have to lay out your views programmatically instead.

Also, iOS-based playgrounds support many, but not all, of the frameworks available in the iOS SDK. Here's a list of the supported frameworks:

```
Accelerate, Accounts, AddressBook, AddressBookUI, AdSupport, AssetsLibrary,
AudioToolbox, AudioUnit, AVFoundation, AVKit, CFNetwork, CloudKit,
CoreAudio, CoreAudioKit, CoreBluetooth, CoreData, CoreFoundation,
CoreGraphics, CoreImage, CoreLocation, CoreMedia, CoreMIDI, CoreMotion,
CoreTelephony, CoreText, CoreVideo, EventKit, EventKitUI,
ExternalAccessory, Foundation, GameController, GameKit, GLKit, HealthKit,
HomeKit, iAd, ImageIO, JavaScriptCore, LocalAuthentication, MapKit,
MediaAccessibility, MediaPlayer, MediaToolbox, MessageUI, Metal,
MobileCoreServices, MultipeerConnectivity, NetworkExtension, NewsstandKit,
NotificationCenter, OpenAL, OpenGLES, PassKit, Photos, PhotosUI, PushKit,
QuartzCore, QuickLook, SafariServices, SceneKit, Security, Social,
SpriteKit, StoreKit, SystemConfiguration, UIKit, VideoToolbox, WebKit
```

There are only three frameworks that are available within an iOS app, but aren't available in an iOS-based playground, and these are as mentioned:

- GSS, which provides a standard set of security-related services
- IOKit, which contains interfaces used by the device, and shouldn't be used directly anyway
- Twitter, which contains interfaces for sending tweets via the Twitter service

There's more...

In the preceding example, and for most of this book, we focused on iOS-based playgrounds, but macOS-based playgrounds are just as useful for the macOS platform and can also be used for UI testing and experimentation.

In the GitHub repository for this chapter, you will find a macOS-based playground called Simple_macOS.playground that also creates a simple bar chart view, at http://swiftbook.link/code/chapter6.

Alternatively, you can create a new macOS-based playground and enter the following code:

```
import PlaygroundSupport
import Cocoa

struct Color {
    let red: CGFloat
    let green: CGFloat
    let blue: CGFloat
    let alpha: CGFloat = 1.0
    var displayColor: NSColor {
        return NSColor(calibratedRed: red, green: green, blue: blue, alpha:
alpha)
    }
}

struct Bar {
    var value: Float
    var color: Color
}

class BarView: NSView {
    let color: NSColor
    init(frame: NSRect, color: NSColor) {
        self.color = color
        super.init(frame: frame)
    }
    required init?(coder: NSCoder) {
        self.color = NSColor.red
        super.init(coder: coder)
    }
    override func draw(_ dirtyRect: NSRect) {
        super.draw(dirtyRect)
        color.set()
        NSBezierPath.fill(dirtyRect)
    }
}

class BarChart: NSView {
    let color: NSColor
    init(frame: NSRect, color: NSColor) {
        self.color = color
        super.init(frame: frame)
    }
    required init?(coder: NSCoder) {
        self.color = NSColor.white
        super.init(coder: coder)
    }
```

```
        var bars: [Bar] = [] {
            didSet {
                self.barViews.forEach { $0.removeFromSuperview() }
                var barViews = [BarView]()
                let barCount = CGFloat(bars.count)
                // Calculate the max value before calculating size
                for bar in bars {
                    maxValue = max(maxValue, bar.value)
                }
                var xOrigin: CGFloat = interBarMargin
                for bar in bars {
                    let width = (frame.width-
(interBarMargin*(barCount+1)))/barCount
                    let height = barHeight(forValue: bar.value)
                    let rect = NSRect(x: xOrigin, y: 0, width: width, height:
height)
                    let view = BarView(frame: rect, color:
bar.color.displayColor)
                    barViews.append(view)
                    addSubview(view)
                    xOrigin = rect.maxX + interBarMargin
                }
                self.barViews = barViews
            }
        }
        var interBarMargin: CGFloat = 5.0
        private var barViews: [NSView] = []
        private var maxValue: Float = 0.0
        override func draw(_ dirtyRect: NSRect) {
            super.draw(dirtyRect)
            color.set()
            NSBezierPath.fill(dirtyRect)
        }
        private func barHeight(forValue value: Float) -> CGFloat {
            return (frame.size.height / CGFloat(maxValue)) * CGFloat(value)
        }
    }
}

let barView = BarChart(frame: CGRect(x: 0, y: 0, width: 300, height: 300),
                       color: .white)
PlaygroundPage.current.liveView = barView
let bar1 = Bar(value: 20, color: Color(red: 1, green: 0, blue: 0))
let bar2 = Bar(value: 40, color: Color(red: 0, green: 1, blue: 0))
let bar3 = Bar(value: 25, color: Color(red: 0, green: 0, blue: 1))
barView.bars = [bar1, bar2, bar3]

PlaygroundPage.current.liveView = barView
```

This macOS version of our custom `BarView` works exactly like the iOS version, and the live view for macOS-based playgrounds works exactly like its iOS-based counterparts. Similar to iOS, macOS-based playgrounds support many, but not all, of the frameworks available in the macOS SDK. Here's a list of the supported frameworks:

```
Accelerate, Accounts, AddressBook, AGL, AppKit, AppleScriptKit,
AppleScriptObjC, ApplicationServices, AudioToolbox, AudioUnit,
AudioVideoBridging, Automator, AVFoundation, AVKit, Carbon, CFNetwork,
CloudKit, Cocoa, Collaboration, Contacts, CoreAudio, CoreBluetooth,
CoreAudioKit, CoreData, CoreFoundation, CoreGraphics, CoreImage,
CoreLocation, CoreMedia, CoreMediaIO, CoreMIDI, CoreServices, CoreText,
CoreVideo, CoreWLAN, CryptoTokenKit, DirectoryService, DiscRecording,
DiscRecordingUI, DiskArbitration, DVDPlayback, EventKit, ExceptionHandling,
FinderSync, ForceFeedback, Foundation, FWAUserLib, GameController, GameKit,
GLKit, GLUT, GSS, Hypervisor, ICADevices, ImageCaptureCore, ImageIO,
IMServicePlugIn, InputMethodKit, IOBluetooth, IOBluetoothUI, IOKit,
IOSurface, JavaScriptCore, LatentSemanticMapping, LocalAuthentication,
MapKit, MediaAccessibility, MediaLibrary, Metal, MetalKit, ModelIO,
MultipeerConnectivity, NetFS, NetworkExtension, NotificationCenter, OpenAL,
OpenCL, OpenDirectory, OpenGL, OSAKit, PreferencePanes, Quartz, QuartzCore,
QuickLook, SceneKit, ScreenSaver, ScriptingBridge, Security,
SecurityFoundation, SecurityInterface, ServiceManagement, Social,
SpriteKit, StoreKit, SystemConfiguration, Tcl, TWAIN, VideoToolbox, WebKit
```

There are, however, quite a few frameworks that are not available in macOS-based playgrounds. Many of these are deprecated frameworks, so it stands to reason that they aren't available. Here's a list of the deprecated frameworks that are unavailable:

```
AppKitScripting, CalendarStore, CoreMIDIServer, InstantMessage, JavaVM,
QTKit, QuickTime, Scripting, SyncServices, vecLib, VideoDecodeAcceleration,
XgridFoundation
```

The rest of the unavailable frameworks are as follows:

- `DrawSprocket`, which contains the game sprocket component for drawing content to the screen
- `DVComponentGlue`, which contains interfaces for communicating with digital video devices, such as video cameras
- `InstallerPlugins`, which contains interfaces for creating plugins that run during software installation sessions
- `JavaFrameEmbedding`, which contains interfaces for embedding Java frames in Objective-C code
- `Kerberos`, which contains interfaces for using the Kerberos network authentication protocol

- `Kernel`, which contains the interfaces for kernel-extension development, including Mach, BSD, libkern, I/O Kit, and the various families built on top of I/O Kit
- `LDAP`, which Apple advises not to use
- `Message`, which contains Cocoa extensions for mail delivery
- `PCSC`, which contains interfaces for interacting with smart card devices
- `PubSub`, which contains interfaces for subscribing to RSS and Atom feeds
- `Ruby`, which contains interfaces for the Ruby scripting language
- `System`, which Apple advises not to use
- `Tk`, which contains interfaces for accessing the system's Tk toolbox from an app

Hopefully, you can see from this recipe that Swift Playgrounds can be really useful to view UI experimentation on both iOS and macOS.

See also

The playgrounds in this recipe can be found in the `http://swiftbook.link/code/chapter6` `GitHub repository`.

Apple's reference for the `PlaygroundSupport` framework can be found at `http://` `swiftbook.link/docs/playgroundsupport`.

Import Resources into Playgrounds

While building apps, we will often need to bundle resources, such as images, with the app. How can we do the same with playgrounds so that our UI can incorporate these images? That is what we will investigate in this recipe.

Getting ready

For this recipe, we will use the playground from the previous recipe. The playground is called `Simple_iOS.playground`, and you can get it from the GitHub repository for this chapter, available at `http://swiftbook.link/code/chapter6`.

This playground demonstrates a simple custom view that shows a bar chart. We will improve this playground by adding a semitransparent image that will act as a texture for the bars in our bar chart.

You can download the semitransparent texture image from `http://swiftbook.link/resources/texture.png`, or you can supply your own.

How to do it...

Let's take a look at the following steps to understand how to add our image to the playground:

1. We need to open up Xcode's project navigator, which is often not visible by default when a playground is opened. To reveal the project navigator, select **View | Navigators | Show Project Navigator** from the menu. Alternatively, you can select the **left pane reveal** button in the top-right corner of the Xcode window:

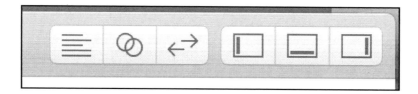

2. The playground will be listed at the top of the project navigator, along with a disclosure triangle; select the triangle to reveal folders named `Sources` and `Resources`. Drag the texture image from Finder into the `Resources` folder:

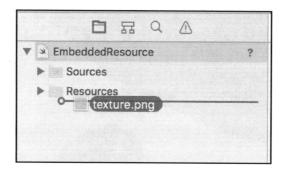

3. Now that we have embedded our texture image within our playground, we need to make use of it. We want each bar in the bar chart to have a settable color, but for the texture to sit on top of that color. Let's update the `BarView` part of our playground to use the texture image; take a look at the given code:

```
class BarView: UIView {
    init(frame: CGRect, color: UIColor) {
        super.init(frame: frame)
        backgroundColor = color
        setupTexture()
    }
    required init?(coder: NSCoder) {
        super.init(coder: coder)
        backgroundColor = UIColor.red
        setupTexture()
    }
    private func setupTexture() {
        guard let textureImage = UIImage(named: "texture") else { return }
        let textureColor = UIColor(patternImage: textureImage)
        let textureView = UIView(frame: CGRect(origin: .zero, size:
bounds.size))
        textureView.backgroundColor = textureColor
        addSubview(textureView)
    }
}
```

4. We can retrieve the image in the same way we would in a full app--by referencing the filename of the image, without the file extension, in a `UIImage` initializer:

```
let textureImage = UIImage(named: "texture")!
```

When the playground is executed, you will see that our bar chart looks a lot more interesting:

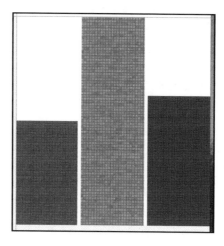

How it works...

To understand where the image that we added is stored, it helps to know how playgrounds are structured. A playground is actually a folder, but with a `.playground` file extension. We can see this by taking a playground file and showing the context menu, which can be done by right-clicking or holding *Ctrl* while clicking on the file. From this menu, select **Show Package Contents**:

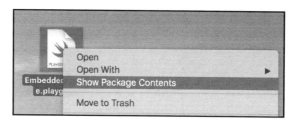

This will open the playground as a folder, showing its contents.

In there, you will find a number of files, including one called `Contents.swift`, which is the Swift file containing the code that is executed. There is also a folder called `Resources`, which contains the texture image we imported:

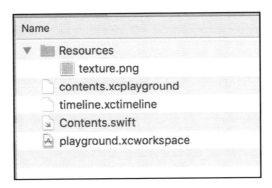

By dragging the image into the file navigator, Xcode created this folder, and placed the image into it. Alternatively, we could have created this folder manually and dropped in the image. Playgrounds will look for a folder named `Resources`, and all the resources in it will be made available from the playground.

See also

The result of this recipe is available as `EmbeddedResources.playground` in the GitHub repository for the chapter, at `http://swiftbook.link/code/chapter6`.

Import Code into Playgrounds

As we have seen throughout this chapter, and this book, playgrounds are a great canvas for exploring APIs, frameworks, and custom code. However, if you want to explore uses for your own code, it appears that you need to include all the code in the playground and that can make it long and unwieldy.

It doesn't need to be that way. In this recipe, we will see how you can embed Swift code in your playground and make use of it from your playground code.

Getting ready

For this recipe, we will use the playground from the previous recipe, called `EmbeddedResources.playground`, which can be retrieved from the GitHub repository for this chapter at `http://swiftbook.link/code/chapter6`.

How to do it...

We will take the `BarChart` custom view and related code, and move it to a separate file embedded within the playground, leaving us free to use the playground to experiment with our custom view. Let's look at these steps:

1. If the playground's project navigator isn't visible, select **View | Navigators | Show Project Navigator** from the menu.
2. We will create a new Swift file, into which we will move some of our code. Select the **Sources** folder and select **File | New | File** from the menu; you will now have a new Swift file in your **Sources** folder:

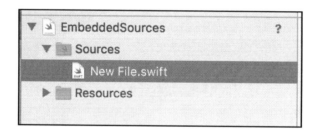

3. If you already have Swift files that you want to embed in a playground, you can drag the files into the `Sources` folder, just like we did with our texture image in the last recipe.
4. Rename the new file `Color.swift`, as we will use this to hold our `Color` struct that is currently in the main playground content.

5. Enter the following code into `Color.swift`:

```swift
import UIKit

public struct Color {
    let red: Float
    let green: Float
    let blue: Float
    let alpha: Float
    public init(red:Float, green:Float, blue:Float, alpha:Float = 1) {
        self.red = red
        self.green = green
        self.blue = blue
        self.alpha = alpha
    }
    var displayColor: UIColor {
        return UIColor(red: CGFloat(red),
                      green: CGFloat(green),
                      blue: CGFloat(blue),
                      alpha: CGFloat(alpha))
    }
}
```

Note that we have added `public` access controls to the `Color` struct and its initializer; we will see more about that as we go ahead.

6. Next, create another new Swift file in the `Sources` folder as we did earlier, called `BarChart.swift`, and enter the rest of the code needed to define the `BarChart` custom view:

```swift
import UIKit

public struct Bar {
    var value: Float
    var color: Color
    public init(value: Float, color: Color) {
        self.value = value
        self.color = color
    }
}

class BarView: UIView {
    init(frame: CGRect, color: UIColor) {
        super.init(frame: frame)
        backgroundColor = color
        setupTexture()
    }
```

```
            required init?(coder: NSCoder) {
                super.init(coder: coder)
                backgroundColor = UIColor.red
                setupTexture()
            }
            private func setupTexture() {
                let textureImage = UIImage(named: "texture")!
                let textureColor = UIColor(patternImage: textureImage)
                let textureView = UIView(frame: bounds)
                textureView.backgroundColor = textureColor
                addSubview(textureView)
            }
        }


        public class BarChart: UIView {
            public var bars: [Bar] = [] {
                didSet {
                    self.barViews.forEach { $0.removeFromSuperview() }
                    var barViews = [BarView]()
                    let barCount = CGFloat(bars.count)
                    // Calculate the max value before calculating size
                    for bar in bars {
                        maxValue = max(maxValue, bar.value)
                    }
                    var xOrigin: CGFloat = interBarMargin
                    for bar in bars {
                        let totalMargin = interBarMargin*(barCount+1)
                        let width = (frame.width - totalMargin) / barCount
                        let height = barHeight(forValue: bar.value)
                        let rect = CGRect(x: xOrigin,
                                          y: bounds.height - height,
                                          width: width,
                                          height: height)
                        let view = BarView(frame: rect,
                                           color: bar.color.displayColor)
                        barViews.append(view)
                        addSubview(view)
                        xOrigin = view.frame.maxX + interBarMargin
                    }
                    self.barViews = barViews
                }
            }
            var interBarMargin: CGFloat = 5.0
            private var barViews: [BarView] = []
            private var maxValue: Float = 0.0
            private func barHeight(forValue value: Float) -> CGFloat {
                return (frame.size.height /
        CGFloat(maxValue))*CGFloat(value)
```

```
        }
    }
```

7. With the `BarChart` implementation code contained in the `Sources` folder, the playground contents can be just for experimenting with the `BarChart` custom view. Remove the code we placed in the other files, and you are left with the following:

```
import PlaygroundSupport
import UIKit

let barView = BarChart(frame: CGRect(x: 0, y: 0, width: 300,
height: 300))
barView.backgroundColor = .white
let bar1 = Bar(value: 20, color: Color(red: 1, green: 0, blue: 0))
let bar2 = Bar(value: 40, color: Color(red: 0, green: 1, blue: 0))
let bar3 = Bar(value: 25, color: Color(red: 0, green: 0, blue: 1))
barView.bars = [bar1, bar2, bar3]
PlaygroundPage.current.liveView = barView
```

How it works...

In moving the `BarChart` implementation to embedded Swift files, we added `public` access control at points where we wanted it to be accessible from the Playground content. This is because code within the **Sources** folder acts as a kind of lightweight module in terms of access control.

Anything with the default `internal` access control is only accessible to other code inside the `Sources` folder; to make it accessible to code in the main playground content, it needs to be declared as `public` or `open`. This is really useful, as it allows you to be in control of what you expose to the playground content; so, you can provide well-designed APIs that don't expose the underlying complexity.

If you need a refresher on access controls or want to learn more, check out the recipe in `Chapter 2`, *Building on the Building Blocks*.

See also

The result of this recipe can be found in `EmbeddedSources.playground` at `http://swiftbook.link/code/chapter6`.

Further information about Swift access controls can be found in `Chapter 2`, *Building on the Building Blocks*.

Multi-Page Playgrounds

We've often discussed how playgrounds can be a great tool for exploring APIs and experimenting with UI; however, playgrounds can also be used for documenting APIs, and providing rich and linkable content. Swift playgrounds provide support for rich text formatting in comments and multiple pages of content, and we will explore these features in this recipe.

Getting ready

In this recipe, we will start with the playground we used in the last recipe, which displayed our custom `BarChart` view. You can get the playground, called `EmbeddedSources.playground`, from the GitHub repository for this chapter, at `http://swiftbook.link/code/chapter6`.

We will use our `BarChart` view to display the price in US Dollars of three different cryptocurrencies over a 6-month period between January 2017 and June 2017. We can show each type of currency on a different playground page.

 If you want to know more about cryptocurrencies, check out the video at `http://swiftbook.link/videos/cryptocurrencies`.

How to do it...

By default, playgrounds have just one Swift content file, but for our purpose, we want to have three pages in our playground--one for each of the three cryptocurrencies we will document: Bitcoin, Etherium, and Lightcoin. Let's get started:

1. If the project navigator isn't visible, you should make it visible using the menu by selecting **View | Navigators | Show Project Navigator**.

2. To create a new playground page, you can click on the plus button in the bottom left-hand corner of the project navigator:

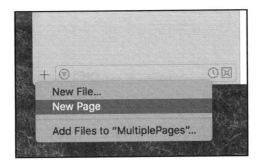

3. Alternatively, from the menu, you can select **File | New | Playground Page**.

4. When creating a new playground page, the existing contents of the playground become a playground page, with another blank page also being created:

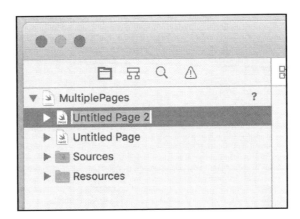

5. Create three pages in total, as we will display data on three different cryptocurrencies, and rename them as follows:

- `Bitcoin`
- `Etherium`
- `Lightcoin`

6. Each of these pages can use the `BarChart` code in the `Sources` folder that we added in the last recipe, so we can create a `BarChart` view on each page to chart the value of each currency.

7. Enter the following code into the `Bitcoin` playground page:

```
import PlaygroundSupport
import UIKit

let barView = BarChart(frame: CGRect(x: 0, y: 0, width: 300,
height: 300))
barView.backgroundColor = .white

let green =  Color(red: 0, green: 1, blue: 0, alpha: 1.0)

let jan2017 = Bar(value: 970.17, color: green)
let feb2017 = Bar(value: 960.05, color: green)
let mar2017 = Bar(value: 1203.02, color: green)
let apr2017 = Bar(value: 1076.90, color: green)
let may2017 = Bar(value: 1390.24, color: green)
let jun2017 = Bar(value: 2414.11, color: green)

barView.bars = [jan2017, feb2017, mar2017, apr2017, may2017,
jun2017]
PlaygroundPage.current.liveView = barView
```

8. Next, enter the following into the `Etherium` playground page:

```
import PlaygroundSupport
import UIKit

let barView = BarChart(frame: CGRect(x: 0, y: 0, width: 300,
height: 300))
barView.backgroundColor = .white

let blue =  Color(red: 0, green: 0, blue: 1, alpha: 1.0)

let jan2017 = Bar(value: 8.06, color: blue)
let feb2017 = Bar(value: 10.70, color: blue)
```

```
let mar2017 = Bar(value: 17.17, color: blue)
let apr2017 = Bar(value: 50.43, color: blue)
let may2017 = Bar(value: 76.85, color: blue)
let jun2017 = Bar(value: 230.15, color: blue)

barView.bars = [jan2017, feb2017, mar2017, apr2017, may2017,
jun2017]
PlaygroundPage.current.liveView = barView
```

9. Lastly, enter the following into the `Lightcoin` **playground page:**

```
import PlaygroundSupport
import UIKit

let barView = BarChart(frame: CGRect(x: 0, y: 0, width: 300,
height: 300))
barView.backgroundColor = .white

let red = Color(red: 1, green: 0, blue: 0, alpha: 1.0)

let jan2017 = Bar(value: 4.32, color: red)
let feb2017 = Bar(value: 3.99, color: red)
let mar2017 = Bar(value: 3.77, color: red)
let apr2017 = Bar(value: 7.43, color: red)
let may2017 = Bar(value: 15.42, color: red)
let jun2017 = Bar(value: 26.44, color: red)

barView.bars = [jan2017, feb2017, mar2017, apr2017, may2017,
jun2017]
PlaygroundPage.current.liveView = barView
```

Now, each page displays the value history as a bar chart, and you can use the project navigator to switch between them.

How it works...

As we did in the previous recipes, we can take a look inside the playground to see how each playground page is represented. Right-click on the playground, or hold *Ctrl* while clicking on it; from this menu, select **Show Package Contents**:

You will see that the `Contents.swift` that we saw earlier has been replaced with a folder containing three `.playgroundpage` files, one for each page in the playground:

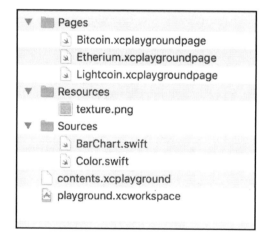

Each of these `.playgroundpage` files is essentially a playground in itself. You can right-click on the `.playgroundpage` and select **Show Package Contents**, and you will see the same playground structure that we saw previously. Much like the normal playground, a `.playgroundpage` file can contain the `Sources` and `Resources` subfolders, and placing code and resources in these will make them visible to just that page.

There's more...

Since we can now add multiple pages of content and have the ability to embed code and resources, Swift Playgrounds look very useful for interactive code documentation. To assist in this use case, it would be great if we could have some control over the presentation of our comments; well we can, as playgrounds support comments in Markdown.

Markdown is a lightweight text formatting syntax, invented by *John Gruber,* and is widely used to write text that can then be rendered with rich text formatting. More details about Markdown can be found at http://swiftbook.link/markdown/docs. We won't delve into the Markdown syntax, but you can find a useful *cheat sheet* at http://swiftbook.link/markdown/cheatsheet.

In our playground, open up the **File Inspector** and look under **Playground Settings**; you will see an option for **Render Documentation**, set it to off while we write some Markdown comments:

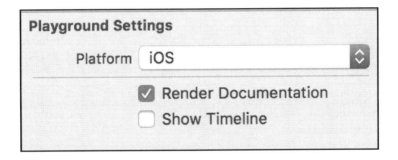

Let's add some comments to our `Bitcoin` page:

```
/*:
 # Crypto Currencies
 ## Bitcoin
 * Create Bar Chart
 * Create Bars and add to chart
 * Make Bar Chart the LiveView
 */

import PlaygroundSupport
import UIKit

/*:
 ## Usage
 * Create Bar Chart
 * Create Bars and add to chart
 * Make Bar Chart the LiveView
```

```
 */
let barView = BarChart(frame: CGRect(x: 0, y: 0, width: 300, height: 300))
barView.backgroundColor = .white
let green =  Color(red: 0, green: 1, blue: 0, alpha: 1.0)

/*:
 * Note:
 Bitcoin Price (in USD)
 - Jan 2017 -  $970.17
 - Feb 2017 -  $960.05
 - Mar 2017 - $1203.02
 - Apr 2017 - $1076.90
 - May 2017 - $1390.24
 - Jun 2017 - $2414.11
 */
let jan2017 = Bar(value: 970.17, color: green)
let feb2017 = Bar(value: 960.05, color: green)
let mar2017 = Bar(value: 1203.02, color: green)
let apr2017 = Bar(value: 1076.90, color: green)
let may2017 = Bar(value: 1390.24, color: green)
let jun2017 = Bar(value: 2414.11, color: green)

barView.bars = [jan2017, feb2017, mar2017, apr2017, may2017, jun2017]
PlaygroundPage.current.liveView = barView
```

To indicate to the playground that your comments contain Markdown formatting, a colon--
:--is added after the opening of the comment block. This works for multiline comments--
/*:--and single line comments--//:.

With these comments in place, let's turn **Render Documentation** back on and see what the
comments look like:

Crypto Currencies

Bitcoin

- Create Bar Chart
- Create Bars and add to chart
- Make Bar Chart the LiveView

```
import PlaygroundSupport
import UIKit
```

Usage

- Create Bar Chart
- Create Bars and add to chart
- Make Bar Chart the LiveView

```
let barView = BarChart(frame: CGRect(x: 0, y: 0, width: 300, height: 300))
barView.backgroundColor = .white

let green =  Color(red: 0, green: 1, blue: 0, alpha: 1.0)
```

> Note
>
> Bitcoin Price (in USD)
>
> - Jan 2017 - $970.17
> - Feb 2017 - $960.05
> - Mar 2017 - $1203.02
> - Apr 2017 - $1076.90
> - May 2017 - $1390.24
> - Jun 2017 - $2414.11

```
let jan2017 = Bar(value: 970.17, color: green)
let feb2017 = Bar(value: 960.05, color: green)
let mar2017 = Bar(value: 1203.02, color: green)
let apr2017 = Bar(value: 1076.90, color: green)
let may2017 = Bar(value: 1390.24, color: green)
let jun2017 = Bar(value: 2414.11, color: green)

barView.bars = [jan2017, feb2017, mar2017, apr2017, may2017, jun2017]

PlaygroundPage.current.liveView = barView
```

In addition, playgrounds also support creating Markdown links between the playground pages; you can link to the next page with @next and to the previous page with @previous. So, in Markdown, the links will be as illustrated:

```
//: [Next page](@next)
//: [Previous page](@previous)
```

It is an exercise left to the reader to add Markdown comments to the other two pages and provide links between the pages.

See also

The result of this recipe can be found in `MultiplePages.playground` at `http://swiftbook.link/code/chapter6`.

Further information about the Markdown syntax can be found at `http://swiftbook.link/markdown/docs`.

7
Server-Side Swift

In this chapter, we will cover the following recipes:

- Swift on Ubuntu
- Building a REST API using Vapor
- Persistence with Vapor using Postgres
- Hosting Your Vapor App on Heroku

Introduction

From its very inception, Swift was intended to be a general-purpose programming language, applicable for multiple use cases and on multiple platforms, not just for building apps for Apple platforms. One of the obvious use cases, other than building apps, is for creating server-side code. After all, interacting with a server is a vital component of almost any app. The vast majority of servers that power the internet run on Linux, which is arguably more suited to the task than any Apple platform. Therefore, being able to run Swift on Linux is vital to the goal of making Swift a viable server-side programming language option.

In this chapter, we will investigate installing the Swift toolchain on Linux, using a web server framework to build a REST API, and hosting our API via a hosting service.

All the code for this chapter can be found in a GitHub repository at `http://swiftbook.link/code/chapter7`.

Swift on Ubuntu

The Linux operating system is a dominant force in the world of backend servers, so to be of any use for server-side development, Swift needs to be available on Linux. Fortunately, part of the open source release of Swift includes the Swift toolchain on Linux. Let's get it up and running with a "Hello World" program in Swift on Linux.

Getting started

This recipe will use Ubuntu 16.04, as this is a very popular and widely used Linux distribution, and 16.04 is the latest **Long-Term Support (LTS)** version. Additionally, pre-built binaries of the Swift toolchain are provided for this distribution by the Swift open source team. As a Mac user, I have tested this process on an instance of Ubuntu, running in the VirtualBox virtualization environment, but there should be no difference when running on bare metal.

How to do it...

Let's install the Swift toolchain and run our first Swift code on Linux:

1. First, we will need to install some dependencies related to the compiler. If you are using Ubuntu with a GUI, open up a Terminal window and run the following from the prompt:

   ```
   sudo apt-get update
   ```

2. The preceding prompt will update the software repositories to ensure that you install the latest versions of the dependencies. Next, run the following command:

   ```
   sudo apt-get install clang libicu-dev
   ```

3. This will download and install **Clang**, which is the Swift compiler and a library that provides Unicode support; these are required for the Swift toolchain that we will install later.

> The Swift team released a prebuilt toolchain for Ubuntu, so we will need to download the latest released version and the associated `signature` file. Links for these releases can be found at `https://swift.org/download/#releases`.

4. The toolchain and signature file can be downloaded using `wget` (with `<BRANCH>`, `<VERSION>`, and `<PLATFORM>` replaced with their relevant values). Fetch the toolchain with the following command:

```
wget
https://swift.org/builds/<BRANCH>/<PLATFORM>/<VERSION>/<VERSION>-<P
LATFORM>.tar.gz
```

Next, fetch the signature file using `wget`:

```
wget
https://swift.org/builds/<BRANCH>/<PLATFORM>/<VERSION>/<VERSION>-<P
LATFORM>.tar.gz.sig
```

5. The `signature` file that we downloaded can be used to verify that the toolchain archive has not been tampered with or modified during the download. The verification will use public PGP keys provided by the Swift project in conjunction with the `signature` file. If you haven't done so before, you can use the following command to retrieve the PGP keys and import them into your keyring:

```
wget -q -O - https://swift.org/keys/all-keys.asc | gpg --import -
```

6. Next, we need to check for any key revocation certificates:

```
gpg --keyserver hkp://pool.sks-keyservers.net --refresh-keys Swift
```

7. With all that done, we can verify the integrity of our downloaded toolchain archive:

```
gpg --verify swift-<VERSION>-<PLATFORM>.tar.gz.sig
```

8. The response should contain the `gpg: Good signature from "Swift Automatic Signing Key #1 <swift-infrastructure@swift.org>"` line; if it does, the archive has been successfully verified, and if not, the download may have been altered and should be retrieved from a trusted source on a trusted network.

 Don't be alarmed if it says the key is not from a trusted `signature`. This is because the system can't find an unbroken chain of certificates from your computer to this key; it's okay to ignore this warning.

9. With our archive verified, let's unzip the archive and see what's inside:

```
tar -xzf swift-<VERSION>-<PLATFORM>.tar.gz
```

Within the archive is a `usr` folder, and within that, a `bin` folder, which contains a number of binaries that are related to building Swift; key among them is the `swift` binary.

10. We want to interact with the Swift toolchain using just the command swift; to do this, we need to tell the system where to look for the Swift binaries. Open up `~/.profile` in your preferred text editor, and add the folder containing your Swift toolchain to the `$PATH` export command. Here's how that will look on a new Ubuntu 16.04 install:

```
PATH="$HOME/bin:$HOME/.local/bin:<path to extracted swift
toolchain>/swift-<VERSION>-<PLATFORM>/usr/bin:$PATH"
```

11. Save your `.profile` file; log out and log back in for the changes to take effect.
12. Now, when you type `swift` and press enter, the Swift REPL will launch. It stands for the **read–eval–print loop (REPL)**; it's a way to interact with the Swift language in a very quick, easy way, much like a Playground.

In the REPL, you can write Swift commands and press enter to have them executed, with each command occurring within the same scope as the previous commands:

1. In the REPL, type as follows:

```
let greeting = "Hello world!"
```

2. Press **Enter**, and the REPL will display the outcome of your command, much like a Playground does:

```
greeting: String = "Hello world!"
```

3. Now we can print our greeting:

```
print(greeting)
```

4. We get the expected response:

```
Hello world!
```

5. To leave the REPL and return to your normal command line, type the following and press Enter:

```
:quit
```

Congratulations! You just executed Swift code on Ubuntu Linux! The world of server-side Swift awaits.

There's more...

It's great to try out Swift code at the command line using the REPL, but what we really require is the ability to compile our code into an executable binary that we can run on demand. Let's take our "Hello world!" example and compile it into a binary:

1. Open your favourite text editor and save the following into a file called `HelloWorld.swift`:

```
print("Hello world!")
```

2. From the command line, in the folder that contains our Swift file, we can compile our binary using `swiftc`:

```
swiftc HelloWorld.swift -o HelloWorld
```

3. You specify the file or files to compile and use the -o flag to provide a name for the output binary.
4. Now, you can execute the binary:

```
> ./HelloWorld
> Hello world!
```

Compiling one file is great, but to perform any useful work, we are likely to have multiple Swift files that define things like models, controllers, and other logic, so how can we compile them into a single, executable binary?

When you have multiple files, which one is the entry point to your application? When compiling a Swift binary with multiple files, one of them should be called `main.swift`, and the code in this file will be executed when the binary is executed; this serves as the entry point to your application.

Let's make two Swift files, first one named `Model.swift`:

```
// Model.swift

class Person {
    let name: String
    init(name: String) {
        self.name = name
    }
}
```

Next, we'll create the `main.swift` file:

```
// main.swift

let keith = Person(name: "Keith")
print("Hello \(keith.name))
```

Now, let's compile these two files into a binary called **Greeter**:

```
swiftc Model.swift main.swift -o Greeter
```

This can then be executed:

```
> ./Greeter
> Hello Keith!
```

We have now written and compiled a multifile binary in Swift on Ubuntu.

Building a REST API using Vapor

One of the main use cases for server-side Swift is for building REST APIs. Interacting with network data is a key function of almost any app, and until now that server-side component had to be built by someone else with the relevant server-side skills, or required an app developer to frequently switch between programming languages and development environments to build both the client-side, and the server-side code in the app.

Swift on the server opens the possibility for a developer to work on everything involved in the app, and move seamlessly between client-side and server-side.

Despite being in its infancy, there is already a vibrant community springing up around server-side Swift, with some impressive open source webserver frameworks from heavy hitters like IBM, in the form of their Kitura framework--`http://www.kitura.io`.

In this recipe, we will use one of the more popular frameworks, Vapor, to build a REST API for an app that stores a user's tasks.

Getting started

Vapor is a Swift framework for building web services, which makes accomplishing common tasks very easy. Vapor is currently at Version 2, which is compatible with Swift 4; more information about Vapor can be found on its website at `http://vapor.codes`.

For this recipe, we will assume that you are developing your Swift web service on a Mac, even if it may eventually be deployed to a Linux server.

 When writing Swift code that will be deployed on Linux, it's very important to test your code by actually running it on Linux, even if it's initially developed on macOS. There are significant differences between Swift's operation on macOS and Linux; often, these differences are due to the different implementation of the `Foundation` framework on the different platforms.

Let's verify that our system is ready to run Vapor; if you have tried any previous recipe, it should be. Run the following command in the Terminal to check for Vapor compatibility:

```
eval "$(curl -sL check.vapor.sh)"
```

We will need to install the Vapor toolbox, which is a set of command-line tools to simplify working with Vapor based projects. The Vapor CLI is available through Homebrew, which is a package manager for macOS; you can find more details about Homebrew at `https://brew.sh`.

If you don't already have Homebrew installed, run the following in the Terminal:

```
/usr/bin/ruby -e "$(curl -fsSL
https://raw.githubusercontent.com/Homebrew/install/master/install)"
```

With Homebrew installed, we can add the `tap` for Vapor:

```
brew tap vapor/homebrew-tap
```

Then, update Homebrew with the information from this new tap:

```
brew update
```

Let's run Vapor to check whether it's installed correctly. You should see instructions on how to use Vapor:

```
vapor version
```

We will create a web service to store and manage tasks from an iOS app. So, let's create a new Vapor project called `TaskAPI` and move to the new folder created:

```
vapor new TaskAPI
cd TaskAPI
```

You can create your Vapor web service using any IDE, but we are familiar with using XCode, so let's use that. Vapor has support for creating an XCode project containing our Vapor code, so let's use that:

```
vapor xcode
```

Answer **y** to the prompt to open the XCode project, and you'll be presented with an XCode project with two schemes: a framework scheme with the name of your project, and a **Run** scheme. Start the **Run** scheme; this will build your project and launch a local webserver, which will handle requests to `http://0.0.0.0:8080`.

Enter `http://0.0.0.0:8080/plaintext` in a browser, and you will see this webpage:

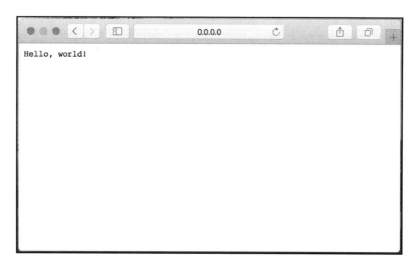

It works! You now have you bare bones Vapor project up and running.

How to do it...

Let's take a look at the XCode project that Vapor has created for us.

In the Project Navigator, you will find a **Sources** group, and two subgroups: **Run** and **App**. The **Run** group contains `main.swift`, the file that will be executed when you run the app. The **App** group contains a number of files with some example code for setting up a REST API.

Open the `main.swift` file; it will contain the following template code:

```
import App

/// We have isolated all of our App's logic into
/// the App module because it makes our app
/// more testable.
///
/// In general, the executable portion of our App
/// shouldn't include much more code than is presented
/// here.
///
/// We simply initialize our Droplet, optionally
/// passing in values if necessary
/// Then, we pass it to our App's setup function
/// this should setup all the routes and special
/// features of our app
///
/// .run() runs the Droplet's commands,
/// if no command is given, it will default to "serve"
let config = try Config()
try config.setup()

let drop = try Droplet(config)
try drop.setup()

try drop.run()
```

As the comments describe, you shouldn't really need to edit this file; it just performs the required setup and starts the web server that serves up our API. What we do need to do is to use this setup process to configure Vapor to provide the API we require.

Let's look at how the default Vapor template sets things up. In the **App** group, open the `Droplet+Setup.swift` file:

```
@_exported import Vapor

extension Droplet {
```

```
        public func setup() throws {
            try setupRoutes()
            // Do any additional droplet setup
        }
    }
```

In this file, the Vapor module is imported with a modifier that we haven't seen before, @_exported, which means that anywhere that the current module is imported will also import the Vapor module. The Vapor module contains all the code to set up and manage the Vapor web server. If you look back at main.swift, you will see that it imports the App module; this is the module that will contain all of your code for setting up the web server and managing requests and responses. Due to the @_exported modifier, when main.swift imports App, it is also importing Vapor.

All that happens in Droplet+Setup.swift is to extend the Droplet class, implement setup(), and have that call setupRoutes(). Droplet as a key class in Vapor; it represents your web server, and through it, we do all our configuration.

Let's switch to Routes.swift, and we will see that this is where setupRoutes() is defined, in another extension of Droplet:

```
import Vapor

extension Droplet {
    func setupRoutes() throws {
        get("hello") { req in
            var json = JSON()
            try json.set("hello", "world")
            return json
        }

        get("plaintext") { req in
            return "Hello, world!"
        }

        // response to requests to /info domain
        // with a description of the request
        get("info") { req in
            return req.description
        }

        get("description") { req in return req.description }
        try resource("posts", PostController.self)
    }
}
```

A number of routes are configured on the `Droplet`. A route defines a type of request that the web server may receive, and the response to send.

You will notice that the `"plaintext"` path is defined, which is the URL we visited to determine that everything was correctly configured:

```
get("plaintext") { req in
    return "Hello, world!"
}
```

This route is for a GET request, with the path string parameter `plaintext`; when our Vapor server was locally run, this related to the URL `http://0.0.0.0:8080`. The process of defining a route in Vapor involves providing a closure that takes a `Request` object and returns something that conforms to `ResponseRepresentable`; Vapor has already defined the String as conforming to `ResponseRepresentable`, so in the String, **Hello, world!** can be returned.

Above this route is one for the path `hello`, which creates an instance of the JSON type, adds some values, and returns it:

```
get("hello") { req in
    var json = JSON()
    try json.set("hello", "world")
    return json
}
```

JSON is the Vapor way of representing the JSON data format, and it also conforms to `ResponseRepresentable`.

Build and run the **Run** scheme, if it's not already running, and visit `http://0.0.0.0:8080/hello` to see the JSON defined.

The last line in the `setupRoutes()` method adds a resource to the `Droplet`:

```
try resource(</span>"posts", PostController.self)
```

Resources are a great way to build a REST API around model objects in Vapor, we will return to these later in the recipe. For now, let's start building our task API.

How it works...

The task API will accept new tasks as POST requests containing JSON representations of the tasks and will return all the existing tasks via GET requests.

First, let's define a task--in the **App** group of your XCode project, create a new file called `Task.swift` in the **Models** group.

After creating this file, ensure that it is a member of the **App** target and not any others. The **Target Membership** panel for our new file should look like this:

Now, let's define our task as having two properties: a `description` and a `category`, plus an identifier:

```
class Task {
    let id: String
    var description: String
    var category: String
    init(id: String, description: String, category: String) {
        self.id = id
        self.description = description
        self.category = category
    }
}
```

We can now create a `Task` in code, like this:

```
let task = Task(id: "1", description: "Remember the milk", category:
"shopping")
```

However, we will always be creating our Task objects from the JSON received by the POST request, so being able to create our task objects directly from JSON will be very helpful, and since we will be returning our `Task` objects as JSON, being able to convert them to JSON will also be helpful.

Vapor has a framework called JSON for dealing with JSON data, and a protocol, `JSONConvertible`, for defining that something can be created from and converted to JSON.

Let's add the `JSONConvertible` conformance to our `Task` model object:

```
import Foundation
import JSON

final class Task: JSONConvertible {
    enum Error: Swift.Error {
        case expectedJSONData
    }
    let id: String
    var description: String
    var category: String
    init(id: String, description: String, category: String) {
        self.id = id
        self.description = description
        self.category = category
    }
    required init(json: JSON) throws {
        guard
```

```
            let description = json["description"]?.string,
            let category = json["category"]?.string else {
                throw Error.expectedJSONData
        }
        self.description = description
        self.category = category

        if let id = json["id"]?.string {
            self.id = id
        } else {
            self.id = UUID().uuidString
        }
    }
    func makeJSON() throws -> JSON {
        var json = JSON()
        try json.set("id", id)
        try json.set("description", description)
        try json.set("category", category)
        return json
    }
}
```

When we are creating a new Task, we don't expect the JSON to include the identifier, so if it is missing, we can generate a UUID using the Foundation framework.

Now that we have our Task model object, which can be converted to and from JSON, let's create some routes for our API.

In Routes.swift, we need an array of Task objects to hold the tasks that get created; for the moment, we can just add that to the top of the file:

```
var tasks = [Task]()
```

Next, we'll add two routes to the setupRoutes() method:

```
post("task") { request in
    guard let json = request.json else {
        throw Abort.badRequest
    }
    let task = try Task(json: json)
    tasks.append(task)
    return try task.makeJSON()
}

get("task") { request in
    return try tasks.makeJSON()
}
```

In the first route, we look for a POST request to the /task path; we check whether the request contains JSON, and if it doesn't, we throw one of Vapor's built-in errors--Abort.badRequest. If the request has JSON, then we can use it to attempt to create a Task object using the JSON; once created, we can store it in the tasks array.

The next route looks for a GET request to that same path--/task--and returns a JSON representation of the tasks we stored in our array. This makes use of the fact that Vapor has an extension on Sequence, which Array conforms to, and if all items in the Sequence conform to JSONRepresentable, then the Sequence can be represented as JSON, too. With these routes defined, let's build and run the **Run** scheme and test them out.

We'll add a task, sending a POST request to http://0.0.0.0:8080/task; we can do this using the curl command:

```
curl -H "Content-Type: application/json" -X POST -d
'{"description":"Remember the milk","category":"shopping"}'
http://0.0.0.0:8080/task
```

This should return a JSON representation of the task we just created, which looks like this, although the id will be different:

```
{
   "id": "CEC93BB9-2487-4207-97D8-E41196B44D24",
   "category": "shopping",
   "description": "Remember the milk"
}
```

Next, let's test our route to show all the existing tasks:

```
curl http://0.0.0.0:8080/task
```

This should return the one Task we created in an array:

```
[
   {
      "id": "CEC93BB9-2487-4207-97D8-E41196B44D24",
      "category": "shopping",
      "description": "Remember the milk"
   }
]
```

We now have a simple API that stores our tasks.

Try adding a few more tasks and check whether they are returned from the GET request.

There's more...

The API we have created so far allows us to perform some operations on a task; namely, to create one and list all the current tasks. Implementing these actions, along with other operations such as modifying, deleting, and listing an individual task, is very common when building a REST API, so Vapor makes this really easy.

In Vapor, you can define a resource that will define how all these operations are performed, and Vapor handles the setting up of routes that follow standard practice for REST APIs.

Let's create a `TaskController` object that conforms to a Vapor protocol-- `ResourceRepresentible`--which will be responsible for creating the Resource for our `Task` model object:

```
import JSON

var tasksByID = [String: Task]()

final class TaskController: ResourceRepresentable, EmptyInitializable {
    typealias Model = Task
    func index(request: Request) throws -> ResponseRepresentable {
        return try tasksByID.values.makeJSON()
    }
    func create(request: Request) throws -> ResponseRepresentable {
        guard let json = request.json else {
            throw Abort.badRequest
        }
        let task = try Task(json: json)
        tasksByID[task.id] = task
        return try task.makeJSON()
    }
    func show(request: Request, task: Task) throws -> ResponseRepresentable
{
        return try task.makeJSON()
    }
    func makeResource() -> Resource<Task> {
        return Resource(index: index,
                        store: create,
                        show: show)
    }
}
```

We will also make `TaskController` conform `EmptyInitializable`, which will make it simpler to instantiate later.

We are storing the created tasks in a dictionary, with the key being the task ID; this allows us to easily retrieve them when the ID is passed as a URL parameter.

To conform to `ResourceRepresentable`, our `TaskController` just needs to implement the `func makeResource() -> Resource<Model>` method, while also defining the `Model` generic type.

To create our resource, we provide functions that provide the response for each REST operation that we would like to support. These are as listed:

- `index`
- `store`
- `show`
- `replace`
- `modify`
- `destroy`
- `clear`
- `aboutItem`
- `aboutMultiple`

Each of these functions must conform to the relevant type definitions, defined by the following `typealias`:

```
typealias Multiple = (Request) throws -> ResponseRepresentable
typealias Item = (Request, Model) throws -> ResponseRepresentable
```

For now, we'll just implement the index, store, and show operations of the resource, matching the routes we manually created earlier. We've defined our methods named `index` and `create`, and we can pass them into the Resource constructor in the `makeResource` method.

This won't currently compile, however, as whatever we define for the generic type Model, in this case, `Task`, must conform to `Parameterizable`.

So, let's extend `Task` to make it conform to `Parameterizable`:

```
extension Task: Parameterizable {
    static var uniqueSlug: String {
        return "task"
    }
    // returns the found model for the resolved url parameter
    static func make(for parameter: String) throws -> Task {
        guard let task = tasksByID[parameter] else {
            throw Abort.notFound
        }
        return task
    }
}
```

Now that we have our `TaskController`, which is a `ResourceRepresentable`, we can replace the two routes we declared in `Routes.swift` with this one line:

```
try resource("task", TaskController.self)
```

This tells Vapor that our `TaskController` will provide a resource to handle requests to the path `"task"`. Vapor will register routes corresponding to the provided operations. Since we provided operations for index and store, this corresponds a GET request and a POST request containing JSON, respectively.

Let's test whether everything still works as expected, let's create a task:

```
curl -H "Content-Type: application/json" -X POST -d
'{"description":"Remember the milk","category":"shopping"}'
http://0.0.0.0:8080/task
```

Then, fetch all task to check our newly created task is returned:

```
curl http://0.0.0.0:8080/task
```

We've now created a simple REST API for storing and retrieving tasks.

In the next recipe, we will build on this to make it truly useful.

See also

More information about the Vapor framework can be found on its website at `https://vapor.codes`.

Here are some other popular Swift web frameworks:

- **Kitura**: `http://www.kitura.io`
- **Perfect**: `http://perfect.org`
- **Zewo**: `http://www.zewo.io`

Persistence with Vapor using Postgres

We saw how we can build a REST API in Swift using the Vapor framework; however, this is of limited use on its own. To provide real utility, we need to store and retrieve our model so that it persists beyond the lifetime of the server.

A common approach is to use a relational database such as **SQLite**, **MySql** or **Postgres**, and **Vapor**, with support for a number of databases through the included `Fluent` framework.

In this recipe, we will build on the REST API for tasks from the last recipe, and persist our model to a Postgres database. We'll choose Postgres because it is a popular relational database for which there is great support in **Heroku**, a hosting service we will use in the next recipe.

Getting started

For this recipe, we need to download, install, and run Postgres, and the easiest way to get Postgres is through the **Homebrew** package manager. We used Homebrew to install the Vapor **CLI** (**Command-Line Interface**), so it very likely that you already have Homebrew setup. If you don't have Homebrew installed, you can follow the given steps.

More information about Homebrew can be found at `https://brew.sh`.

Brew can be installed by running the following command and following the instructions:

```
/usr/bin/ruby -e "$(curl -fsSL
https://raw.githubusercontent.com/Homebrew/install/master/install)"
```

With Homebrew, or `brew`, installed, we can install `Postgres`:

```
brew install postgres
```

Now that we have `Postgres` installed, we can use brew to start the database as a background service:

```
brew services start postgresql
```

When we want to stop the database service, we can do so with the following command:

```
brew services stop postgresql
```

However, we want to leave it running while we work on this recipe.

The database service is running, but we need a database to use for our REST API, so let's create one from the Terminal:

```
createdb TaskAPI
```

We now have `Postgres` ready; next, we need to get Vapor ready to work with `Postgres`.

Vapor has a modular approach to persistence, interfacing with databases through the `Fluent` framework. Support for different database types has to be added in the form of provider modules. The available provider modules can be found in separate repositories under the Vapor organization on GitHub, or the Vapor Community organization, which has a number of third-party providers.

Go to `https://github.com/vapor` or `https://github.com/vapor-community` and search for repositories containing the word **provider** to see all the options:

We are interested in the Postgres provider, which can be found at `https://github.com/vapor-community/postgresql-provider`.

The repository landing page provides the structure and location of the JSON configuration files, that we will need to provide so that the provider can connect to the database; take note of this under **Configure PostgreSQL**, as we will need it soon:

```
{
    "hostname": "127.0.0.1",
    "user": "postgres",
    "password": "hello",
    "database": "test",
    "port": 5432
}
```

Copy the HTTPS git reference for the repository; we will use this to import the provider framework using the Swift Package Manager:

The git reference should be this:

```
https://github.com/vapor-community/postgresql-provider.git
```

Switch back to XCode and open Package.swift, which is at the top of the **Project Navigator**.

We need to add the Postgres provider package as a dependency within this app's package declaration. Update your Package.swift to read as follows:

```
import PackageDescription

let package = Package(
    name: "TaskAPI",
    targets: [
        Target(name: "App"),
        Target(name: "Run", dependencies: ["App"]),
    ],
    dependencies: [
        .Package(url: "https://github.com/vapor/vapor.git", majorVersion:
2),
        .Package(url: "https://github.com/vapor/fluent-provider.git",
majorVersion: 1),
        .Package(url:
"https://github.com/vapor-community/postgresql-provider.git", majorVersion:
        2, minor: 0)
            ],
        exclude: [
```

```
            "Config",
            "Database",
            "Localization",
            "Public",
            "Resources",
        ]
    )
```

When we next run `swift build`, `vapor build`, or `vapor xcode`, our new dependency will be downloaded and linked.

Next, we need to define our config JSON file as described in the repository. The provider framework is expecting to find a file called `postgresql.json` in the `<Project Folder>/Config/secrets` folder, so let's create that file, also creating the secrets folder if it doesn't already exist, and paste in the example JSON from the `Postgresql` Provider GitHub README file:

```
{
    "hostname": "127.0.0.1",
    "user": "postgres",
    "password": "hello",
    "database": "test",
    "port": 5432
}
```

We need to change the user to match the local user of your machine, and the name of the database to match the database we created earlier:

```
{
    "hostname": "127.0.0.1",
    "user": "keefmoon",
    "password": "",
    "database": "TaskAPI",
    "port": 5432
}
```

Next, we have to tell Vapor to use the PostgreSQL driver for persistence. To do this, open the file `fluent.json` in the `Config` folder, and change the value of `driver` to `postgresql`. You should now have a line in the file, as shown:

```
"driver": "postgresql",
```

Finally, we need to set up our PostgreSQL provider on our `Droplet`. Open `Config+Setup.swift` in XCode, and import the `PostgreSQL` provider module:

```
import PostgreSQLProvider
```

We can replace the `FluentProvider` configured in our Vapor template with the `PostgreSQL` provider, so the `setupProvides()` method now looks like this:

```
private func setupProviders() throws {
    try addProvider(PostgreSQLProvider.Provider.self)
}
```

Now, we can run `vapor xcode` to fetch the dependencies, and regenerate the XCode project.

How to do it...

Now that we have a database to persist our model, let's ensure that our model object can use that database. In Vapor, this is done by making the model type conform to the `Model` protocol, and if you look at the definition of the Model, you'll see that it simply requires conformance to two other protocols:

```
protocol Model: Entity, Parameterizable
```

Let's take a look at these protocols, one at a time:

- `Entity`: This governs how our model object interacts with the database. We will come back to this, as our Task object does not currently conform to it.
- `Parameterizable`: We added conformance to this protocol for `Task` in the last recipe. If you need a refresher, refer to the *There's more...* section of the last recipe, which used resources to implement our Task API.

By importing `FluentProvider` and adding `Model` conformance, our `Task.swift` now looks like this:

```
import Foundation
import JSON
import FluentProvider

final class Task: JSONConvertible, Model {
    enum Error: Swift.Error {
        case expectedJSONData
    }
    var id: String
```

```
    var description: String
    var category: String
    init(id: String, description: String, category: String) {
        self.id = id
        self.description = description
        self.category = category
    }
    required init(json: JSON) throws {
        guard
            let description = json["description"]?.string,
            let category = json["category"]?.string else {
                throw Error.expectedJSONData
        }
        self.description = description
        self.category = category
        if let id = json["id"]?.string {
            self.id = id
        } else {
            self.id = UUID().uuidString
        }
    }
    func makeJSON() throws -> JSON {
        var json = JSON()
        try json.set("id", id)
        try json.set("description", description)
        try json.set("category", category)
        return json
    }
}
```

Currently, this won't compile, as Task doesn't yet conform to Entity, so let's add the properties and methods that are required by Entity; we can also remove our id property from Task, as Entity provides a unique identifier:

```
import Foundation
import JSON
import FluentProvider

final class Task: JSONConvertible, Model {
    // MARK: - Entity Conformance
    var storage = Storage()
    init(row: Row) throws {
        description = try row.get("description")
        category = try row.get("category")
    }
    func makeRow() throws -> Row {
        var row = Row()
        try row.set("id", id)
```

```
            try row.set("description", description)
            try row.set("category", category)
            return row
        }
        // MARK: -
        enum Error: Swift.Error {
            case expectedJSONData
        }
        var description: String
        var category: String
        init(description: String, category: String) {
            self.description = description
            self.category = category
        }
        required init(json: JSON) throws {
            guard
                let description = json["description"]?.string,
                let category = json["category"]?.string else {
                    throw Error.expectedJSONData
            }
            self.description = description
            self.category = category
        }
        func makeJSON() throws -> JSON {
            var json = JSON()
            try json.set("id", id)
            try json.set("description", description)
            try json.set("category", category)
            return json
        }
    }
}

extension Task: Preparation {
    static func prepare(_ database: Database) throws {
        try database.create(self) { builder in
            builder.id()
            builder.string("description")
            builder.string("category")
        }
    }
    static func revert(_ database: Database) throws {
        try database.delete(self)
    }
}
```

We've added a property called `storage`, and two methods--`init(row: Row) throws` and `func makeRow() throws -> Row`--which will convert our task object to and from an instance of `Row`, which is used to represent a record in the database.

In addition to these changes, Entity requires conformance to `Preparation`. This protocol defines how the database should be prepared to work with our model object and has two method requirements:

```
static func prepare(_ database: Database) throws
```

Within this method, we will need to define how our model will be stored in the database. Since we are dealing with a relational database, Postgres, this will take the form of a database table with fields corresponding to the properties of the model:

```
static func revert(_ database: Database) throws
```

For the `revert` method, we need to tell the database how to revert the changes made in the `prepare` method. For our use of a relational database, this simply involves dropping the database table that was created for our model.

We can extend our model object to add this conformance to `Preparation`:

```
extension Task: Preparation {
    static func prepare(_ database: Database) throws {
        try database.create(self) { builder in
            builder.id()
            builder.string("description")
            builder.string("category")
        }
    }
    static func revert(_ database: Database) throws {
        try database.delete(self)
    }
}
```

Now that we have our Task object conforming to `Model`, let's open `TaskController.swift` to see how we can use the functionality in `Fluent` to save to and retrieve from our database.

We have methods for creating a Task as the result of a request, and listing all tasks as the result of the request. Let's rewrite these to use the database, and remove our Task dictionary, as it's no longer needed; we also need to update our extension of Task that adds conformance to `Parameterizable`, which should now find a task in the database:

```
import Vapor
import HTTP
```

```
import JSON

extension Task: Parameterizable {
    static var uniqueSlug: String {
        return "task"
    }
    // returns the found model for the resolved url parameter
    static func make(for parameter: String) throws -> Task {
        guard let task = try Task.find(parameter) else {
            throw Abort.notFound
        }
        return task
    }
}

final class TaskController: ResourceRepresentable, EmptyInitializable {
    typealias Model = Task
    func index(request: Request) throws -> ResponseRepresentable {
        let tasks: [Task] = try Task.all()
        return try tasks.makeJSON()
    }
    func create(request: Request) throws -> ResponseRepresentable {
        guard let json = request.json else {
            throw Abort.badRequest
        }
        let task = try Task(json: json)
        try task.save()
        return try task.makeJSON()
    }
    func show(request: Request, task: Task) throws -> ResponseRepresentable
    {
        return try task.makeJSON()
    }
    func makeResource() -> Resource<Task> {
        return Resource(index: index,
                        store: create,
                        show: show)
    }
}
```

By conforming to Model, Task now has some functionality to get information to and from the database. All static functions will return from the database all task entries as an array of Task objects. The save method will save the values in the model object to the database; as this is a newly created object, it is saved as a new record in the database table, and the id property is given a new value. Also, the find(_ id: NodeRepresentable?) static method will return the Model for a given id.

The last step to getting database support with Vapor is to configure our `Droplet` to use the database, which we do in `Config+Setup.swift`.

During our `Droplet` setup, we need to do two things: add `PostgreSQL` as a provider, and prepare the database to work with the `Task` model object. We have already added `PostgreSQL` as a provider, and the template code adds preparations for the `Post` model, so we can just change that to `Task`:

```
/// Configure providers
private func setupProviders() throws {
    try addProvider(PostgreSQLProvider.Provider.self)
}

/// Add all models that should have their
/// schemas prepared before the app boots
private func setupPreparations() throws {
    preparations.append(Task.self)
}
```

The first part instructs the `Droplet` to use the `Postgres` provider to set up a database; the provider will use the JSON file we set up earlier to create a connection to the database, so you will need to ensure that the database is running locally before testing the API.

The second part will, when needed, call the `Preparation` methods that we added to `Task` earlier, to create a database table to store the task information.

With everything in place, run the **Run** scheme and use the same CURL commands as in the previous recipe to test the API:

- To create a task, run the following:

    ```
    curl -H "Content-Type: application/json" -X POST -d
    '{"description":"Remember the milk","category":"shopping"}'
    http://0.0.0.0:8080/task
    ```

- To list all tasks, run this:

    ```
    curl http://0.0.0.0:8080/task
    ```

However, you can now quit the app and run it again, and when you list all tasks, the one we just created will still be returned, as it was persisted to the database across the separate executions of the API.

There's more...

Let's return to `TaskController` and provide more resource capabilities as part of the API. Currently, we have provided functions to handle the index and store and show capabilities; let's add resource capabilities to modify and destroy.

In `TaskController`, we'll review the function for returning a single task for a given ID:

```
func show(request: Request, task: Task) throws -> ResponseRepresentable {
    return try task.makeJSON()
}
```

Our function matched the `Item` signature that the show parameter requires:

```
typealias Item = (Request, Model) throws -> ResponseRepresentable
```

In this case, Vapor does the heavy lifting and retrieves the task from the database based on the `id` provided in the URL, so we can simply return the JSON representation of the task.

This function is provided when we create the resource:

```
func makeResource() -> Resource<Task> {
    return Resource(index: index,
                    store: create,
                    show: show)
}
```

Build and run the `App` scheme, and we can test it with this CURL command, assuming that you have previously created a task:

```
curl http://0.0.0.0:8080/task/1
```

Next, we want to be able to update a task using a PATCH request. Vapor simplifies this with use of the `Updatable` protocol; let's add conformance for the `Task`:

```
extension Task: Updateable {
    public static var updateableKeys: [UpdateableKey<Task>] {
        return [UpdateableKey("description", String.self) { (task,
description) in
                task.description = description
            },
                UpdateableKey("category", String.self) { (task, category)
in
                task.category = category
            }]
    }
}
```

For each property that we want to be updated, we proved an `UpdateableKey` that provides the key to expect in the JSON, the type to expect, and a closure that performs the update.

This is conformance; adding support for updating a Task in our `TaskController` is simple:

```
func update(_ req: Request, post: Post) throws -> ResponseRepresentable {
    try task.update(for: req)
    try task.save()
    return try task.makeJSON()
}
```

Our `Updatable` conformance provides an update method that we can call with the request; then, we just need to save the changes, and return the newly modified task in the response for convenience.

Now, we can provide this function when creating the resource:

```
func makeResource() -> Resource<Task> {
    return Resource(index: index,
                    store: create,
                    show: show,
                    update: update)
}
```

Build and run, and you can modify a task using a PATCH request:

```
curl -H "Content-Type: application/json" -X PATCH -d
'{"description":"Remember the strawberry milk","category":"shopping"}'
http://0.0.0.0:8080/task/1
```

Finally, let's create a function to delete a task:

```
func delete(request: Request, task: Task) throws -> ResponseRepresentable {
    try task.delete()
    let tasks: [Task] = try Task.all()
    return try tasks.makeJSON()
}
```

We can use the `delete helper` function to remove the task from the database, and then return all the remaining tasks as a response. Let's provide our `delete` function for the resource's destroy functionality:

```
func makeResource() -> Resource<Task> {
    return Resource(index: index,
                    store: create,
                    show: show,
```

```
                    modify: modify,
                    destroy: delete)
    }
```

We can test it by sending a `DELETE` request using curl:

```
curl -X DELETE http://0.0.0.0:8080/task/1
```

We now have a really useful REST API for our tasks. Next, we will look hosting our REST API to make it useful outside of our local machine.

See also

Vapor provides a number of other database providers that can be used instead of `Postgres`:

- **MySQL**: https://github.com/vapor/mysql-provider
- **SQLite**: https://github.com/vapor-community/sqlite-provider
- **Redis**: https://github.com/vapor/redis-provider
- **Mongo**: https://github.com/vapor-community/mongo-provider

Hosting your Vapor app on Heroku

In the previous recipes in this chapter, we created a REST API that stores and retrieves information from a Postgres database. We have our Vapor web server running on our local machine and can interact with it over HTTP requests; however, unless you plan on making your machine available to the public internet, this is of limited use, and we need to find somewhere to host our data and REST interface.

At the time of writing, Swift support on hosting services is the exception rather than the norm; however, support is growing. Heroku is a popular hosting service that provides dynamic scaling of resources and a really simple deployment mechanism. It also has support for Swift and Postgres, so in this recipe, we will deploy our REST API to Heroku.

Getting started

Heroku provides simple and scalable infrastructure for your server-side projects. Once deployed, instances of your app are called Dymos, and additional Dymos can be started to cope with increased load.

Deployment to Heroku happens through a remote Git repository; when you are ready to deploy your app, simply push the code to Heroku.

First, visit http://www.heroku.com and sign up for a free account. Next, we will install the Heroku CLI (**Command-Line Interface**), as this is helpful for interacting with Heroku. Since we installed Homebrew in the previous recipes, we can use it to get the Heroku CLI:

```
brew install heroku
```

Next, we need to login to the Heroku CLI with the account that we just created. Run the login command and follow the instructions:

```
heroku login
```

We now have our Heroku CLI set up and ready to use.

How to do it...

Since the deployment mechanism for Heroku is git, we need to create a local git repo.

In the Terminal, navigate to the folder containing our TaskAPI app that we built in the previous recipes, and create a local git repo:

```
git init
```

Now we need to stage all the files:

```
git add .
```

Then, commit all the code:

```
git commit -m "Initial commit"
```

Next, we will set up this Vapor project to use Heroku, and follow the instructions:

```
vapor heroku init
```

You will be asked if you would like a custom name for your app. If you choose not to have a custom app name, then a random app name will be assigned in the form of two words and a number; for example, afternoon-bastion-18185. Therefore, the app's URL will be https://afternoon-bastion-18185.herokuapp.com.

You will also be asked if you want to provide a custom build pack and a custom executable name. You can answer no to both of these.

We need to associate our local git repository with the Heroku app we just created. Run the following command, replacing the final parameter with the name of the app that Heroku just created for you:

```
heroku git:remote -a afternoon-bastion-18185
```

To get our database backed API up and running on our local machine, we ran a `Postgresql` service and configured Vapor's connection to it using a configuration JSON file in `Config/secret`. However, this configuration is specific to our local machine, and so we need to start a `PostgreSQL` database service on Heroku and configure Vapor to connect to it.

Luckily, Heroku CLI makes this really easy; just run the following:

```
heroku addons:create heroku-postgresql:hobby-dev
```

In this command, `hobby-dev` is the pricing plan to use for the database, which is free for up to 10,000 database rows.

This will cause the database to be made available to your Heroku Dymo whenever your app is deployed. By running `heroku config`, we can see that an environment variable called `DATABASE_URL` is created, containing the connection URL for the database.

Now, we need to ensure that Vapor knows how to connect to the database when it's running on Heroku. To do this, we will add a configuration to the `Procfile` which is used by Heroku to set up the environment.

In the root of the project, create a file named `Procfile`; open this file and add the following:

```
web: App --env=production --workdir=./ --config:servers.default.port=$PORT
--config:postgresql.url=$DATABASE_URL
```

This will allow Vapor to use the PostgreSQL database set up on Heroku.

Now, let's commit the change:

```
git add .
git commit -m "Added Procfile with databse URL"
```

We are now ready to push our code to Heroku, which will then be deployed:

```
git push heroku master
```

It may take a while, but eventually, Heroku will report that the code has been deployed and will provide the URL for the deployed app, which will look similar to this:

```
https://afternoon-bastion-18185.herokuapp.com
```

You have a deployed version of our `TaskAPI` running on Heroku. You can rerun all the CURL tests from the last recipe, but with the preceding hostname in the place of `http://0.0.0.0:8080`.

See also

What we have built in this chapter is just the tip of the iceberg of what Vapor is capable of. Vapor has built-in support for authentication, templating, and much more, so check out `http://vapor.codes` for full documentation.

The team behind Vapor has launched their own hosting service, Vapor Cloud. This really simplifies the process of getting your Vapor app online. At the time of writing, this service is in open beta; you can find out more and sign up at `https://vapor.cloud`.

8

Performance and Responsiveness in Swift

In this chapter, we will cover the following recipes:

- Value and reference semantics
- Dispatch Queues
- Concurrent queues and dispatch groups
- Operations

Introduction

We have covered a lot of ground in the previous chapters, and we have a lot of Swift tools in our toolbelt. Now it's time to delve into more advanced topics, to look at how certain Swift types are implemented, how they can be used, and their performance characteristics. We will also look at how we can perform asynchronous tasks using **Grand Central Dispatch (GCD)** through the *Dispatch* framework and the higher-level operations in the Foundation framework that are also built on GCD.

Understanding the multithreaded environment available on all Apple platforms, as well as the performance profile of the Swift constructs you use, is vital to building a fast and responsive app.

Value and reference semantics

We saw back in Chapter 1, *Swift Building Blocks*, that certain Swift types behave differently from others, specifically regarding ownership and the mutation of properties. We even defined this difference, saying that classes are *reference* types, while structs and enums are *value* types.

Getting ready

In this recipe, we will examine why these types behave differently and the performance implications this entails.

Let's create the model for an app that allows a user to schedule events that they do every day and reminds them when these events should occur.

Therefore, we need to decide how we will model our daily event; the key to this decision is whether we want our event to have reference semantics or value semantics. We discussed the differences between the two in Chapter 1, *Swift Building Blocks*, but let's reexamine the differences.

How to do it...

Value types are simple data structures that you can think of as just bundles of data; Swift makes these types more useful by allowing them to have methods, but any change or *mutation* of the underlying data results in a whole new bundle of data. In contrast, *reference* types are more complex data structures that have an identity outside of their component properties; therefore, a change in the component properties will be available via any references to the object.

A value type's simple composition has the advantage of being very cheap on resources to create and maintain; however, this simplicity comes at the expense of dynamic dispatch, which enables sub-classing.

Given this distinction, what behaviour do we want for our daily event? If we change the name of our event, should we expect anything that has a reference to it to also see that change? That sounds like the behaviour we want, so our daily event should be a reference type:

```
class DailyEvent {
    var name: String
    init(name: String) {
        self.name = name
    }
}
```

Let's check that this gives us the behaviour we expect:

```
var event1 = DailyEvent(name: "have bath")
var event2 = event1
print("Event 1 - \(event1.name)") // have bath
print("Event 2 - \(event2.name)") // have bath
event1.name = "have shower"
print("Event 1 - \(event1.name)") // have shower
print("Event 2 - \(event2.name)") // have shower
```

We want to be reminded of our event every day at a certain time, but for our purpose, Date in Foundation is a bit of an overkill, since it contains both date and time information, and we only need to maintain time information. Let's create something to represent the time, irrespective of the date. What behaviour is most appropriate for our time model; should it have reference semantics or type semantics?

Let's try both and see which seems to most accurately model the situation we are after.

First, we'll create time as a class, with reference semantics:

```
class ClockTime {
    var hours: Int
    var minutes: Int
    init(hours: Int, minutes: Int) {
        self.hours = hours
        self.minutes = minutes
    }
}
```

Now, let's see how this will behave when its properties are changed:

```
let defaultEventTime = ClockTime(hours: 6, minutes: 30)
var event1Time = defaultEventTime // 6:30
var event2Time = defaultEventTime // 6:30
// Event 2 has been moved to 9:30
event2Time.hours = 9
print("Event 1 - \(event1Time.hours):\(event1Time.minutes)") // Event 1 -
9:30
print("Event 2 - \(event2Time.hours):\(event2Time.minutes)") // Event 2 -
9:30
```

When we change the properties of an instance of `ClockTime`, it has the unintended consequence of changing all references to that same instance of `ClockTime`.

Since reference semantics aren't a perfect fit for `ClockTime`, let's change it to a value type and see if that is more appropriate. We now have two options for value types in Swift; we can model `ClockTime` as a `struct` or an enum. Enums are great for modeling concepts that have a small number of finite values; while there are a finite number of minutes in a day, it's not a small number, and we might want to do math calculation on the hours and minutes in `ClockTime`, so a `struct` is more appropriate:

```
struct ClockTime {
    var hours: Int
    var minutes: Int
}
```

Let's see how this changes the behaviour when we change the properties of a `ClockTime` instance:

```
let defaultEventTime = ClockTime(hours: 6, minutes: 30)
var event1Time = defaultEventTime // 6:30
var event2Time = defaultEventTime // 6:30
// Event 2 has been moved to 9:30
event2Time.hours = 9
print("Event 1 - \(event1Time.hours):\(event1Time.minutes)") // Event 1 -
6:30
print("Event 2 - \(event2Time.hours):\(event2Time.minutes)") // Event 2 -
9:30
```

With ClockTime as a value type, changing a property of a ClockTime instance results in a new instance, so the change doesn't have the unintended consequences that we saw when it was a reference type.

Lastly, let's consider some of the dynamic features that we will give up by making ClockTime a value type. Will we ever want to subclass ClockTime? This doesn't seem likely, and it is right to characterize ClockTime as a simple bundle of data; so in this scenario, modeling ClockTime as a value type is the right decision.

To complete the model, we will add a ClockTime property to the DailyEvent class:

```swift
class DailyEvent {
    var name: String
    var time: ClockTime
    init(name: String, time: ClockTime) {
        self.name = name
        self.time = time
    }
}
```

How it works...

We've already covered how value types differ from reference types; now, let's examine why they behave differently.

When storing new instances of a type in memory, Swift has two different data structures that it can use for storage: the **Stack** and the **heap**. These structures are common to many programming languages. Value types are stored on the **Stack**, and reference types are stored on the *heap*. Understanding how data is stored in these structures, even at the superficial level that we will cover, it will help us understand why value types and reference types have differing behavior.

The stack can be thought of as sequential blocks of data; an instance of a type may be represented by multiple blocks of data, and an instance can be referenced using the memory position of its first piece of data. A **Stack Pointer**, which is a reference to the memory position at the end of the stack, is maintained; new instances are always added to the end of the stack, and then the stack pointer's position is updated to the new end of the stack.

Let's go through adding a value type instance using a simplified diagram of the stack:

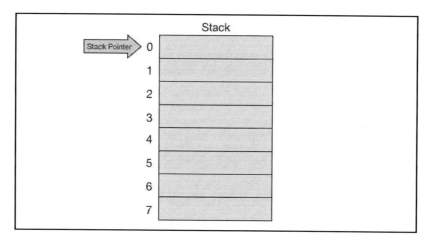

Before anything is added, the stack pointer is at the top of the stack:

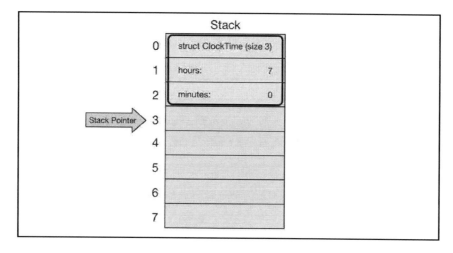

A `ClockTime` struct for 7:00 is added to the stack; this takes up three blocks, and the stack pointer moves to the next empty block on the stack:

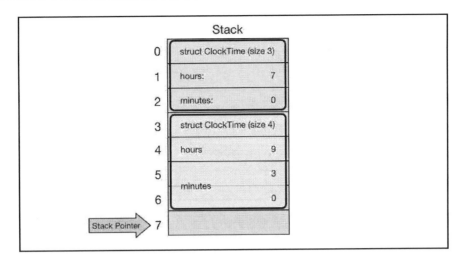

Another `ClockTime` struct for 9:30 is added to the stack; this has a size of four blocks, and the stack pointer moves to the next empty block on the stack.

Once data is placed on the stack, it is immutable; to see why this is an important restriction, let's try and change our first `ClockTime` instance on the stack:

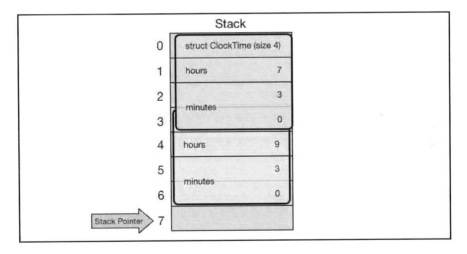

The simplicity and efficiency of the stack is predicated on the fact that it is a continuous block of memory. If we try and change any data already on the stack, it may take up more space, which will cause data in the subsequent blocks to be overwritten.

Therefore, any change to a `struct` results in a new, changed version of the `struct` appended at the end of the stack.

Let's mutate a `ClockTime` instance and see how that looks in our simplified stack representation by taking it step by step:

```
var event1Time = ClockTime(hours: 9, minutes: 0)
```

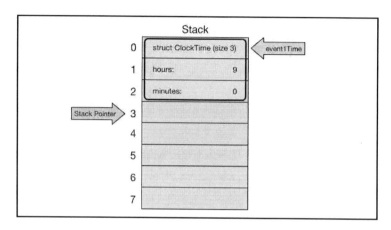

We have a `ClockTime` struct for 9:00 assigned to the variable named `event1Time`:

```
var event2Time = event1Time
```

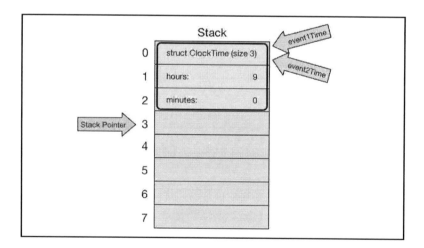

The value of event1Time is also assigned to a new variable, called event2Time:

```
event2Time.minutes = 30
```

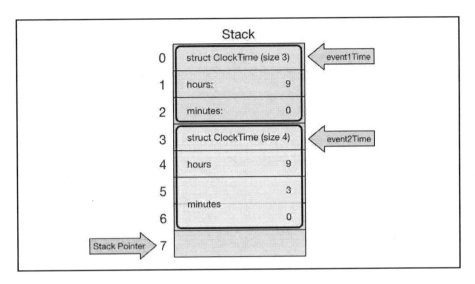

When we mutate event2Time, changing the minute value to 30, a new ClockTime instance with the changed minute value is placed at the end of the stack. The event2Time variable now points to this new stack position, while event1Time continues to point at the stack position of the original ClockTime struct for 9:00.

As the preceding examples show, the stack is a very simple and efficient data structure, and its properties explain the behavior we see when we use value types such as struct and enums.

In contrast, reference types, such as class objects, are stored on the heap, which enables more dynamic and complex behavior at the expense of efficiency.

An accurate look at heap allocations is beyond the scope of this book, but let's take a very simplified look at how a reference type instance is stored on the **Heap**:

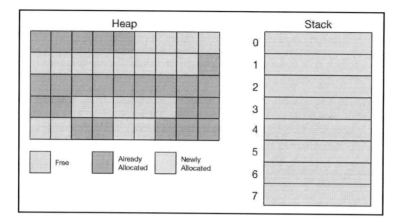

The heap is not a continuous chain of blocks, but an area of memory that can be free or already allocated:

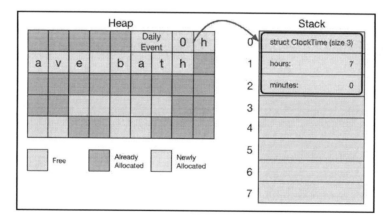

When a class is allocated to the **Heap**, it must search through the heap to find a set of free blocks appropriate for its size. The reference type instance may include references to other reference types or value types by storing their stack positions:

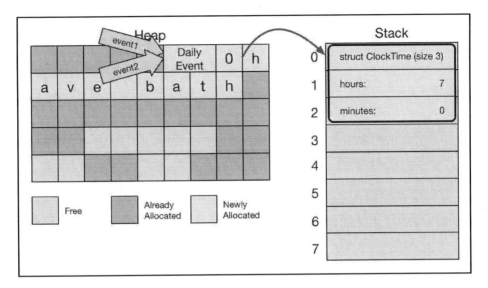

Multiple variables can hold references to the same instance:

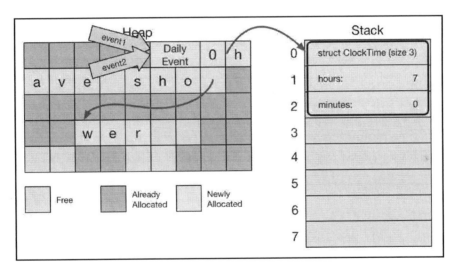

When reference types are modified, they aren't copied; instead, extra space must be found to accommodate the extra information. All references to the instance have the changed information.

This recipe describes the difference between reference semantics and value semantics, and hopefully illustrates that these behaviours arise out of the way they are stored in memory.

Both have their uses, and it's important to choose the right type when building your model.

See also

- **Swift blog**: Value and reference types: `http://swiftbook.link/blog/type-semantics`
- **Apple Developer Videos (Developer account needed)**:
    - WWDC 2015 - Building Better Apps with Value Types in Swift:
        - `https://developer.apple.com/videos/play/wwdc2015/414`
    - WWDC 2016 - Protocol and Value Oriented Programming in UIKit Apps:
        - `https://developer.apple.com/videos/play/wwdc2016/419`

Dispatch Queues

We live in a multicore computing world; multicore processors are found in everything, from our laptops and mobile phones to our watches. With these multiple cores come the abilities to work parallelly. These concurrent streams of work are known as *threads*, and programming in a multithreaded way enables your code to make the best use of the processor's cores. Deciding how and when to create new threads and managing the available resources are complex tasks, so Apple built a framework to do the hard work for us; it's called *Grand Central Dispatch*.

Grand Central Dispatch (GCD) handles the thread maintenance and monitors the available resources while providing a simple, queue-based interface for getting concurrent work done. With the open sourcing of Swift, Apple also open sourced GCD in the form of `libdispatch`, since Swift does not yet have built-in concurrency features.

In this recipe, we will explore some of the features of `libdispatch`, also known as the Dispatch framework, and see how we can use concurrency to build apps that are efficient and responsive.

Getting ready

We will see how we can improve the responsiveness of an app using GCD; so first, we need to start with an app that needs some improvement. Go to:

`https://github.com/SwiftProgrammingCookbook/PhotobookCreator`; here, you will find the repository of an app that takes a collection of photos and turns them into a PDF photo book. You can download the app source files directly from GitHub or using `git`:

```
git clone https://github.com/SwiftProgrammingCookbook/PhotobookCreator.git
```

If you build and run the app, you will see a collection of sample images, with the ability to add more:

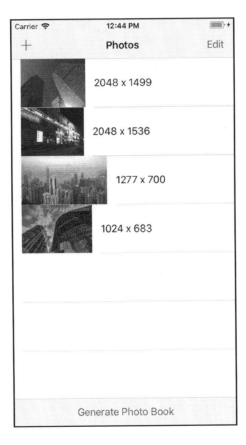

When you tap on **Generate Photo Book**, the app will take the photos you have chosen, resize them to the same size, and save them as a multipage PDF that can then be exported or shared. Depending on how many photos are included and the performance of the device, this process can take a little time to complete During this time, the whole interface is unresponsive; for example, you can't scroll through the pictures.

How to do it...

Let examine why the app is unresponsive during photobook generation, and how we can fix this.

Open up the `PhotoBookCreator` project and navigate to `PhotoCollectionViewController.swift`; in this file, you will find the following method:

```
func generatePhotoBook(with photos: [UIImage]) {
    let resizer = PhotoResizer()
    let builder = PhotoBookBuilder()
    // Scale down (can take a while)
    var photosForBook = resizer.scaleToSmallest(of: photos)
    // Crop (can take a while)
    photosForBook = resizer.cropToSmallest(of: photosForBook)
    // Generate PDF (can take a while)
    let photobookURL = builder.buildPhotobook(with: photosForBook)
    let previewController = UIDocumentInteractionController(url:
photobookURL)
    previewController.delegate = self
    previewController.presentPreview(animated: true)
}
```

In this method, we call three functions that can take quite a long time to complete; we take the output of one function and feed it into the next function, and the result is a URL for our photobook, which we then launch some UI to preview and export.

This work to resize and crop the photos, and then generate the photo book, is taking place on the same queue where UI touch events are processed, the main queue, which is why our UI is unresponsive. To free up the main queue for UI events, we can create our own private queue, which we can use to execute our long-running functions:

```
import Dispatch

class PhotoCollectionViewController: UIViewController {
    //...
    let processingQueue = DispatchQueue(label: "Photo processing queue")
```

```
func generatePhotoBook(with photos: [UIImage]) {
    processingQueue.async { [weak self] in

        let resizer = PhotoResizer()
        let builder = PhotoBookBuilder()

        // Get smallest common size
        let size = resizer.smallestCommonSize(for: photos)

        // Scale down (can take a while)
        var photosForBook = resizer.scaleWithAspectFill(photos, to:
                                                         size)
        // Crop (can take a while)
        photosForBook = resizer.centerCrop(photosForBook, to: size)
        // Generate PDF (can take a while)
        let pbURL = builder.buildPhotobook(with: photosForBook)
        // Show preview with export options
        let previewController = UIDocumentInteractionController(url:
                                                               pbURL)
        previewController.delegate = self
        previewController.presentPreview(animated: true)
    }
  }
}
```

By calling the `async` method on our `DispatchQueue` and providing a block of code, we are scheduling that block to be executed; GCD will execute that block when resources are available. Now our long-running code isn't blocking the main queue, so our UI will remain responsive; however, if you were to run the app with only this change, you would get some very odd behavior when the app tried to show the preview view controller.

We just discussed that UI touch events are delivered to the main queue, which is why we wanted to avoid blocking it; however, `UIKit` expects *all* UI events to happen on the main queue. Since we are currently creating and presenting the preview view controller from our private queue, we are defying this `UIKit` expectation, which can produce a number of bugs, including UI elements that never appear, or appear long after they were presented.

To solve this problem, we need to ensure that when we are ready to present our UI, we do that operation on the main queue:

```
func generatePhotoBook(with photos: [UIImage], using builder:
PhotoBookBuilder) {
    processingQueue.async { [weak self] in

        let resizer = PhotoResizer()
        let builder = PhotoBookBuilder()
```

```
    // Get smallest common size
    let size = resizer.smallestCommonSize(for: photos)

    // Scale down (can take a while)
    var photosForBook = resizer.scaleWithAspectFill(photos, to: size)
    // Crop (can take a while)
    photosForBook = resizer.centerCrop(photosForBook, to: size)
    // Generate PDF (can take a while)
    let pbURL = builder.buildPhotobook(with: photosForBook)
    DispatchQueue.main.async {
      // Show preview with export options
      let previewController = UIDocumentInteractionController(url:
      pbURL)
      previewController.delegate = self
      previewController.presentPreview(animated: true)
    }
  }
}
```

Now if you run the app you will find that you can generate a photo book while still being able to interact with the UI; for instance, being able to scroll the table view.

How it works...

GCD uses queues to manage blocks of work in a multithreaded environment; queues operate on a **first in first out (FIFO)** policy. When GCD determines that resources are available, it will take the next block from the queue and execute it; once the block has finished executing, it will be removed from the queue:

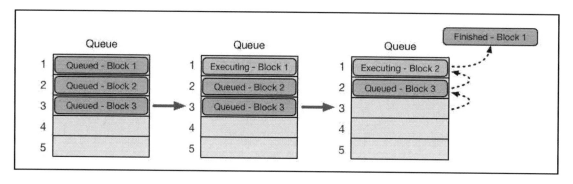

There are two types of `DispatchQueue`: *serial* and *concurrent*. With the simplest form of a queue, a serial queue, GCD will only execute one block at a time from the top of the queue. When each block finishes executing, it is removed from the queue, and each block moves up one position.

The main queue, which processes all UI events, is an example of a serial queue, and this explains why performing a long-running operation on the main queue will cause your UI to become unresponsive. While your long-running operation is executing, nothing else on the main queue will be executed until the long-running operation has finished.

With the second type of queue, a concurrent queue, GCD will execute as many blocks as resources allow on different threads. The next block to execute will be the block closest to the top of the stack that isn't already executing, and blocks are removed from the stack when finished:

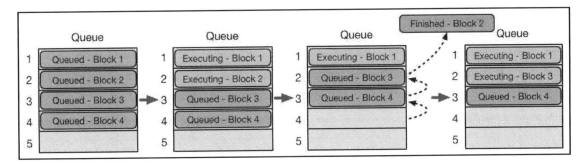

Concurrent queues can be really useful when you have numerous operations that are independent of each other. We will look into concurrent queues further in the next recipe.

See also

- The GitHub repository for `libdispatch`:
  `https://github.com/apple/swift-corelibs-libdispatch`
- Documentation for Dispatch Queues: `http://swiftbook.link/docs/dispatchqueue`

Concurrent queues and dispatch groups

In the last recipe, we looked into using a private serial queue to keep our app responsive by moving long-running operations off the main queue. In this recipe, we will break our operations down into smaller, independent blocks and place them on a concurrent queue.

Getting ready

We are going to build on the app we improved in the last recipe, which is an app that will produce a PDF photo book from a collection of photos. You can get the code for this app at `https://github.com/SwiftProgrammingCookbook/PhotobookCreator` and choose the branch `start-dispatch-groups`, or you can use `git`:

```
git clone https://github.com/SwiftProgrammingCookbook/PhotobookCreator.git
git checkout start-dispatch-groups
```

Open the project in XCode, and navigate to the `PhotoCollectionViewController.swift` file.

How to do it...

We saw in the last recipe how Dispatch Queues operate on a *first in first out* policy; **Grand Central Dispatch** (GCD) will execute a block from the top of the queue, and remove it from the queue when it has finished executing. The number of blocks that GCD will allow to execute at the same time will depend on the type of queue being used. *Serial* queues will only have one block of code being executed at any time; other blocks in the queues will have to wait until the block at the top of the queue has finished executing. However, for a *concurrent* queue, GCD will concurrently execute as many blocks as there are resources available. We can make more efficient use of a concurrent queue by breaking down the work into smaller, independent blocks, allowing them to be executed concurrently.

Take a look at the current implementation of the generatePhotoBook method; the only thing changed since the last recipe is that we now present the preview UI within a completion that is passed to the generatePhotoBook method. This simplifies the method and prevents us from needing to weakly capture self within the async block:

```
func generatePhotoBook(with photos: [UIImage], completion: @escaping (URL)
-> Void) {
    processingQueue.async {
        let resizer = PhotoResizer()
        let builder = PhotoBookBuilder()
        // Get smallest common size
        let size = resizer.smallestCommonSize(for: photos)
        // Scale down (can take a while)
        var photosForBook = resizer.scaleWithAspectFill(photos, to: size)
        // Crop (can take a while)
        photosForBook = resizer.centerCrop(photosForBook, to: size)
        // Generate PDF (can take a while)
        let photobookURL = builder.buildPhotobook(with: photosForBook)
        DispatchQueue.main.async {
            // Fire completion handler which will show the preview UI
            completion(photobookURL)
        }
    }
}
```

The work we are doing is in one block of code that we place on a queue. Let's see whether we can break this down into smaller, independent pieces of work that can be executed concurrently. We can't perform the scale and crop operations concurrently, as they will be operating on the same UIImage objects, and we will not get the intended result if the image is cropped before it's scaled.

However, we can apply the scale and crop operation to each photo separately and perform that operation concurrently on the other photos. Once each photo has been scaled and cropped, we can use the processed images to generate the photo book:

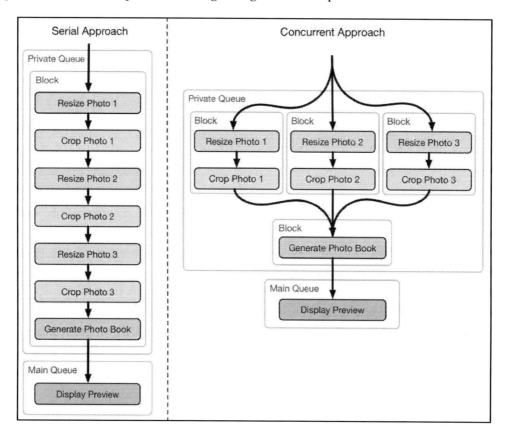

 Splitting the work up in this way may not make the overall operation faster, as there is overhead to each block of work. The efficiency improvement of dividing the work into concurrent blocks will depend on the operation involved, and how many concurrent operations can run.

We now have blocks of work that can run concurrently, but we have given ourselves a new problem; how do we coordinate all these concurrent pieces of work so that we know they are all completed and we can start generating the photo book? Here, GCD can help us; we can use a DispatchGroup to coordinate our operations on each of the images and be notified when they are all completed.

A dispatch group is like a turnstile at a stadium; every time someone enters the stadium, they pass through the turnstile and one extra person is counted as being in the stadium, and at the end of the day, as people leave the stadium and pass through the turnstile, the number of people in the stadium decreases. Once there is no one left in the stadium, the lights can be turned off.

Let's use a dispatch group to coordinate the work of our photo book creator:

1. First, we will create a dispatch group:

    ```
    let group = DispatchGroup()
    ```

2. Every time we start a block work to resize a photo, we will `enter` the group:

    ```
    group.enter()
    ```

3. Once the work is finished, we will `leave` the group:

    ```
    group.leave()
    ```

4. Finally, we will ask the group to notify us when the last resize operation has finished and left the group. Then, we can take the processed files and generate the photobook:

    ```
    group.notify(queue: processingQueue) {
        //.. generate photo book
        //.. execute completion handler
    }
    ```

5. Let's take a look at our `generatePhotoBook` method, now using a concurrent queue and dispatch groups:

    ```
    let processingQueue = DispatchQueue(label: "Photo processing
    queue",
                                    attributes: .concurrent)

    func generatePhotoBook(with photos: [</span>UIImage], completion:
    @escaping (URL) -> Void) {
        let resizer = PhotoResizer()
        let builder = PhotoBookBuilder()
        // Get smallest common size
        let size = resizer.smallestCommonSize(for: photos)
        let processedPhotos = NSMutableArray(array: photos)
        let group = DispatchGroup()
        for (index, photo) in photos.enumerated() {
            group.enter()
    ```

```
        processingQueue.async {
            // Scale down (can take a while)
            var photosForBook =
resizer.scaleWithAspectFill([photo], to: size)
            // Crop (can take a while)
            photosForBook = resizer.centerCrop([photo], to: size)
            // Replace original photo with processed photo
            processedPhotos[index] = photosForBook[0]
            group.leave()
        }
    }
    group.notify(queue: processingQueue) {
        guard let photos = processedPhotos as? [UIImage] else {
return }
        // Generate PDF (can take a while)
        let photobookURL = builder.buildPhotobook(with: photos)
        DispatchQueue.main.async {
            completion(photobookURL)
        }
    }
}
```

How it works...

Dispatch Queues are serial by default, so to create a concurrent queue instead, we pass the
.concurrent attribute when it is created:

```
let processingQueue = DispatchQueue(label: "Photo processing queue",
                                    attributes: .concurrent)
```

Before we loop through all the photos, we set up anything that isn't specific to each photo:

```
let resizer = PhotoResizer()
let builder = PhotoBookBuilder()
// Get smallest common size
let size = resizer.smallestCommonSize(for: photos)
let processedPhotos = NSMutableArray(array: photos)
let group = DispatchGroup()
```

This includes creating the DispatchGroup, which we will use to coordinate the work. Since
our photo resizing will now be happening concurrently, we need a place to collect the
photos once they have been processed. We can use a Swift array for this; however, a Swift
array is a value type, so we can't use it from within multiple blocks, as each block will be
taking a copy of the array, not the original array itself.

To solve this with a Swift array, we would need to make the `processedPhotos` array a property on the view controller, which would mean we would have to weakly capture self in the blocks that we would need to unwrap. A simpler way to solve this problem is to use a collection that has reference semantics; the `Foundation` framework provides that in the forms of `NSArray` and `NSMutableArray`. As we saw earlier in this chapter, it's important to understand the semantics of the construct being used and pick the right tool for the right job:

```
for (index, photo) in photos.enumerated() {
    group.enter()
    processingQueue.async {
        // Scale down (can take a while)
        var photosForBook = resizer.scaleWithAspectFill([photo], to: size)
        // Crop (can take a while)
        photosForBook = resizer.centerCrop([photo], to: size)
        // Replace original photo with processed photo
        processedPhotos[index] = photosForBook[0]
        group.leave()
    }
}
```

For each photo, we enter the group and place the resize work on the concurrent queue. We can use the same scale and crop methods that we used previously, just passing an array containing one photo. Once the work is completed, we'll replace the original photo with the processed photo in the array and leave the group.

Once every block has left the group, this `notify` block will execute. We retrieve the processed photos and use them to generate the photo book. Finally, we ensure that the completion handler is executed on the main queue:

```
group.notify(queue: processingQueue) {
    guard let photos = processedPhotos as? [UIImage] else { return }
    // Generate PDF (can take a while)
    let photobookURL = builder.buildPhotobook(with: photos)
    DispatchQueue.main.async {
        completion(photobookURL)
    }
}
```

If you build and run the app, you can still generate a photo book and the UI is still responsive, and now GCD can make the best use of the available resources to generate our photobook.

See also

- Documentation for Dispatch Queues: `http://swiftbook.link/docs/dispatchqueue`
- Documentation for Dispatch Groups: `http://swiftbook.link/docs/dispatchgroup`

Operations

In this chapter so far, we have taken our long-running operations and scheduled them as blocks of code, called **closures**, on Dispatch Queues. This has made it really easy to move long-running code off of the main queue, but if we intend to reuse this long-running code, pass it around, track its state, and generally deal with it in an object-orientated way, a closure is not ideal.

To solve this, the `Foundation` framework provides an object, `Operation`, that allows us to wrap up our block of work within an encapsulated object.

In this recipe, we will take the photo book app we used throughout this chapter, and convert our long-running blocks to `Operations`.

Getting ready

You can get the code for our photo book app by visiting:
`https://github.com/SwiftProgrammingCookbook/PhotobookCreator`, and choosing the `start-operations` branch, or you can use git:

```
git clone https://github.com/SwiftProgrammingCookbook/PhotobookCreator.git
git checkout start-operations
```

Open the project in Xcode, and navigate to the `PhotoCollectionViewController.swift` file.

How to do it...

Let's recap how we broke the work down into independent parts:

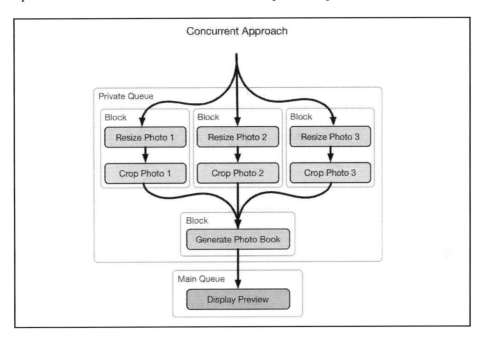

We can turn each of these blocks of work into separate operations. First, let's create an operation to scale and crop each photo. We define an operation by sub-classing the Operation class, so in the project, create a new Swift file and call it PhotoResizeOperation.swift.

In the simplest Operation implementation, we only need to override one method, main(), so let's copy and paste the relevant code from our generatePhotobook method. This main() method will be executed when the operation starts:

```
import UIKit

class PhotoResizeOperation: Operation {
    override func main() {
        // Scale down (can take a while)
        var photosForBook = resizer.scaleWithAspectFill([photo], to: size)
        // Crop (can take a while)
        photosForBook = resizer.centerCrop([photo], to: size)
        // Replace original photo with processed photo
        processedPhotos[index] = photosForBook[0]
```

```
        }
    }
```

Copying and pasting the code is not enough, as there are a number of dependencies that were previously being captured by the block; now we have to explicitly provide these dependencies to the operation:

```
class PhotoResizeOperation: Operation {
    let resizer: PhotoResizer
    let size: CGSize
    let photos: NSMutableArray
    let photoIndex: Int
    init(resizer: PhotoResizer, size: CGSize,
        photos: NSMutableArray, photoIndex: Int) {

        self.resizer = resizer
        self.size = size
        self.photos = photos
        self.photoIndex = photoIndex
    }
    override func main() {
        // Retrieve the photo to be resized.
        guard let photo = photos[photoIndex] as? UIImage else { return }
        // Scale down (can take a while)
        var photosForBook = resizer.scaleWithAspectFill([photo], to: size)
        // Crop (can take a while)
        photosForBook = resizer.centerCrop(photosForBook, to: size)
        photos[photoIndex] = photosForBook[0]
    }
}
```

We have converted our resize block to an operation. We now need to do the same for the block that generates the photo book:

```
import UIKit

class GeneratePhotoBookOperation: Operation {
    let builder: PhotoBookBuilder
    let photos: NSMutableArray
    var photobookURL: URL?
    init(builder: PhotoBookBuilder, photos: NSMutableArray) {
        self.builder = builder
        self.photos = photos
    }
    override func main() {
        guard let photos = photos as? [UIImage] else { return }
        // Generate PDF (can take a while)
        photobookURL = builder.buildPhotobook(with: photos)
```

```
        }
    }
```

We pass the dependencies into the operation just like in `PhotoResizeOperation`. The output of this operation is a URL for the resulting photobook. We expose that as a property on the operation, so it can be retrieved outside the operation.

With our blocks of work converted to operations, let's switch over to `PhotoCollectionViewController.swift` and update our `generatePhotoBook` method to use this new operation:

```swift
let processingQueue = OperationQueue()

func generatePhotoBook(with photos: [UIImage], completion: @escaping (URL)
-> Void) {
    let resizer = PhotoResizer()
    let builder = PhotoBookBuilder()
    // Get smallest common size
    let size = resizer.smallestCommonSize(for: photos)
    let processedPhotos = NSMutableArray(array: photos)
    let generateBookOp = GeneratePhotoBookOperation(builder: builder,
                                                    photos:
processedPhotos)
    for index in 0..<processedPhotos.count {
        let resizeOp = PhotoResizeOperation(resizer: resizer,
                                            size: size,
                                            photos: processedPhotos,
                                            photoIndex: index)
        generateBookOp.addDependency(resizeOp)
        processingQueue.addOperation(resizeOp)
    }
    generateBookOp.completionBlock = { [weak generateBookOp] in
        guard let pbURL = generateBookOp?.photobookURL else {
            return
        }
        OperationQueue.main.addOperation {
            completion(pbURL)
        }
    }
    processingQueue.addOperation(generateBookOp)
}
```

Let's walk through the changes step by step:

```swift
let processingQueue = OperationQueue()
```

Where we were previously using a `DispatchQueue` to manage the execution of our blocks, operations are managed with an `OperationQueue`:

```
func generatePhotoBook(with photos: [UIImage], completion: @escaping (URL)
-> Void) {
    let resizer = PhotoResizer()
    let builder = PhotoBookBuilder()
    // Get smallest common size
    let size = resizer.smallestCommonSize(for: photos)
    let processedPhotos = NSMutableArray(array: photos)
```

The method signature and the dependencies we need to generate upfront remain the same:

```
let generateBookOp = GeneratePhotoBookOperation(builder: builder,
                                                photos: processedPhotos)
```

Next, we create the operation to generate the photo book, passing in the dependencies. Although the operation will be executed last, we create it first, so that we can make it dependent on the resize operations we are about to create. An operation does not execute immediately upon creation; it will only execute when the `start()` method of `Operation` is called, which can be called manually, or, if an `Operation` is placed on an `OperationQueue`, it will be called by the queue as appropriate:

```
for index in 0..<processedPhotos.count {
    let resizeOp = PhotoResizeOperation(resizer: resizer,
                                        size: size,
                                        photos: processedPhotos,
                                        photoIndex: index)
    generateBookOp.addDependency(resizeOp)
    processingQueue.addOperation(resizeOp)
}
```

Now, we loop through the number of photos that we intend to process and create a resize operation for each, passing in the dependencies.

With our move to use `Operation`, one thing we have lost is the use of `DispatchGroup`, which we used to ensure that we only generated the photo book once all the photo resize block had completed. We can, however, achieve the same goals using operation dependencies. An operation can be declared as dependent on a set of other operations, so it will not begin executing until the operations it depends on have finished. To ensure that the `generateBookOp` operation, which we just created, only executes when all the `PhotoResizeOperation` operations are complete, we add each of them as a dependency of `generateBookOp`.

With this done, we can place each `PhotoResizeOperation` on the `OperationQueue`:

```
generateBookOp.completionBlock = { [weak generateBookOp] in
    guard let pbURL = generateBookOp?.photobookURL else {
        return
    }
    OperationQueue.main.addOperation {
        completion(pbURL)
    }
}
```

`Operation` has a `completionBlock` property; any block set here will be executed once the operation has completed. We can use this to fire our completion handler on the main queue. Since we need to provide the completion handler with the URL to the photo book created by `generateBookOp`, we can retrieve this from within the block, as we know that the operation will be finished and the URL will be there. However, we need to be careful. We are providing a closure to `generateBookOp`, which will be retained, and we are using, and therefore capturing and retaining, the `generateBookOp` operation in the same block. This will lead to a retain cycle, and `generateBookOp` will never get released from memory. To avoid this retain cycle, we specify that we want to weakly capture `generateBookOp` in the block we provide, using the `[weak generateBookOp]` capture list. This won't increment the retain count, preventing the retain cycle from happening.

Much like `DispatchQueue`, `OperationQueue` has an available property that provides a reference to the main queue, upon which the UI events are processed. Also, `OperationQueue` has a convenience method that will take a block of code, wrap it in an `Operation`, and add it to the queue; we use this to ensure that the completion handler is executed on the main queue:

```
processingQueue.addOperation(generateBookOp)
```

As the last step, we put the `generateBookOp` operation on the processing queue. It's important that we do this as the last step, because once placed on the queue, the operation may be executed immediately, but we don't want it executed immediately. We only want `generateBookOp` executed once all the resize operations are complete, and if we placed the operation on the queue before setting up the dependencies, this could happen.

Now that we have transitioned our app over to using `Operation`, let's build and run and verify that everything works just as it did before.

How it works...

How does `OperationQueue` know when to start an operation and when to remove it from the queue? It knows by monitoring the operation's state. The `Operation` class goes through a number of state transformations during its life cycle; the following diagram describes how these state transformations occur:

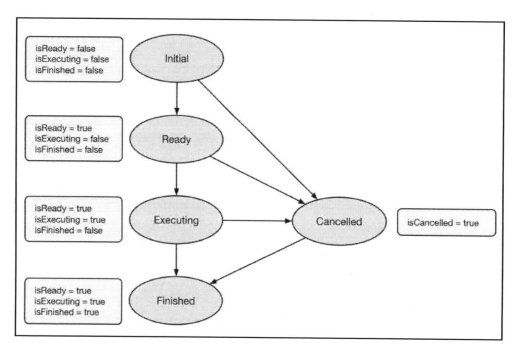

Information about the operation's state is exposed through a number of boolean properties on `Operation`, and the operation queue uses the properties to know when to perform certain actions on the operations. Let's look at these properties one by one:

```
var isReady: Bool
```

An operation will return `true` for `isReady` when all its dependencies are finished; if it doesn't have any dependencies, it will always return `true`. The queue will only start executing an operation if `isReady` is true:

```
var isExecuting: Bool
```

Once `start` is called on an operation, either manually or by a queue, `isExecuting` will return true, and when the operation has finished executing, `isExecuting` will revert to returning `false`.

Since operations remain on the queue until they have finished, the queue uses the `isExecuting` property to ensure that it doesn't call `start` on an operation that has already started:

```
var isFinished: Bool
```

Once the operation has finished doing whatever processing is required, `isFinished` should return true. When `isFinished` starts to return true, it will be removed from the queue, and the queue will no longer maintain a reference to the operation. For the simplest implementation of `Operation`, as we implemented earlier, `isFinished` returns true automatically when the `main()` method has finished executing:

```
var isCancelled: Bool
```

Operations can be cancelled by calling the `cancel()` method on the operation. Once called, the `isCancelled` property will return true. This can be used to exit early from a long-running operation, but it is up to you to check the `isCancelled` method and interrupt any long-running code if it returns true.

There's more...

Users of our photo book app currently do not have the ability to cancel the generation of a photo book once the process has started, so let's add that functionality.

First, we will examine our two operations and look for opportunities to check the `isCancelled` property and exit early. Switch to `PhotoResizeOperation.swift` and add `isCancelled` checks to the `main()` method:

```
override func main() {
    // Check if operation has been cancelled
    guard isCancelled == false else { return }
    guard let photo = photos[photoIndex] as? UIImage else { return }
    // Scale down (can take a while)
    var photosForBook = resizer.scaleWithAspectFill([photo], to: size)
    // Check if operation has been cancelled
    guard isCancelled == false else { return }
    // Crop (can take a while)
    photosForBook = resizer.centerCrop(photosForBook, to: size)
    photos[photoIndex] = photosForBook[0]
}
```

Before each piece of long-running work, we check the `isCancelled` property, and if it is true, we return early, which will finish the operation. We can do the same in `GeneratePhotoBookOperation.swift`:

```
override func main() {
    // Check if operation has been cancelled
    guard isCancelled == false else { return }
    guard let photos = photos as? [UIImage] else { return }
    // Generate PDF (can take a while)
    photobookURL = builder.buildPhotobook(with: photos)
}
```

Next, we will need to add some UI that allows the user to cancel the photo book generation once it is in progress. This is an exercise for the reader, or you can switch to the `end-operations` branch to see how I have implemented it.

Once the user chooses to cancel generating a photo book, we can call this:

```
processingQueue.cancelAllOperations()
```

This will fire the `cancel()` method on all the operations in the queue.

We now have an app with a cancelable, long-running operation.

See also

Documentation for the `Operation` class: `http://swiftbook.link/docs/operation`

Index

M

markdown
  about 291
  references 291
Model View Controller (MVC) 244
Mongo
  URL 326
multi-page playgrounds 286, 294
mutating 44
MySQL
  about 313
  URL 326

N

namespace 188
nested types
  about 188
  defining 190, 191, 192
networking, components
  URL 198
  URLRequest 199
  URLResponse 199
  URLSession 199
  URLSessionDataTask 199
networking
  in Foundation 198, 200, 202
  reference 202
nil coalescing operator 28

O

object classes
  about 36, 37, 40
  reference 42
  reference types 42
Object Oriented Programming 36
operations
  about 354
  URL 362
operators
  advanced operators 176, 177, 178
  AND operation 178
  AND operator 179
  bit shift operator 178
  OR operation 179

  reference 180
  XOR (exclusive or) operation 179
option set
  about 180
  reference 181
optionals
  about 25, 26, 28
  URL 31

P

parameter overloading 35
Perfect
  URL 313
Playgrounds
  code, importing 281, 286
  references 278
  resources, importing 277, 281
Postgres
  about 313
  URL 315
  using, for model persistence 313, 326
precondition
  using 154, 156, 157
property observers
  property changing notifications, obtaining with
    96, 97
  reference 98
protocols
  about 58
  conformance 60
  definition 59
  reference 61
  Saveable protocol 59
pure function 33

R

RaptureXML
  URL 240
read-eval-print loop (REPL) 298
Really Simple Syndication (RSS) 221
Redis
  URL 326
reference semantics
  about 332
  references 342

Z

Zewo
URL 313